ART BOOKS

FROM CRESCENT MOON PUBLISHING

Leonardo da Vinci
by James Pearson

Early Netherlandish Painting
by Rosalind Mutter

Piero della Francesca
by Naomi Haskell

Fra Angelico: Art and Religion in the Renaissance
by Rosalind Mutter

Eric Gill: Nuptials of God
by Anthony Hoyland

Minimal Art and Artists in the 1960s and After
by Laura Garrard

Postwar Art
by George Knighton

Vincent van Gogh: Visionary Landscapes
by Stuart Morris

Max Beckmann
by Stuart Morris

Egon Schiele: Sex and Death in Purple Stockings
by D. Simon Eade

Mark Rothko: The Art of Transcendence
by Julia Davis

Jasper Johns
by L.M. Poole

Brice Marden
by Laura Garrard

Frank Stella
by James Pearson

The Light Eternal: J.M.W. Turner
by Jeremy Mark Robinson

Maurice Sendak and the Art of Children's Book Illustration
by L.M. Poole

Sex in Art: Pornography and Pleasure in Painting and Sculpture
by Cassidy Hughes

Glorification: Religious Abstraction
in Renaissance and 20th Century Painting
by Jeremy Mark Robinson

The Art of Andy Goldsworthy
by William Malpas

Andy Goldsworthy: Touching Nature
by William Malpas

Andy Goldsworthy In Close-Up
by William Malpas

Richard Long: Pocket Guide
by William Malpas

The Art of Richard Long
by William Malpas

Constantin Brancusi: Sculpting the Essence of Things
by James Pearson

Alison Wilding: The Embrace of Sculpture
by Susan Quinnell

The Erotic Object: Sexuality in Sculpture
From Prehistory to the Present Day
by Susan Quinnell

Land Art: A Complete Guide to Landscape, Environmental,
Earthworks, Nature, Sculpture and Installation Art
by William Malpas

Land Art In Close-Up
by William Malpas

Colorfield Painting: Minimal, Cool, Hard Edge, Serial
and Post-Painterly Abstract Art From the Sixties to the Present
by Laura Garrard

Sacred Gardens: The Garden in Myth, Religion and Art
by Jeremy Mark Robinson

LEONARDO DA VINCI

LEONARDO DA VINCI

James Pearson

CRESCENT MOON

CRESCENT MOON PUBLISHING
P.O. Box 1312, Maidstone
Kent, ME14 5XU
Great Britain
www.crmoon.com

First published 1994. Second edition 2008. Reprinted with additions 2014/ 2018.

Printed and bound in the U.S.A.
Set in Bodoni Book 10 on 14pt.
Designed by Radiance Graphics.

British Library Cataloguing in Publication data

Pearson, James
Leonardo da Vinci
I. Title
759.5

ISBN-13 9781861717429

Contents

Abbreviations

L Leonardo, *Leonardo On Painting*

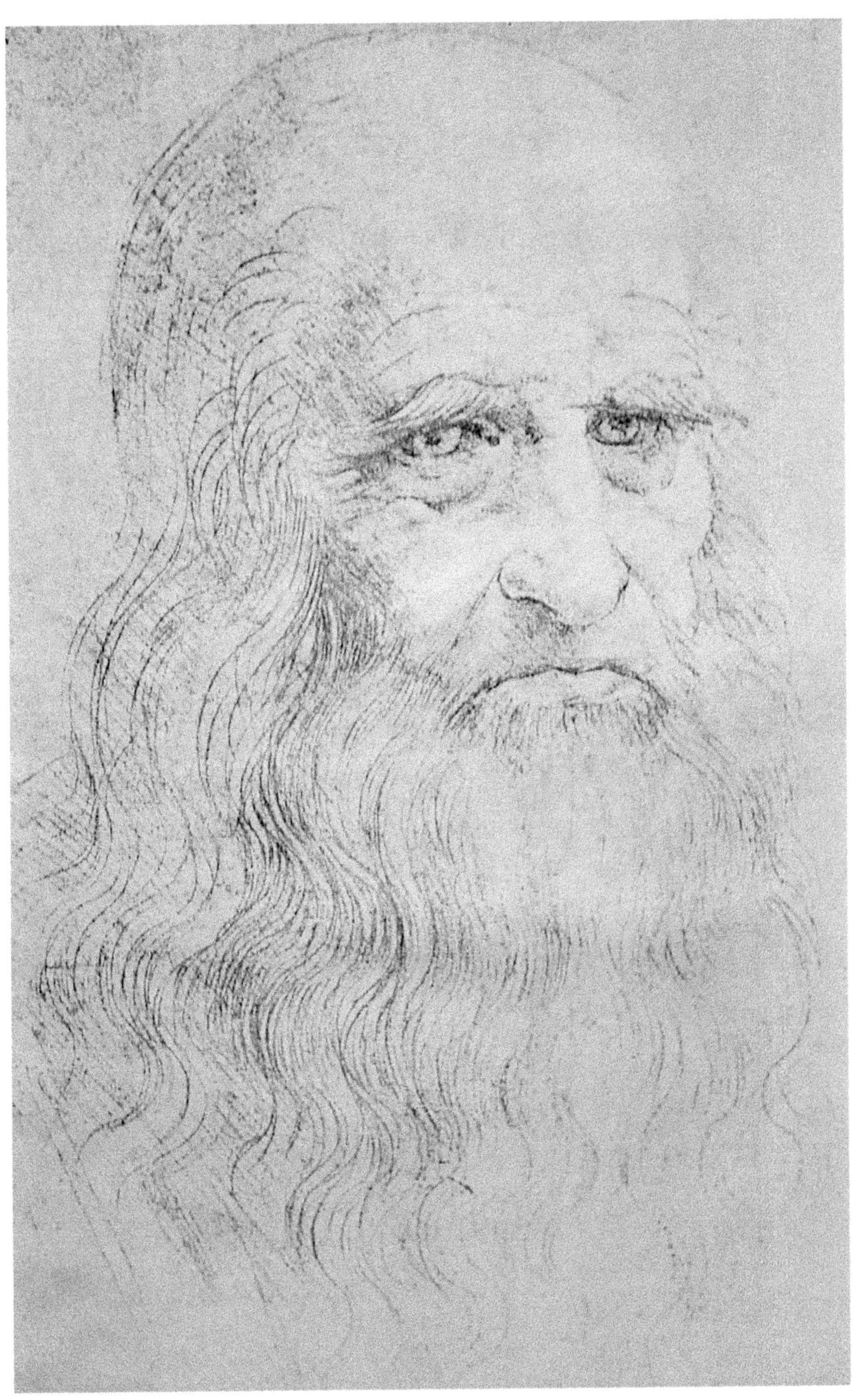

Leonardo, Self-Portrait

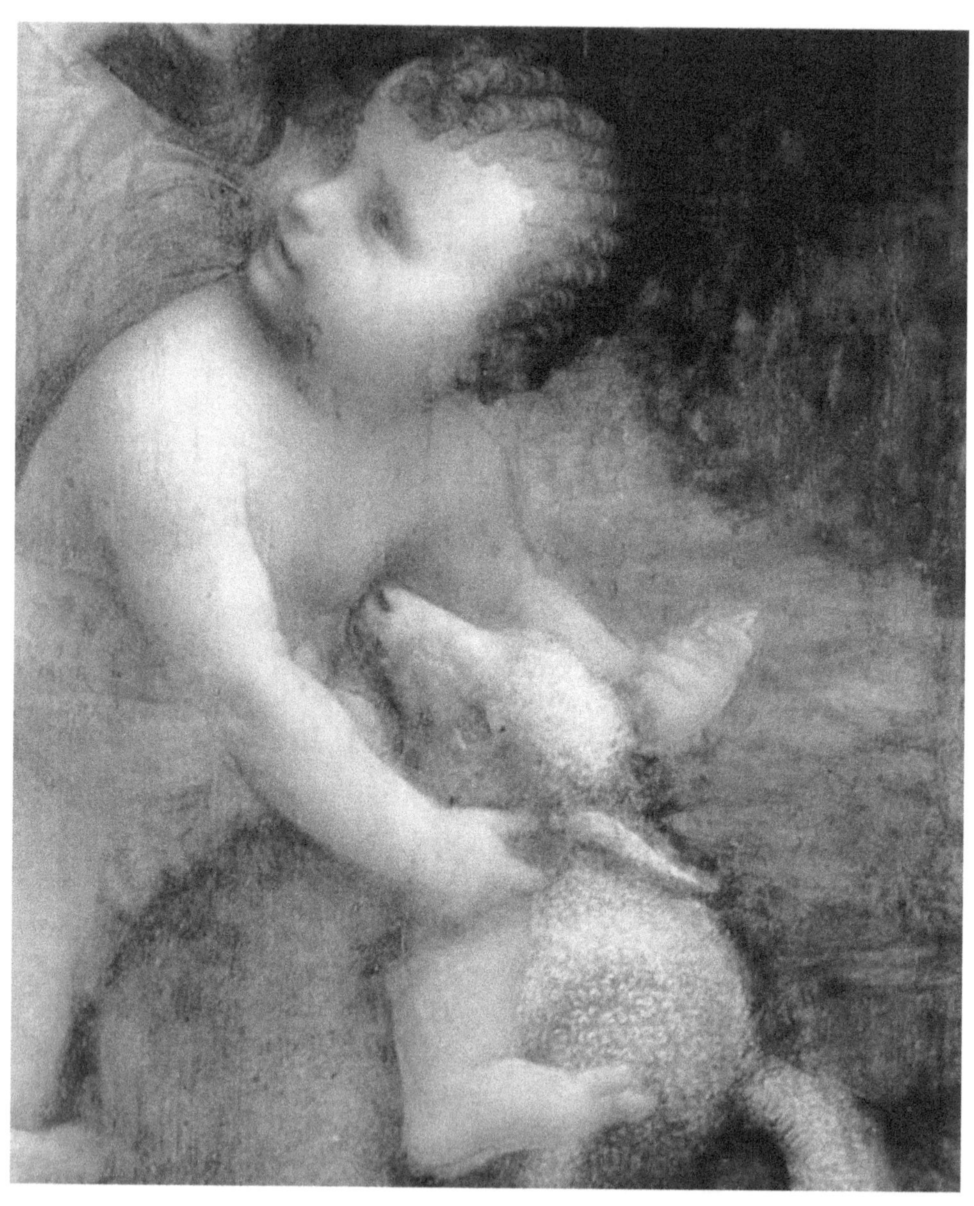

Leonardo da Vinci, detail from The Virgin and Child With St Anne, Louve, Paris

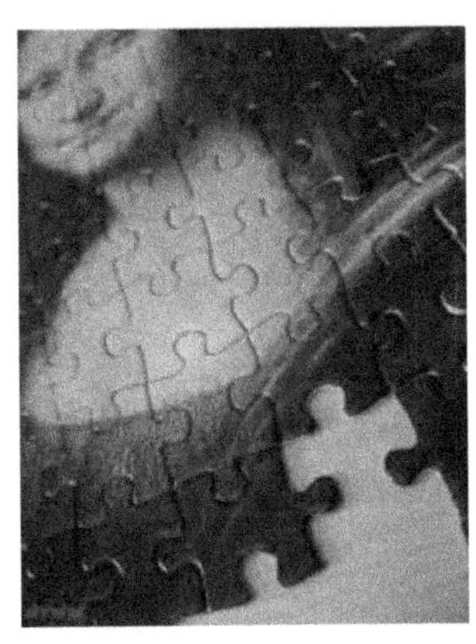

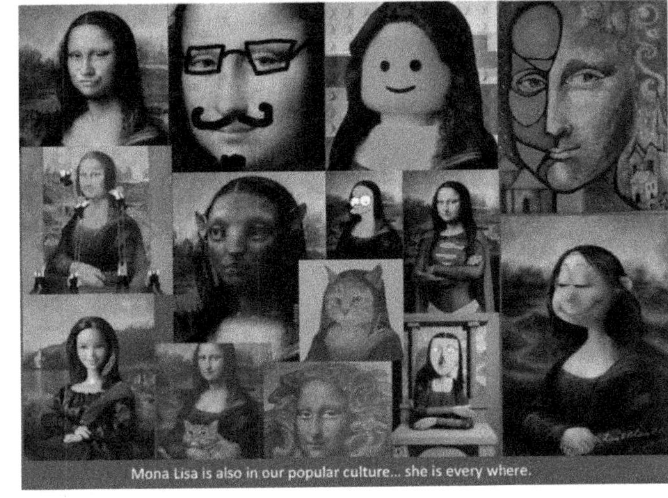

Leonardo da Vinci in popular culture, including toys, movies, cartoons and merchandizing.

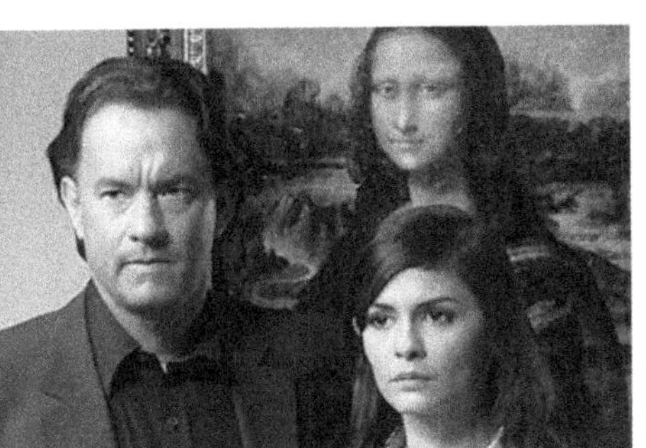

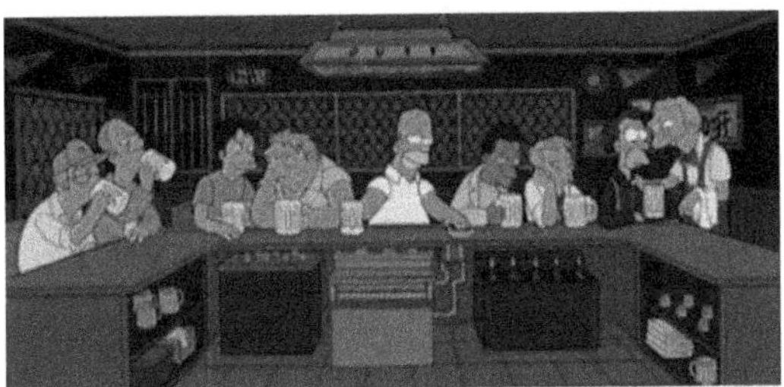

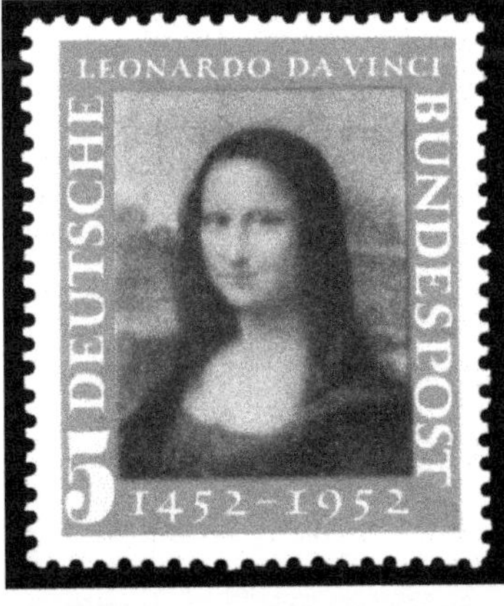

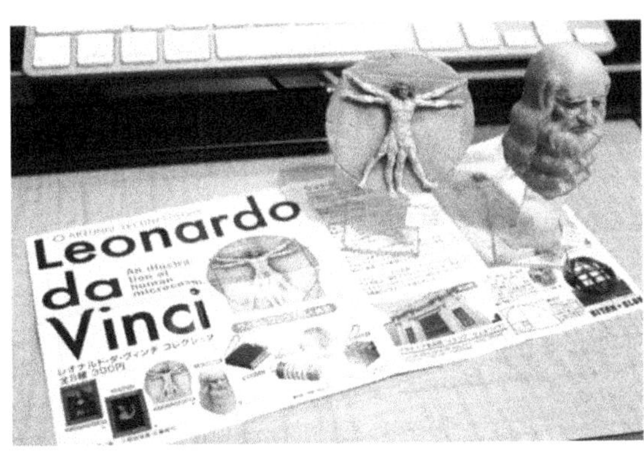

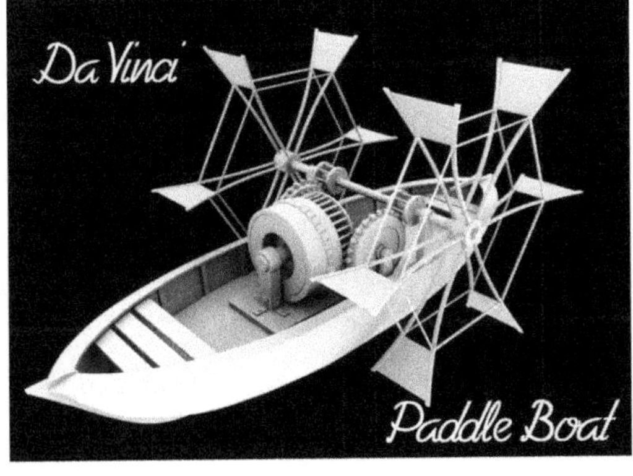

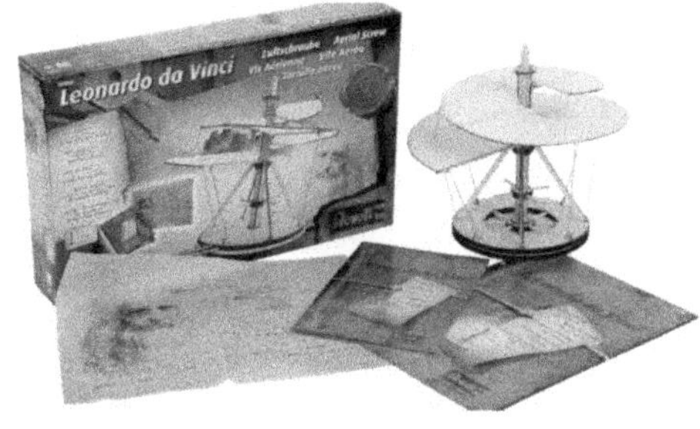

Introduction

The art of painting embraces and contains within itself all visible things.

Leonardo da Vinci, notebooks[1]

The most erotic artist of the Renaissance, the one who created the darkest and the strangest images, who created the most hypnotic smile in art, who took Western painting to the highest point it has reached, was not Michelangelo Buonarroti, Andrea del Sarto, Fra Angelico, Sandro Botticelli, Piero della Francesca, Andrea Mantegna, Giovanni Bellini, Raphael, Titian, Caravaggio, Simone Martini, Fra Bartolommeo, Lucas Cranach or Masaccio, but Leonardo da Vinci. He is the creator of the *Mona Lisa*, and '[t]he *Mona Lisa* is without doubt the most famous work in the entire forty-thousand year history of the visual arts' writes Roy McMullen (1). There are any number of descriptions of the *Mona Lisa*. This extract from Théophile Gautier's 1858 article will suffice:

> We have seen these faces before, but not upon this earth: in some previous existence perhaps, which they recall to use vaguely. How can we explain otherwise the singular charm, almost magic, which the *Mona Lisa* exercises

1 Leonardo: *Treatise on Painting*, in *Leonardo on Painting*, 40.

on even the least enthusiastic natures? Is it her beauty?...She is no longer even young; her age must be that loved by Balzac, thirty years; through the subtle modelling we divine the beginnings of fatigue, and life's finger has left its imprint on the peachlike cheek. Her costume, because of the darkening of the pigments,has become almost that of a widow, a crêpe veil falls with the hair along her face; but the expression, wise, deep, velvety, full of promise, attracts you irresistibly and intoxicates you, while the sinuous, serpentine mouth, turned up at the corners, in the violet shadows, mocks you with so much gentleness, grace, and superiority, that you feel suddenly intimidated, like a schoolboy before a duchess. The head with its violet shadows, seen as through black gauze, arrests one's dreams as one leans on the museum railing before her, haunts one's memory like a symphonic theme. Beneath the form *expressed*, one feels a thought that is vague, infinite, *inexpressible*, like a musical idea. One is moved, troubled, images *already seen* pass before one's eyes, voices whose note seems familiar whisper languorous secrets in one's ears; repressed desires, hopes that drive one to despair stir painfully in the shadow shot with sunbeams; and you discover that your melancholy arises form the fact that Mona Lisa three hundred years ago greeted your avowal of love with this same mocking smile which she retains even today on her lips.[2]

Leonardo da Vinci inspires these sensual, poetic responses time after time. Something in his work excites people tremendously. Pierre-Paul Prud'hon wrote in Rome in 1785:

I have just come from seeing the admirable tapestries done from the cartoons of the famous Raphael; in my opinion they are without doubt the most beautiful things he did, the most deeply felt and the most expressive. But one who far surpassed him in precision, pithiness, and force of execution, and in harmony of chiaroscuro and perspective, etc, is the inimitable Leonardo da Vinci, the father, the prince, and the first of painters, after whom one can also see a single tapestry done from his famous *Last Supper* painted in Milan in a Dominican refectory. This is the world's outstanding picture, the masterpiece of painting.[3]

Leonardo da Vinci is one of the most celebrated of artists. He is the artist-as-hero, the artist-as-genius, undisputed genius (like William Shakespeare or Sophocles). Leonardo is exalted for his amazing mind, his scientific curiosity, his ideas on botany, anatomy, architecture, weaponry, engineering, etc. He wrote copiously, on art and painting, on philosophy; subjects studied in his notebooks include geology, optics,

2 Théophile Gautier: *Les Dieux et les demi-dieux de la peinture*, 1863, quoted in McMullen, 172-3.
3 Prud'hon, in Goldwater, ed, 176-7.

acoustics, music, mathematics, anatomy, hydraulics, ballistics, weight, movement, naval armaments, flight and so on. He 'invented', or rediscovered, the bicycle, an early form of military tank, the helicopter, he understood the principle of gravity before Newton, and explained why stars twinkled before Kepler; he prefigured Bacon, Galileo, Pascal, Huygens, Cuvier and Halley, among others. Nothing is neglected from Leonardo's 'scientific' curiosity about the world. Artists have long studied all manner of things, despising the relatively recent notion of 'specialization', where people should 'specialize' in this or that. The Renaissance character looks at all sort of areas of knowledge. Poets such as Shakespeare, Spenser, Dante, Vaughan, Rimbaud and Keats drew on all sorts of traditions and ways of thinking. Like Leonardo, they absorbed elements of botany, meteorology, anatomy, psychology, zoology, and so on. The poet or artist draws everything together – by the powers of her/ his imagination and creativity. All things are connected with everything else: this is basic Western philosophy, a key part of the Renaissance, Neoplatonic tradition which informed Leonardo's art. Novalis, the German poet, wrote:

> In our mind, everything is connected in the most peculiar, pleasant, and lively manner. The strangest things come together by virtue of one space, one time, an odd similarity, an error, some accident. In this manner, curious unities and peculiar connections originate – one thing reminds us of everything, becomes the sign of many things. Reason and imagination are united through time and space in the most extraordinary manner, and we can say that each thought, each phenomenon of our mind is the most individual part of an altogether individual totality. (1960-88, 3, 650-1)

We return again and again when discussing Leonardo da Vinci to the problem of attribution. Very few of Leonardo's paintings are definitely by his own hand. Or at least, very few that critics and art historians agree on. *The Adoration of the Magi, Mona Lisa, St Jerome* and *The Last Supper* are pretty much undisputed now. As for the others, well, nothing is certain. It's the same with Shakespeare: people seem to want to debunk the legend and the achievement of the artist. Thus, Shakespeare did not write the plays, some people say, but a group of people did. Or Queen Elizabeth I did, and so on. Leonardo's paintings caused controversy even when they were in his studio.

The *Benois Madonna* in St Petersburg seems to be by Leonardo da Vinci, and critics are nearly unanimous about it. It accords with Leonardo's descriptions in his notebooks of producing various early Madonnas. The Munich *Madonna* too seems to be a Leonardo painting. Others are more problematic in their attributions: the *Madonna Litta*, in St Petersburg, has an awkwardly posed head, which does not seem to square with Leonardo's handling of poses and heads. Even in the clumsy early works – in *The Annunciation*, for instance – Leonardo is not as awkward as in the *Madonna Litta*. *The Madonna of the Yarn-Winder*, for some by Leonardo, also seems too awkward.[4] Mary has the the hand gesture from *The Virgin of the Rocks,* and the usual Leonardoan headdress and costumes. The face is not right, though, and the pose, with one shoulder much lower than the other, and the other turned round towards the child, doesn't seem quite right. The space between viewer and Madonna is distorted, the perspective of the two bodies is twisted, so that *The Madonna of the Yarn-Winder* seems to be inspired by but not by Leonardo.

The portraits are also problematic: the *Portrait of Ginerva Benci (?)* is regarded as by Leonardo da Vinci. The openness of the face set against the dark conifer seems to be particularly Leonardoan. Something about this youthful face suggests Leonardo and no other painter. It is the precision of the lines, and the somewhat stern, distant expression. The arrangement of the hair accords with Leonardo's idiosyncratic treatment of hair, found through his work. Indeed, with the *Leda* sketches, he spent much of his time trying out different ways of drawing Leda's hair. The space of the *Ginerva Benci (?)* portrait is powerful: she is seen in quarter-length, very close to the picture plane. The viewer is standing maybe two or three feet away from the woman: it is thus an intimate portrait, for the viewer is brought into the personal space of the sitter, as with the *Mona Lisa.* Leonardo was particularly good at this: it is part of his power as an artist, to involve the viewer directly with his subjects. The viewpoint in the large crowd scenes of

4 Follower of Leonardo: *The Madonna of the Yarn-Winder*, Deleuch Collection, Boughton, Kettering

The Last Supper and *The Adoration of the Magi* has to be distant, to incorporate all the figures. In *The Virgin of the Rocks* we seem to be the only viewer present in this sacred space in the mountains. There is no town in the distance in *The Virgin of the Rocks* as there is in *St Jerome* or the *Portrait of Ginerva Benci (?)*.

Leonardo da Vinci has always been brilliant with landscapes, and the background of the *Portrait of Ginerva Benci (?)* is no exception. There is a lake, perhaps a river too, to the right of the woman. It is an autumnal, overcast scene, in blues and browns, where the shimmering water fuses with the trees and bushes seamlessly. It is the depiction of the background landscape that so many painters found difficult to emulate in Leonardo's art when they came to copy him or be inspired by him. Copies of Leonardo are often let down by bad landscapes. The cave and mountainscape of *The Virgin of the Rocks* is particularly dazzling, with its complex series of rocks and many beautifully painted plants. In *The Virgin of the Rocks* Leonardo displays his brilliant grasp of botany and natural forms. The landscape of the *Mona Lisa* is similarly celebrated, with its dark browns giving way to the ærial perspective of the azures. Even the interior of *The Last Supper* allows for a landscape, seen behind Christ's head. The background of the Louvre *Virgin and Child with St Anne* is, again, constructed out of predominantly blues and sepias. The landscape is lighter than in the *Mona Lisa* or *The Virgin of the Rocks* with a vast mountainscape seen in delicate greys and blues.

The head of Ginerva Benci (?) against the tree is an amazing juxtaposition of dark and light tones. The identification here, as throughout Leonardo da Vinci, is between the notion of 'woman' and 'Nature'. The tree frames the whitish face, and the woman is firmly identified with Nature and the feminine principle. The background of *The Annunciation*, being an early work, is disappointing. It features a city by the sea complete with whales in the sea. The background of the early *Madonnas* is, again, that rocky, dusty world of low hills giving way to high blue mountains.

The Lady With an Ermine seems also to be very Leonardoan – a woman with an animal is one of Leonardo's favourite motifs. Yet there is something about *The Lady With the Ermine*, as with the *Portrait of a Musician*, *La Belle Ferronnière* and Milan *Portrait of a Lady*, that seems to suggest other contributors. As with the London *The Virgin of the Rocks*, other artists probably helped with these portraits; or they were painted over in later years by other people. The black chalk and pastel *Portrait of Isabella d'Este* is almost certainly by Leonardo. It features many Leonardoan stylistic aspects.

In laying claim to a painting, or discrediting a painting, art historians and critics are proving or propounding certain theories, protecting certain ideas, playing powergames, getting back at certain people.

Looking at the many many 'followers' of Leonardo da Vinci, one is struck by the amazing accuracy of their copies. Considering they did not have photographs, the artists who studied the *Mona Lisa* or the Louvre *Virgin and Child with St Anne* looked long and hard at Leonardo's paintings. Sometimes the copiers get things very wrong, but just as often they get it very close. The many copies of the *Mona Lisa* capture so much of Leonardo's original painting: the pose, the eyes, the landscape. They lack the subtleties of the Leonardo Smile, though, and his softly glowing lighting.

The copies of Leonardo da Vinci reveal to us what the artists thought was important or fascinating about Leonardo's paintings. The artists emphasize certain features while neglecting others. Many artists are intrigued by the way Leonardo groups together the four figures in the *Virgin and Child with St Anne and John the Baptist*. How does he get them all so close together, so entwined? The copies of the Louvre painting grapple with this complex problem of pose and the meanings poses conjure up.

The copies of the lost paintings are more problematic. With the copies of the *Mona Lisa*, there is no argument about the original: it's the painting in the Louvre Museum. With the lost *Leda* or the *Battle of Anghiari*, we can only get *quite* close to Leonardo da Vinci's original. There are copies of them, and contemporary accounts of the pictures, plus Leonardo's own sketches and writings. The rest must be our imagination in piercing together the lost works.

2

Sfumato

But it is Leonardo da Vinci's *sfumato* painterly technique, his brilliant manipulation of oil colours, that makes him so profusely erotic. He used a fine white ground, made of a mixture of lime, lead, turpentine, arsenic and corrosive sublimate. He then put on a reddish colouring, and began working in blue, red and white colours. He worked up the painting through a glazing method similar to that of Flemish painters, and a translucent varnish covered the top layers. The technique of glazes produces those shimmering, glowing effects, where the layers beneath glow through the upper layers. In *The Virgin of the Rocks* this layering of oil paint enhances those contrasts of tone which are so much a part of the Leonardoan magic. As with *Portrait of Ginerva Benci (?),* Leonardo expands the range of tones until he is moving from deep black to brilliant white. Yet he knows how to control the mid-tones brilliantly. You only have to compare Leonardo with, say, Poussin, to see how skillful Leonardo is with tones. Poussin works within a narrow range of tones, and is not particularly subtle. Leonardo, however, is more delicate, tonally, than almost any other painter. Like Vermeer,

Bosch, Van Eyck, Roger van der Weyden and Velasquez, Leonardo inhabits a world of painterly shadows. While the Quattrocento painters in Italy were still painting bright, nearly shadowless paintings, the Early Netherlandish painters were deepening tones to their fullest. Leonardo partakes of this Northern European tonal approach, which is perhaps partly why his paintings look un-Italian at times.

The Leonardo da Vinci painting technique finds its fullest expression in the Louvre *Virgin and Child with St Anne*, despite other artists (possibly) contributing to it. This is an astonishing painting. It is overshadowed on the walls of the Louvre Museum in Paris by the star attraction, the most popular fine art image in history, the *Mona Lisa*. Yet, if you can tear yourself away from the *Mona Lisa*, as few tourists seem to be able to do, you'll find *The Virgin and Child with St Anne* an equally rich, equally mysterious and equally powerful painting as the *Mona Lisa*. There are the colours of the painting, for a start, from that panorama of grey mountains to the warm hues of skin. The enmeshment of limbs is constantly intriguing: how one body grows out of the other, and asserts itself in its own psychic and physical space while retaining a deep connection with each figure. Then there are the facial expressions, ranging from the lamb and Christ, to the Virgin and St Anne. The Virgin smiles with total love at her offspring: she is constantly forgiving of her son. But the most extraordinary element of this painting is St Anne's face. She smiles softly, with absolute knowingness and self-consciousness. She is the wise crone, the Goddess as eternal wisdom, all-knowing, yet hopeful. For, despite knowing everything, St Anne is not saddened: total knowledge does not make her melancholy, as it might. For St Anne, more than her daughter on her lap, knows the fate of the child playing with the lamb. The presence of the lamb emphasizes the sense of sacrifice in the painting, and, though the Madonna clearly knows this, she smiles at her son. There is a forgiveness in the Mother of God, for it is her role as bearer of the Son of Man to be the passive nurturer, to give give give no matter what the cost. She is glorified because she gives up everything: she gives up her life for her child. Christ, meanwhile, has a 'higher' duty, in the eyes of the Church: he is to give up his whole life not for another life, as the

Mother of God does, but for all of humanity. St Anne sees all this religious complexity enriching and, despite the overall sadness and suffering, she smiles.

That smile really is extraordinary. No amount of painterly technique could emulate it, and no amount of critical waffle will take away its fundamental profundity and mystery. You can't boil Leonardo da Vinci's smiling mother of the Mother of Jesus down to nothing. It won't get reduced. It remains solid. It will not be explained away.

In the *Burlington Cartoon*, St Anne is even more mysterious, for she is clearly the dark side of the Virgin. Leonardo da Vinci sets the two mothers side by side, face turned towards each other. They are set up as complimentary beings, and their bodies are fused, so that the Virgin's torso and legs melds with St Anne's torso and legs. In this preliminary drawing, as with *The Adoration of the Magi* and *St Jerome*, the lack of oil paint does not detract for a second from the power of the picture. Unfinished these works may be, but they are no less fabulous for all that. *The Virgin and Child with St Anne and St John the Baptist* is an artwork that continues to beguile people. The lines of black chalk here are as assured as in Leonardo's other drawings, but the heightening with white makes parts of the drawings seem as 'full' or rich as a painting. The Madonna is all glowing light, the shadows on her face are delicate, designed to emphasize her youthfulness and purity. For hers is a blemishless face, open and young, smooth and soft, gently curved and quietly relaxed as she smiles at the two boys.

St Anne's face, on the other hand, is full of darkness. It is all shadows and depth: deep shadows under the cheeks, under the nose, around the sides of the faces and – most prominently – in the eye sockets. St Anne's left eye can be made out: we can see the white of it, but her right eye is dissolved just about completely in shadow. In every way St Anne is the dark side or mirror image of the Madonna. You could place a mirror between the two faces and see each reflected as they are drawn here. Perhaps Leonardo did use a mirror for this cartoon, as he used a mirror often for other things. You can of course read anything you like into St Anne's expression, the way she smiles at her daughter, while her eyes seem to ask if the Madonna understands the full import of her fate. For St Anne points upwards, a gesture which everywhere in Renaissance art denotes divinity and heavenly origins. St Anne seems to be imploring the Virgin to understand that her son comes from Above. The Virgin, meanwhile, understands but chooses to ignore this information, concentrating on the joy of being with her son, of the joy of motherhood. St Anne is the darkness in the drawing, as she is in the Louvre painting. She is the one who reminds the figures present of the divine nature of this situation. While the two mothers are smiling, the two children are solemn: Jesus blesses John with that same childish solemnity we find in *The Virgin of the Rocks* But any *gravitas* the two *Virgin and Child with St Anne* images have comes mainly from St Anne. Smiling though she is, she is deadly serious. Even though she smiles softly – *so softly* in the Louvre painting – she is the rock, the foundation, the solid base of Nature upon which the other figures, and the religion of Christianity, is built. If his horror at the violence of Botticelli's *The Annunciation* is an indicator of his religiosity, Leonardo was vehemently anti-heretical: he despised blasphemy. For all his scientific explorations, Leonardo seems to have had deep religious feelings. It comes out in his paintings. And the means of translation of religious feeling and mystery is his painterly *sfumato* technique, to which we return time after time.

Stendhal wrote of Leonardo da Vinci's 'soft, melancholy tones, full of shadows'.[5] The most common adjective applied to Leonardo's art is 'mysterious'. Each era reinvents Leonardo, or any artist. The most astonishing mythicization of an artist is undoubtedly that of van Gogh, so that van Gogh's works sell for millions and millions of dollars, far exceedingly (nearly) all other artists.

Leonardo da Vinci is and is not typical of the Renaissance. There is no one else quite like him. His art transcends time and place, and becomes a symbol of all that is 'great' and to be strived for in art. His erotic *sfumato* technique stems from his manipulation of oil glazes, similar to those employed by the Early Flemish painters (Jan van Eyck, Roger van der Weyden and Hans Memling, among others).

In his *Treatise on Painting*, Leonardo da Vinci set out his notion of

5 Stendhal: *Histoire de la peinture en Italie*, 1877

the aims of the painter:

> The first intention of the painter is to make a flat surface display a body as if modelled and separated from this plane, and he who most surpasses others in this skill deserves most praise. This accomplishment, with which the science of painting is crowned, arises from light and shade, or we may say *chiaroscuro*.[6]

Here Leonardo da Vinci targets the central aim of painting, of figurative painting in particular: the problem of *illusion*, of producing a three dimensional illusion on a two dimensional surface. Surveying Quattrocento art, from Masaccio to Piero della Francesca, Leonardo might have seen how 'flat' it was, how spaceless, on one level, how devoid of real *shadows*. Leonardo's painterly technique was to deepen shadows to their utmost. In Piero's Arezzo fresco cycle we find very light shadows, shadows that are sometimes so faint Piero's worlds seem lit by an all-over, total illumination. Leonardo, however, cultivates, at length, a deep, shadowy luminescence, so that when he paints lighter parts of the painting, they glow. Leonardo's darks are only one part of the technique: the darker the darks the lighter the lights. Thus, his painted skin glows with a phosphorescence that seems unearthly at times. In fact, the glow is quite 'natural', that is, is naturalistic, for skin really does glow like that – at times. Also, this dark/ light glow fits in with Leonardo's painterly æsthetics.

Always Leonardo da Vinci emphasizes Nature and the natural. The painter, he says, must describe the natural world as accurately as possible. In his notebooks he wrote:

> Therefore painter, you should know that you cannot be good if you are not a master universal enough to imitate with your art every kind of natural form, which you will not know how to do unless you observe them and retain them in your mind...[the painter] should be like a mirror which is transformed into as many colours as are placed before it, and, doing this, he will seem to be a second nature.[7]

Mark Rothko put a parachute over the windows of his New York

---

6 Leonardo: *Leonardo on Painting*, 15. Subsequent quotes are from this edition.
7 Leonardo: *Codex Urbinas Latinus*, Vatican 1270, 33 v.

studio: Leonardo da Vinci recommended doing the same thing in his notebooks:

> If you have a courtyard which you could for your purpose cover with a linen awning, the light there will be good. Otherwise, when you wish to portray someone, do it in dull weather or towards evening, and have the person to be portrayed keep his back to one of the walls of the courtyard. Pay attention in the street towards evening, when the weather is bad, to how much grace and sweetness can be seen in the faces of the men and women. (215)

Leonardo da Vinci is clearly alive to life, for his notebooks are full of the thoughts and insights of someone acutely aware of the world around him – and not just visually. On the visual side, though, he is detailed and loquacious. He speaks again of those faces half-glimpsed in the half-dark, a situation he clearly adores:

> The utmost grace in the shadows and the lights is added to the faces of those who sit in the darkened doorways of their dwellings. Then the eye of the beholder observes the shaded part of the face thrown into deeper shade by the shadows from the aforesaid dwellings, and sees brightness added to the illuminated part of the face by the radiance of the atmospheres. (215)

You see this twilight most obviously in the two *Virgin of the Rocks* paintings, where the oil glazes push the darks back and further back, until some of the shadow areas seem to fade totally to black. Leonardo da Vinci speaks of this visual aspect:

> Because of such increases in the shadows and lights the face acquires great relief, and in the illuminated part the shadows are almost indistinguishable, and in the shaded part the lights are almost indistinguishable. The face depicted in this way acquires much beauty with the increase in shadows and lights. (215-6)

In the late *St John the Baptist*, the background darkens totally. The effect of the figure against blackness is extremely stark, and rarish in Italian Renaissance art. Spanish painters used the black background – such as in Ribera and Zurbarán, or Velasquez in his *Christ Crucified*. Even in his drawings Leonardo da Vinci deepens his shadows. While other painters made do with finely, lightly done drawings, Leonardo kept going over his shapes again and again until he found the right combination of lines. To make sense of his many lines, one drawn on top of the other, he used to prick the paper with a pin, to see the design on the other side. Drawings such as *Virgin and Child with a Cat* use a wash to ink in the tones, so crucial to Leonardo's painterly vision. (Just for his drawings and sketches Leonardo would be among the greatest artists ever lived.)

There is a section of the drawing/ painting *The Adoration of the Magi* which is full of Leonardo da Vinci's shadows and *chiaroscuro*, to the right of the Virgin and Child. Leonardo has worked over this area, beyond the kneeling Magi, where those half-angelic half-demonic figures flit between the onlookers. As Cecil Gould writes: 'Leonardo allowed the strange and marvellous creatures of his subconscious to surface momentarily and mingle with the projections of his geometry.' (47) This is also the area of the *Adoration* where that beautiful figure stands that is thought to be a portrait of Leonardo, much as Botticelli appears in his *Adoration of the Magi* as a figure, again the right hand side of the crowd.

Leonardo da Vinci spoke of the importance of contemplation, of doing nothing but looking, calmly, quietly, meditatively. In his *Precetti* he wrote:

> I have seen shapes in clouds and on patchy walls which have roused me to beautiful inventions of various things, and even though such shapes totally lack finish in any single part they were yet not devoid of perfection in their gestures or other movements.[8]

Sit and look, Leonardo da Vinci advised. He did this himself many times, it seems. In the notebooks he wrote:

> ...our Botticelli said such study was of no use because by merely throwing a sponge soaked in a variety of colours at a wall there would be left on the wall a stain in which could be seen a beautiful landscape. He was indeed right that in such a stain various inventions are to be seen. I say that a man may seek out in such a stain heads of men, various animals, battles, rocks, seas, clouds, woods and other similar things. It is like the sound of bells

8 Leonardo: *Treatise on Painting*, 1956, fol. 62 r.

which can mean whatever you want it to. (L, 201)

Leonardo da Vinci was described thus by Matteo Bandello during the painting of *The Last Supper*:

> It was his habit, as I myself have witnessed and observed on several occasions, to come here in the early hours of the morning and mount the scaffolding, for the *Cenacolo* is somewhat high above the ground; he was accustomed (I say) to remain there brush in hand from sunrise to sunset, forgetting to eat or drink, painting continually. Then he might stay away for two, three or four days without setting hand to it, or he would remain in front of it for one or two hours and contemplate it in solitude, examining and criticizing to himself the figures he had created. I have also seen him (as caprice or fancy took hold of him) departing in the middle of the day when the sun was in Leo from the Corte Vecchia, where he was working on his stupendous clay Horse and he would come straight to Delle Grazie; and he would climb the scaffolding, seize a brush, apply a brush stroke or two to one of the figures, and suddenly depart and go elsewhere.[9]

Here is a picture of Leonardo da Vinci as the archetypal artist, obsessed with his work. An interior monologue goes in his head, which others only get glimpses of. We see the thoughts of Leonardo acted out as he sits gazing at *The Last Supper*, or when he returns for a moment then leaves it again. All the while, we can suppose, he was thinking about the problems each work created.

9 Badello, in Robert Payne, 14.

3

Deep Space

Leonardo da Vinci creates very deep space, deep shadows, sculptural forms, dark tones and glowing lights. His art is 'deep', you might say: artistically, psychologically, emotionally and spiritually.

Leonardo da Vinci created a new sense of space, inaugurating High Renaissance space, and the space that is the basis of much of painting to this day. Frank Stella, the American abstract painter, has the notion of 'working space', which is not to do with perspective, line, atmosphere or flatness, but is about the space the painting makes for itself, the space the artist intends for the painting, a 'space in which the subjects of painting can live' (*Working Space*, 5). Painters before Leonardo had 'accepted the given surface and made the best of it', Stella contends, but Leonardo broke with Quattrocento space and æsthetics. Stella writes:

> Leonardo signals the beginning of painting's attempt to free itself from architecture. The *Mona Lisa* tells us about landscape space, about modelling the human figure, about atmospheric perspective and *sfumato* – all the things that begin to separate sixteenth-century painting from the painting that went before it. But the best news is that the *Mona Lisa* comes in a tidy

package, a marvellous, a manageable rectangle. How wonderful it would be to see it in the Uffizi, in Florence, where it really belongs, rather than in Paris in the Louvre. In the Uffizi it would be a new dawn, a glass house rising above the jagged Levittown of gold altar pieces. In the Uffizi's opening rooms its simple rectilinearity would rest our eyes after their arduous tour around the crazy edges of early Italian painting. (6)

4

The Shock of the New

Really good new art does tend to sweep aside everything that came before it. See an Ingmar Bergman film (*Through a Glass, Darkly,* for instance) and every other film ever made is swiftly forgotten. Bergman's cinema is total art, art that fills up space and time completely, allowing nothing else in its world. It's the same with a really good piece of music, or a really good new painting. Leonardo da Vinci's art does this. With the arrival of Leonardo, the apotheosis of Western art is ushered in; not just the High Renaissance, but all art, ever. Heinrich Wöfflin writes of that much faded but oft celebrated painting, *The Last Supper*:

> An immense fund of new expression is added to art, and although Leonardo does not lose touch with his predecessors, it is the unheard-of intensity of expression which makes his figures appear to have no parallels. (26)

In that serene architectural space, Leonardo da Vinci's version of the Last Supper is full of frenzied emotion. It is a mass of hand gestures, all manner of gesticulations. Peter grabs a knife, Johns swoons, Thomas raises a finger, James is horrified, Andrew (?) raises his hands, and so on. In this panoply of hands and gestures, Leonardo's theories of the relation between gesture and meaning are most dynamically expressed. He had many thoughts on the expressionism of bodies. This is from his notebooks:

> That figure is most praiseworthy which best expresses through its actions the passion of its mind. The movement which is depicted must be appropriate to the mental state of the figure. It must be made with great immediacy, exhibiting in the figure great emotion and fervour, otherwise this figure will be deemed twice dead, inasmuch as it is dead because it is a depiction, and dead yet again in not exhibiting motion either of the mind or of the body. The motions and postures of figures should display the true mental state of the originator of these motions, in such a way that they could not signify anything else.[10]

Seen from a distance, *The Last Supper* looks much better than in close-up. Close to, the decay is saddening. Few other major works by major painters are so decayed. 'At least eight, and perhaps a dozen, separate efforts were made to restore the painting,' writes Robert Payne, 'and inevitably every restoration partook of a further act of destruction. Each time the painting was killed; each time the painting refused to die.' (113)

Johann Wolfgang von Goethe wrote enthusiastically about it, though it was in his time in a better state of preservation, perhaps. The painting is a ghost of its former self. In fact, it seems that Leonardo da Vinci, who knew so much about technical and scientific matters, got his fresco materials very wrong. Other painters did OK with their frescoes – Giotto, Piero, Botticelli. Sadly, Leonardo did not get *The Last Supper* right. But, even in its ghostly, deteriorated state, it is still marvellous.

Michael Levey writes of *The Virgin of the Rocks*, that painting that really does sweep away all that was produced before it. And there was some excellent painting done before Leonardo da Vinci's *Virgin of the Rocks* (Fra Angelico's San Marco frescoes, for instance, or Piero della Francesca's *Madonna del Parto*, or Giotto's *Pietà*, or Simone Martini's Uffizi *Annunciation*). Yet, Levey is right, Leonardo does 'outwork and kill' all other painters, to use J.M.W. Turner's phrase:

10 Leonardo, *Codex Urbinas Latinus 1270, Vatican*, 123 r, in L, 144-6.

> Its realism positively eclipses reality. Its nature is so natural that most other fifteenth-century pictures look stiff and contrived beside it, dry against its liquid atmosphere, harsh against its subtly muted light. And its ambition is tremendous... after such a creative act, art could not be the same again. (M. Levey, 1967, 177)

Heinrich Wöfflin also writes of the startling, innovative nature of Leonardo da Vinci's *The Virgin of the Rocks* 'how entirely unique is a picture like that of the *Madonna of the Rocks* in a company of Florentine Quattrocento Madonnas!' (18). Wöfflin continues:

> Here, everything is new and significant – in motive as well as in treatment: the freedom of movement in details, and the orderly disposition of masses in the whole; the infinitely subtle animation of the forms; the new, painterly, use of light clearly intended to give the figures a strongly plastic effect against the dark ground and, at the same time, to lead the imagination into depth in an unexpected way. (18)

For Robert Payne, 'Of all Leonardo's paintings it is the most visionary', it is a 'a vision, something seen outside of time and outside of space', and we must remember, says Payne, that the painting would originally have been viewed by candlelight, in some dark church interior: 'Candlelight will give a trembling to the figures. The spring will seem deeper, the billowing gown and wings will extend further, and the Baptist will be more at ease when there is more space around him.' (73-75) The idea of an exhibition of Leonardo da Vinci being candlelit is inspiring. How incredible some of his paintings would be if viewed in succession by the flickering light of candles. The light would return the viewer to the shadowy realms of Leonardo's painterly spaces. Candle-light would also evoke the first Leonardo painting, that Medusa he painted to scare his father. Candlelight might imbue the viewer with an atmosphere of mystery so important to Leonardo's work.

Of course, some museums already light paintings dimly, so as not to 'harm' them. Direct sunlight hurts artworks, we're told. But the gloomy lighting also gives the paintings an aura of reverence, as if we are in the presence of something incredible. In the new wing of the National Gallery in London, the curators and designers have done just this with Leonardo. His *Burlington Cartoon* is housed in a small dark space, like the *camera obscura*. The viewer enters the room as if entering a small chapel. The *Cartoon* is framed by paper, then wood, then glass. The lighting suggests awe, and there is a little bench to sit on. The suggestion is that one gasps quietly, 'Wow!', then sits down and contemplates the drawing at length.

Wrongly, perhaps, the *Virgin of the Rocks* in London is placed high on the wall outside the little *Burlington Cartoon* chapel. Of all the paintings in the National Gallery, London, *The Virgin of the Rocks* should be housed in a dark, intimate space. while the *The Virgin and Child with St Anne and the Baptist* cartoon requires brighter lighting, in order to fully appreciate Leonardo da Vinci's immense drawing skills.

Leonardo da Vinci's art is one of the richest there is. You can return to it again and again, and still find new things there. It is not a limited art; its scope is vast. This is partly because it suggests so much. Despite producing a tiny amount of paintings (compared to, say, Turner or Warhol), Leonardo's paintings remain, like the tiny quantity of Vermeers, very inspiring. It is this richness, this sense of expansion, that makes Leonardo fascinating, and so popular with critics and public alike.

5

The Adoration of the Magi

The Adoration of the Magi is worth looking at many times. It is one of those rich artworks that can withstand many visits. Any artwork can have any number of readings, as Roland Barthes says. Leonardo da Vinci's *Adoration*, like all his paintings, gives you a lot of richness to work on in the first place. There are many layers to it, yet each layer can also be seen on the top layer, so to speak. Leonardo makes the deepest layers visible, as well as the upper layers. If the artwork is a lake, with the deep meanings at the bottom, in the dark, unconscious zones, Leonardo makes these visible. He makes mystery visible, as Paul Valéry says.

No matter how deeply you trawl Leonardo da Vinci's *Adoration of the Magi*, you never quite explain away its sense of mystery. The mystery remains present to the end. The drawing *suggests* so much, without, finally, being specific about its content. The meanings it suggests change, softly and subtly, exactly like the play of light over its sublime surface.

There is the mystery of that tree, rising from roots directly above the head of Christ. The tree is clearly the Tree of Life, and Christ is the shaman who will later, as a grown man, become the shaman of his tribe, climbing the cosmic Tree, and bringing back news of the otherworld. Leonardo's picture is also, of course, the World Tree on which Christ is crucified. Significantly, there are angels on either side of the tree trunk, the angels are guardians of the tree, and they also remind us of its miraculous nature.

There is the mystery of the crowds of figures, interweaving, limbs merging into limbs in the shadows. There is the mystery of that background architecture, with its grand steps and arches, worked out so carefully in the sketch for this scene.[11]

The abasement of Balthazar, Caspar and Melchior is total: one of the kings kneels down so low his head nearly touches the ground. The child soaks up this adoration, while the Virgin deflects it with her expression of humility. She is absolutely the centre of the painting, visually, although the child is the centre, spiritually, in the orthodox view.

Early sketches for an *Adoration* show the Virgin doing all the adoring; she kneels with her arms outspread before the child,[12] as in the *Adorations* of Early Netherlandish art. In the *Adorations* or *Nativities* of Fra Filippo Lippi, Piero della Francesca, and the Early Flemish painters, the Madonna holds her hands together in humble prayer before the majesty of the child. In Leonardo da Vinci's drawings, her arms are outspread: her awe at the child below her is also a self-glorification.

The central act is the giving and receiving of the gift of the Magi to the child. It is this portion of the picture that Andrei Tarkovsky used as the title sequence of his last film, *The Sacrifice*.

It is quite right that Oswald Spengler calls the *Adoration* 'the most daring painting of the Renaissance' (155). It depicts a moment of epiphany, where the child's divine majesty is revealed. Here the

11 Leonardo: Study of the Perspective of the Adoration of the Magi, 16.5 x 29cm, pen and ink over metalpoint, with some wash, Uffizi, Florence.

12 Leonardo: Madonna Adoring the Infant Christ, 11.9 x 13.5cm, pen and ink over metal-point, Academy, Venice; Adoration of the Shepherds, 21.3 x 15.2cm, pen and ink over lead-point, Musée Bonnat, Bayonne; Studies for a Virgin Worshipping the Child, pen and lead-point, 19.5 x 17cm, Metropolitan Museum, New York.

deification is enacted, with a host of witnesses, the witnesses being a cross-section of humanity, from the lowly sub-proletariat in the background, around the horses, to the royal figures in the foreground. All are witnesses of *mana*, which Weston La Barre defines thus:

> Mana is a projection of our awe at the spectacle of the "holy", the uncannily unknown, the *mysterium tremendum et alienum*, the unreachable other. Subjectivity experienced, the numinous is taken for an external epiphany of mana. (368)

The 'spectacle of the holy' is a useful term, and Leonardo da Vinci makes a spectacle of the revelation of holiness: there is no other picture like the *Adoration* in Leonardo's art, and indeed, in all Renaissance art. It is one of the few images that is 'unique'. Although this term – 'unique' – is much abused, and means little in our era of advertizing, where everything is 'special', 'fabulous', 'unique', 'wonderful'.

Yet, this is the point: that Leonardo da Vinci makes 'special' or 'miraculous' events or emotions that by his day had become tired and well-used cliches. Before his time, there had already been hundreds, if not thousands, of *Adorations* painted. There had already been hundreds and thousands of religious images made. Leonardo's task, as a religious painter, was to imbue the religious subject matter with the sense of mystery and transcendence that it first had. He has to re-invent the presence of the eternal and the Divine. It's not easy. This is every religious artist's task. Yet he succeeds, and his *Adoration* is once again miraculous and transcendent.

This is the talent of the brilliant painter: to revivify the subject again, to make the world seem miraculous, to make religious events that occurred eons ago fresh and meaningful. This is what the brilliant performer does on stage, makes a work come alive again.

Energy resounds off the surface of *The Adoration of the Magi*. It is an amazingly energetic, even chaotic, picture. As Lionello Venturi said, 'modelling is swept away on a tide of emotion' (1979, 11). Only the lost *Battle of Anghiari* would have had a similar frenetic energy as the *Adoration*.

6

Sexual Surfaces

Like high or intellectual 'erotic art', Leonardo da Vinci's art hides as much as it reveals. Leonardo's paintings are mysterious, difficult to 'penetrate', to use the terminology of pornography. In Leonardo's work, the visible is self-consciously obscured. There are veils which have to be lifted aside, to uncover the mysteries and beauties within. This is the process of eroticism – all tantalizing anticipations – while pornography shows everything at once. Leonardo's art is *occult* in its eroticism: it hides its essence in cloaks of superbly-crafted presence. Something is there, the viewer knows, but it is not readily available, it is not presented in daylight. If the manufacture of high art is a crucial element in its power, then Leonardo's paintings are the most sublimely sensuous of all high art works. The skin on his figures – in the two *Virgin of the Rocks* paintings, for instance, is in one glance like cold marble, then in the next glance like snakeskin, then like living flesh, moving gently, reflecting back the light of the room.

Leonardo da Vinci's painterly surfaces are among the most erotic in all art (one thinks of Jasper Johns with his oil and wax surfaces, or van Gogh with his heavily impastoed surfaces). In Leonardo's art, surface is sublime. Frank Stella says this of Caravaggio's surfaces: the same can be said of Leonardo:

> The second miracle of Caravaggio is the miracle of surface. Skin, flesh, and pigment blend into reality. Painting is acknowledged as an act and as a physical fact, but immediately afterward, almost simultaneously, the presence of the human figure is felt as real, touchably there. (11)

Leonardo da Vinci's figures too have that miraculous sense of *presence*, of actually *being there*. This is what takes the breath away when one contemplates Leonardo. If Vasari is to be believed, people were astonished by Leonardo's works, filing past them in awe when they were displayed. Vasari writes:

> The people, when they beheld the new and living beauty [of Francia of Bologna and Pietro Perugino], ran madly to see it, thinking that it would never be possible to improve upon it. But the works of Leonard da Vinci clearly proved how much they erred, for he began the third style, which I will call the modern, notable for boldness of design, the subtlest imitation of nature in trifling details, good rule, better order, correct proportion, perfect design, and divine grace, prolific and diving to the depths of art, endowing his figures with motion and breath.[13]

As a painter of three dimensional illusions, Leonardo da Vinci has no equal. He does everything painters try to do, and, despite the many lost pictures, and the controversial attributions, he remains *the* Western painter. He is more 'superreal' than the Superrealists or Photorealists (Estes, Goings, Close), he is more 'surreal' than the 'Surrealists' (Dali, Magritte, Tanguy, Delvaux, Breton, Buñuel), he is more 'expressive' than the Expressionists (Kirchner, Jawlensky, Mueller, Pechstein), he is more 'naturalist' than the Naturalists or 'Realists' (Courbet, Manet), he is more 'decadent' and 'symbolic' than the Decadents and Symbolists (Moreau, Redon, Böcklin, Rops), he is more 'baroque' than the Baroque artists (Pozzo, Bernini, Caravaggio), more 'neo-classical' than the Neo-Classicists (David, Canova, Mengs), more 'mannerist' than the Mannerists (Vasari, Rosso, Parmigianino, Pontormo).

In eroticism, *nearly* seeing the erotic is the key experience. People

13 Vasari, *Lives*, quoted in R. Goldwater, 97.

don't want to see sex, says Paul Shrader, the American filmmaker, they want to nearly see sex. And people speak of (partially) clothed bodies being more erotic than naked ones. Eroticism trades on glimpses of the body, on fragments of scenes being revealed. Leonardo is the master of such erotic glimpses. As Paul Valéry wrote of Leonardo in a famous essay: '[h]e feels a desire to picture the invisible wholes of which he has been given some visible parts.' (54)

7

The Unknown

The innnerness or interiority that Leonardo da Vinci depicts has been the province of poets for centuries. It is the unknown, dark, nighttime, inner space of poetry, symbolized by the night, by stars, blackness, and infinite spaces. Novalis, the German Romantic poet, wrote:

> Toward the Interior goes the arcane way. In us, or nowhere, is the Eternal with its worlds, the past and future...The seat of the world is there, where the inner world and the outer world touch...The inner world is almost more mine than the outer. It is so heartfelt, so private – man is given fullness in that life – it is so native. (*Pollen and Fragments* , 503).

Leonardo da Vinci reaches the innerness that Max Beckmann, the German Expressionist painter, spoke of: it was Beckmann's goal to reach that invisible realm and to paint it. Leonardo does this, and marvellously.

The figure of the angel is a key element in Leonardo da Vinci's depiction of the 'invisible'. The angel, as Rilke noted, is that presence that can move between this and the Otherworld, between light and dark, between the living and the dead, between Heaven and Earth. Leonardo's angels are the most terrifying figures in Renaissance art. They are human and more-than-human, they are softly smiling, they are sunken in shadow, they are sumptuously androgynous, both male and female, and more than either, like the divine being of alchemy. Leonardo's angels are at the height of their mystery in *The Adoration of the Magi*, a truly magnificent drawing, and so frightening in its inexplicableness, its miraculous ability to hypnotize the viewer, its astonishing power and frenetic energy. Leonardo's angels move amongst humans in that shadowy zone below the tree. It is a vision of humanity in a whirlpool of religious energy, the focus of which is the epiphany of the Virgin and Child, who sit so calmly still in the centre. As Robert Payne writes:

> A bomb is dropped. Everything is uprooted and hurled into the air... There has been an explosion of spiritual energy, and the people are jolted, alarmed, terrified, happy, wildly joyful, and swept outside of themselves by the appearance of the Virgin and Child... In Leonardo's *Adoration* we are made aware that an event of unprecedented and incalculable importance is taking place and the people are excited beyond measure. (36-37)

In the two *Virgin of the Rocks*, the Leonardoan angel appears at its most voluptuous. The sketch of Leonardo's angel is extraordinary in itself, but when Leonardo's unsurpassed graphic abilities are combined with his deeply erotic *sfumato* lighting and oil technique, the result is dazzling. Leonardo's painted angel is, to use Spengler's term, 'indescribable' (154). So the art critic moves into superlative overload, as Walter Pater or John Ruskin often did, and comes out with a load of over-lyrical hyperbole. The gushing style of some art historians helps to emphasize the erotic nature of art and art criticism.

Leonardo da Vinci's angels certainly have a 'terrifying ethereality', to use a term typical of the more Romantic branches of art criticism. Leonardo's 'genius' is more than a thaumaturgic ability to manipulate paint and tone and colour, but this does help. The American painter Adolph Gottlieb wrote: '[p]aint quality is meaningless if it does not express quality of feeling.'[14] Gottlieb announces again the connection between the materiality of painting and the emotionalism of it. Certainly Leonardo knows how to modulate expressiveness and feeling through

14 A. Gottlieb in *The New Decade*, Whitney Museum of Art, New York 1955, 36.

paint and line. Nowhere is this more apparent than in the famous Leonardo Smile. Many painters attempted the Leonardo Smile – Correggio, Luini, Sodoma, Boltraffio, Solario and many anonymous artists – but only Leonardo could make it work successfully.

Illustrations

Some of the immortal faces created by Leonardo da Vinci.

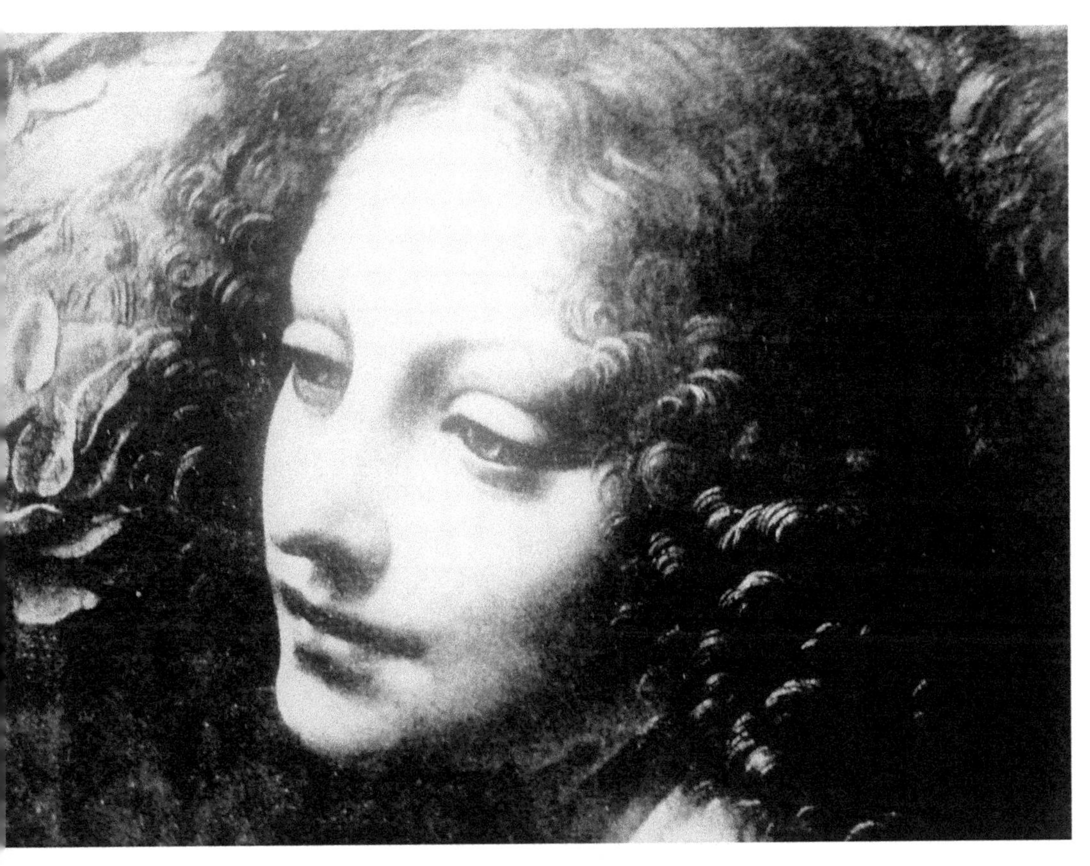

Some of the immortal faces created by
Leonardo da Vinci on the following pages.
Above: the angel from The Virgin of the Rocks

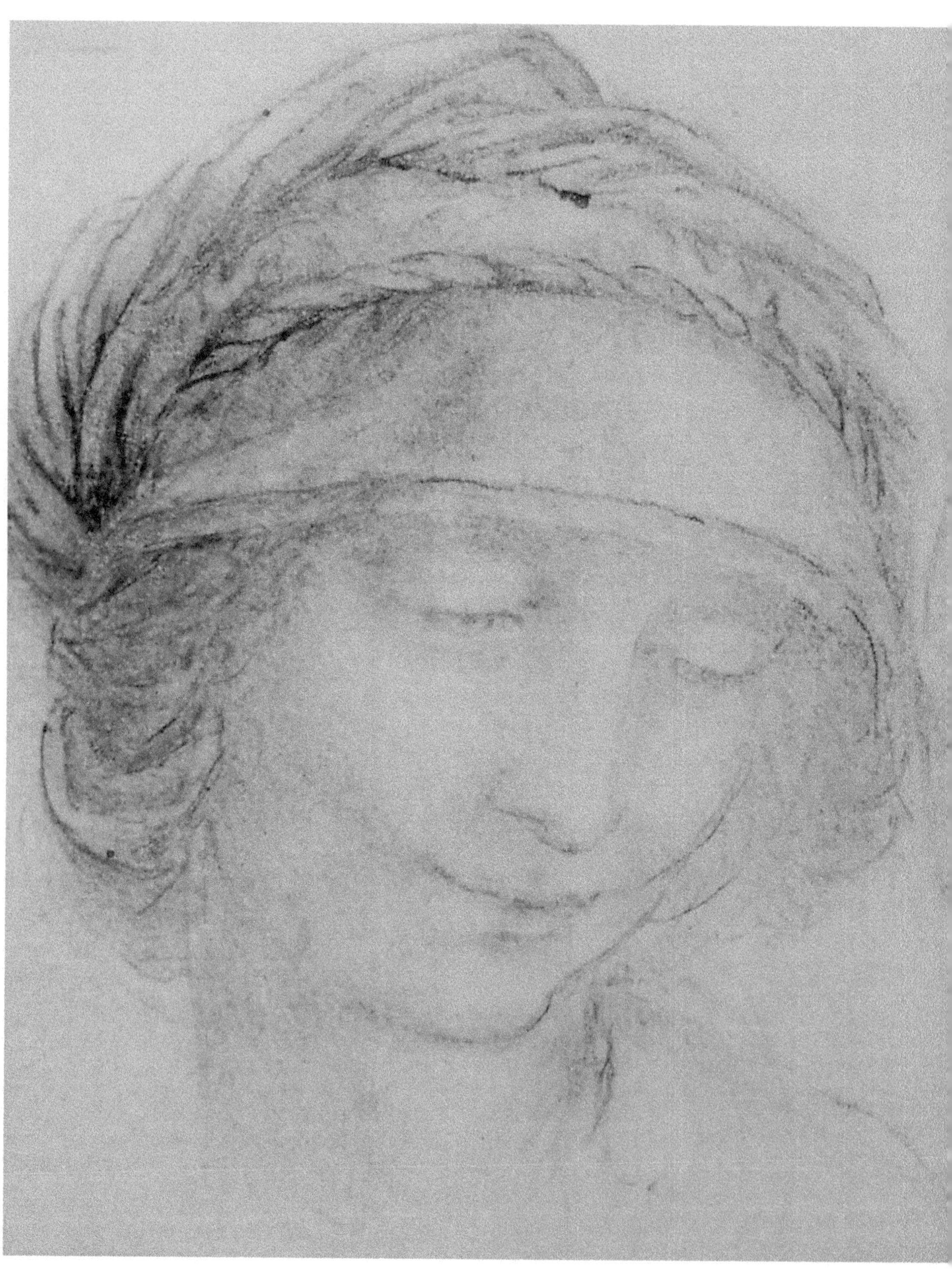

Leonardo, Study for The Virgin and Child With St Anne

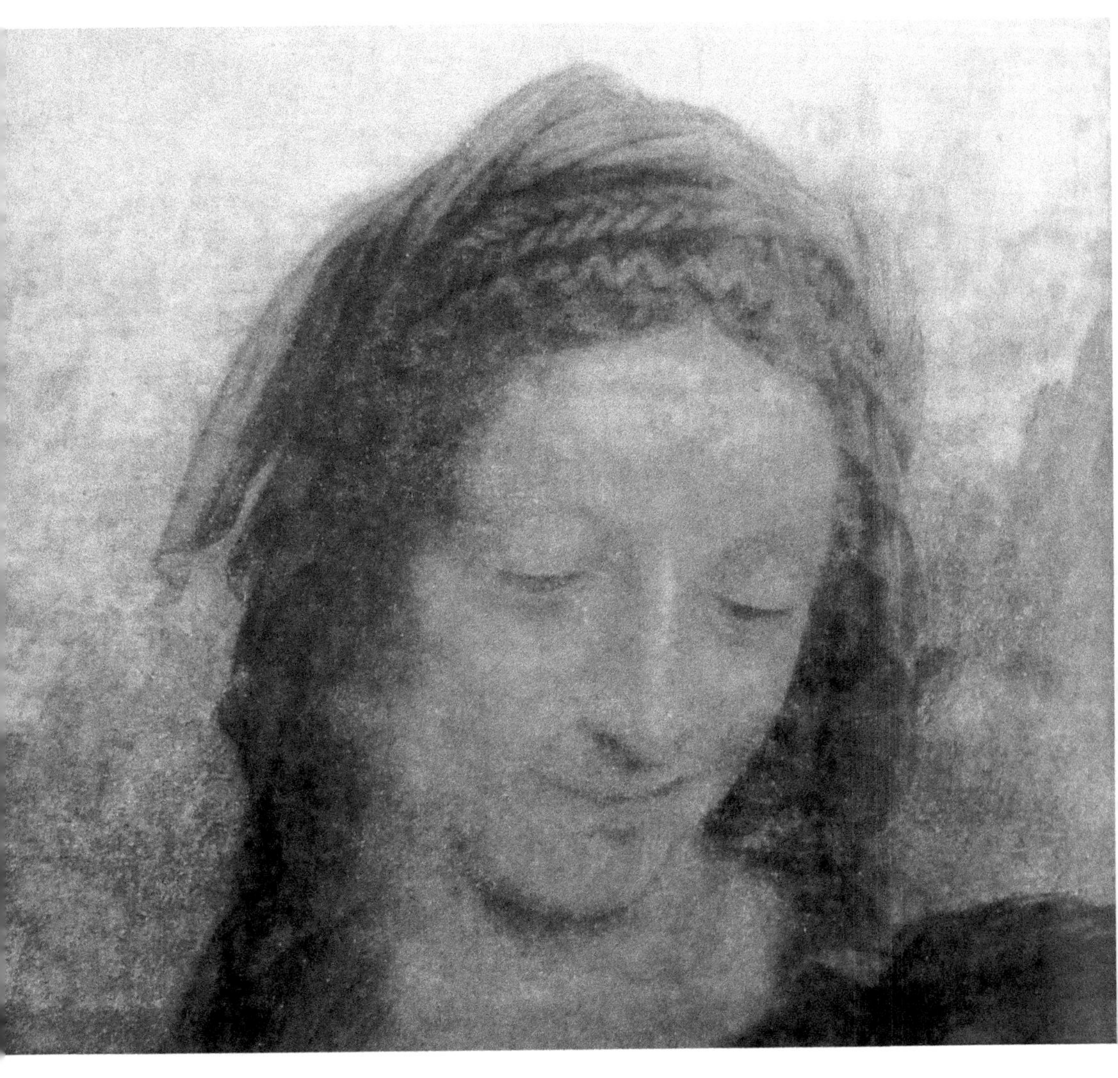

Leonardo da Vinci, Head of St Anne, from The Virgin and Child With St Anne, Louvre Museum

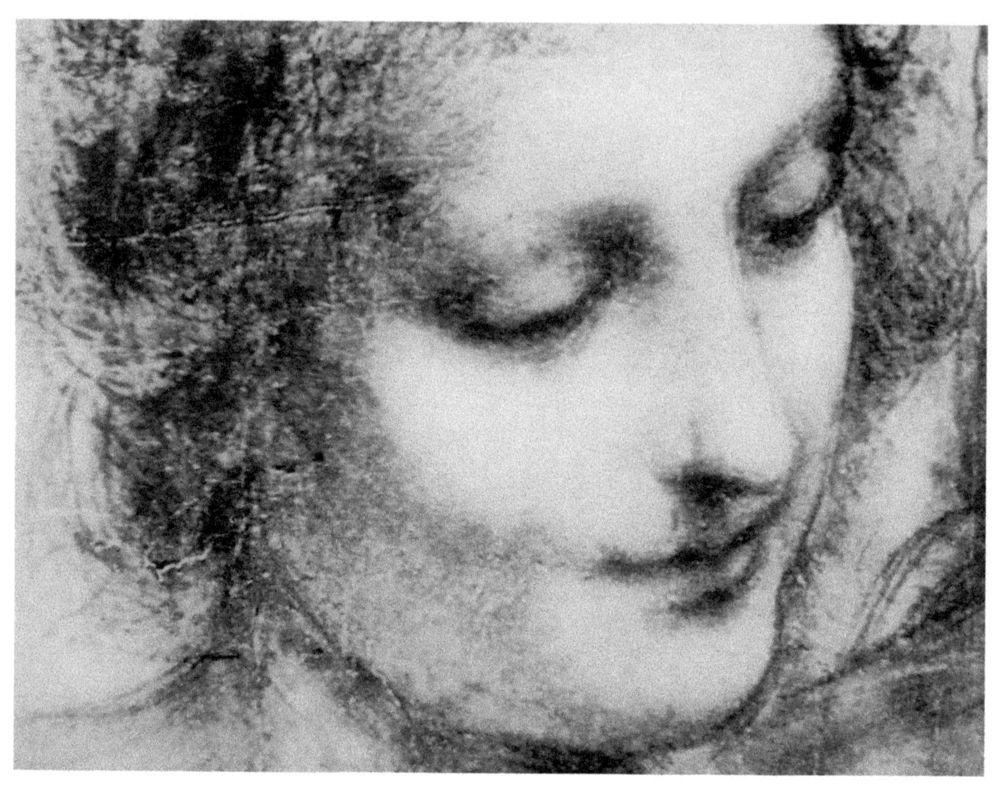

The Head of the Virgin Mary
from The Virgin and Child With St Anne in London

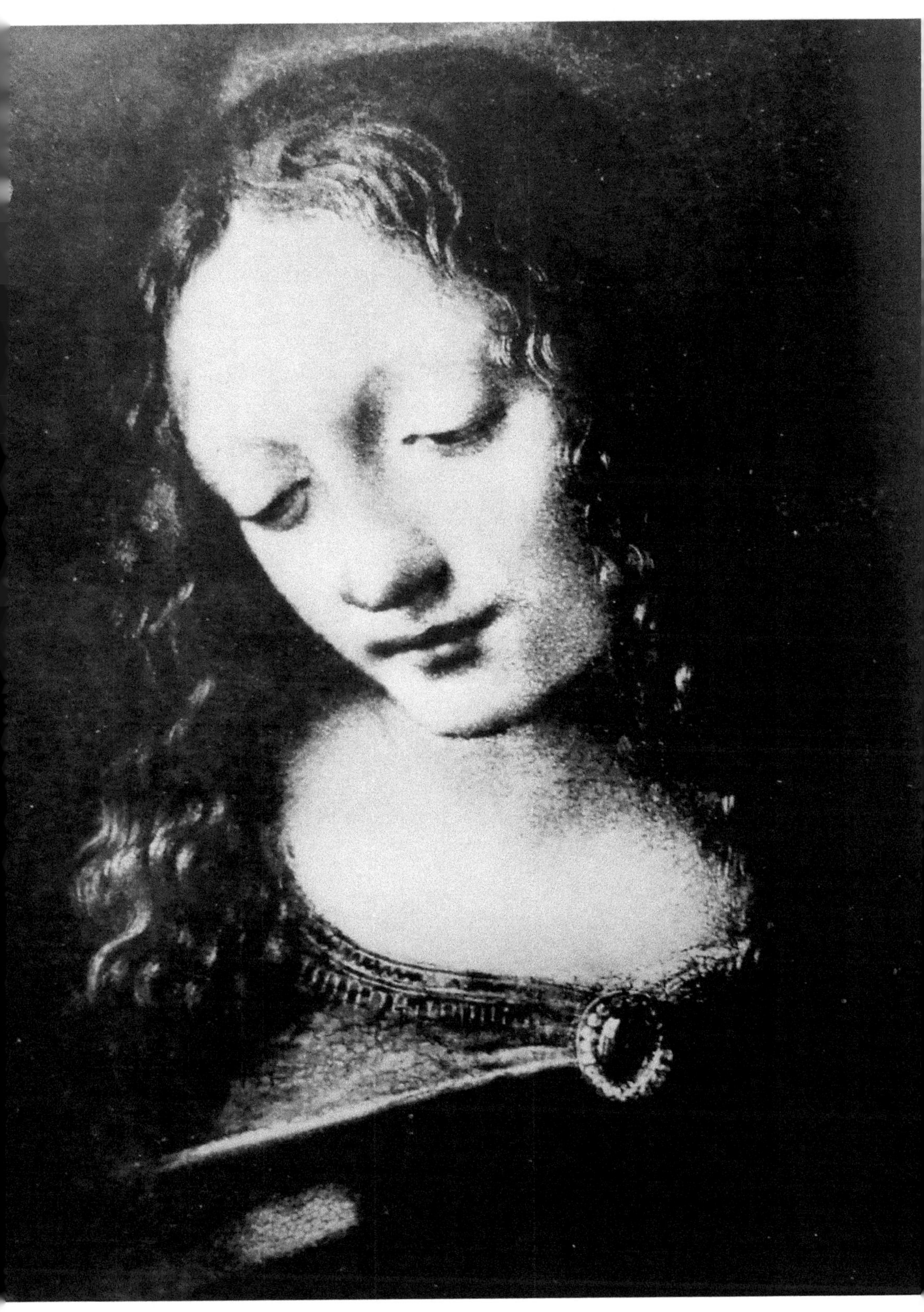

Head of the Virgin Mary from Leonardo's Paris Virgin of the Rocks

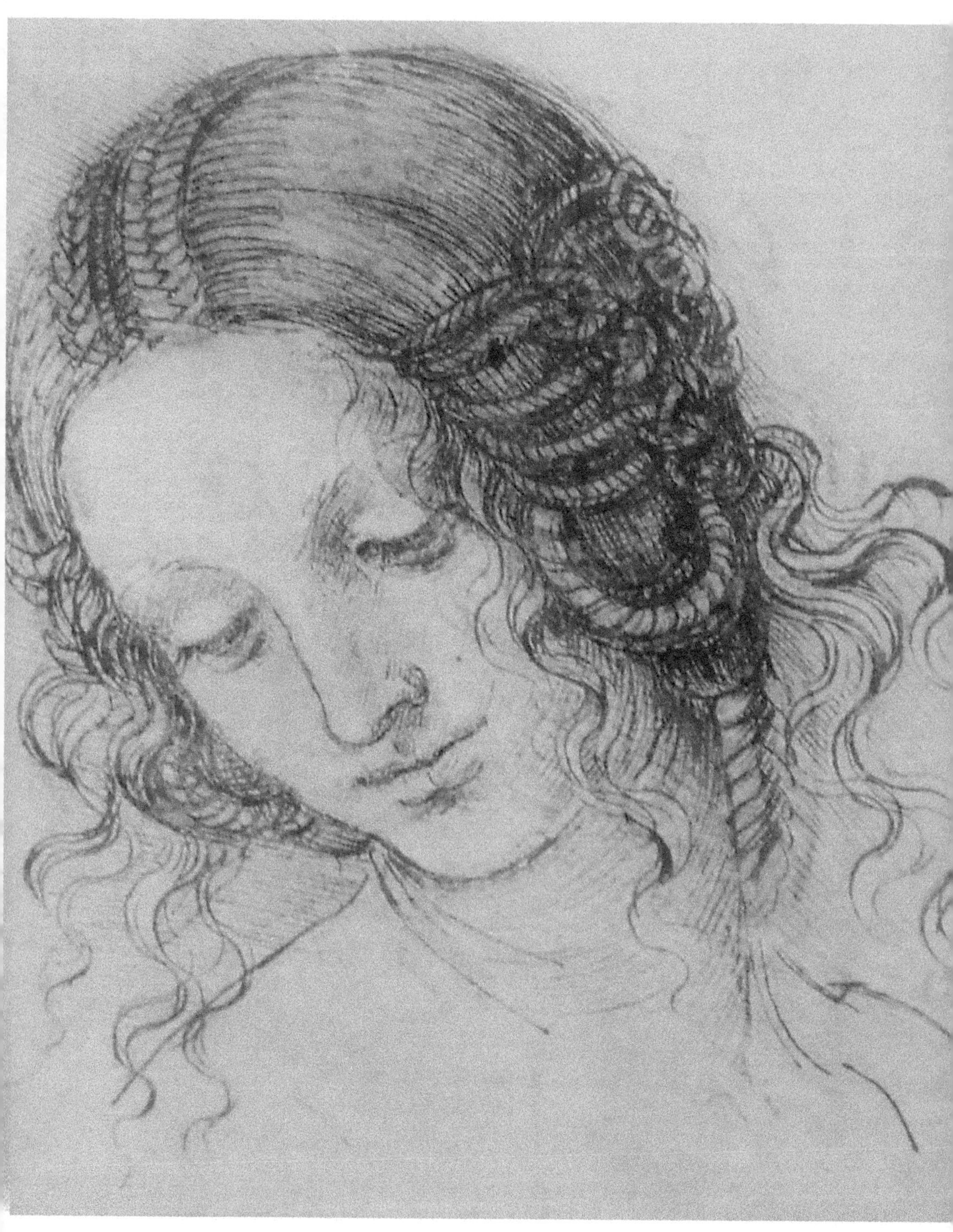

Leonardo, Study For the Leda and the Swan

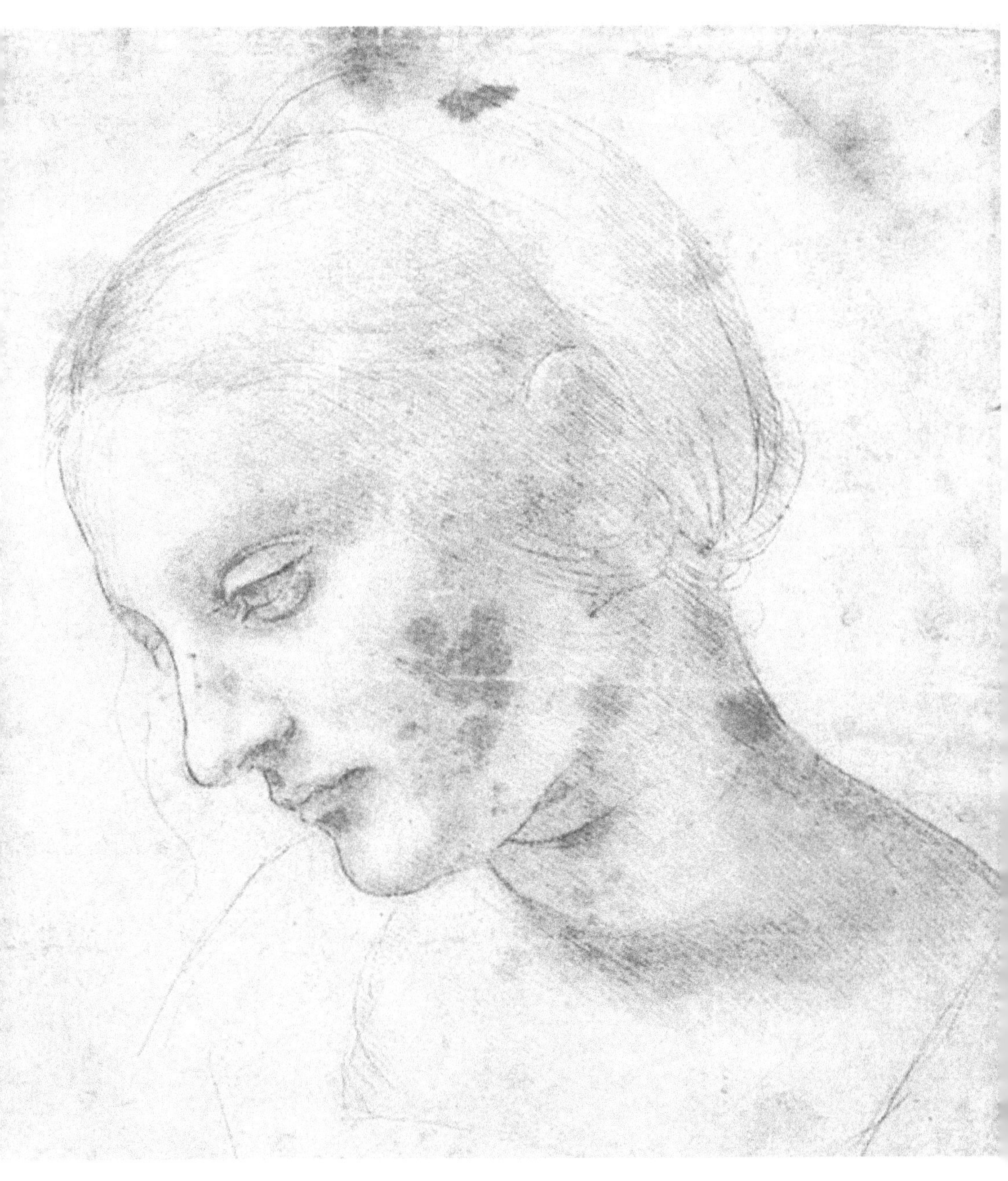

Leonardo da Vinci, Study of a Woman's Head, 1490,
Louvre, Paris

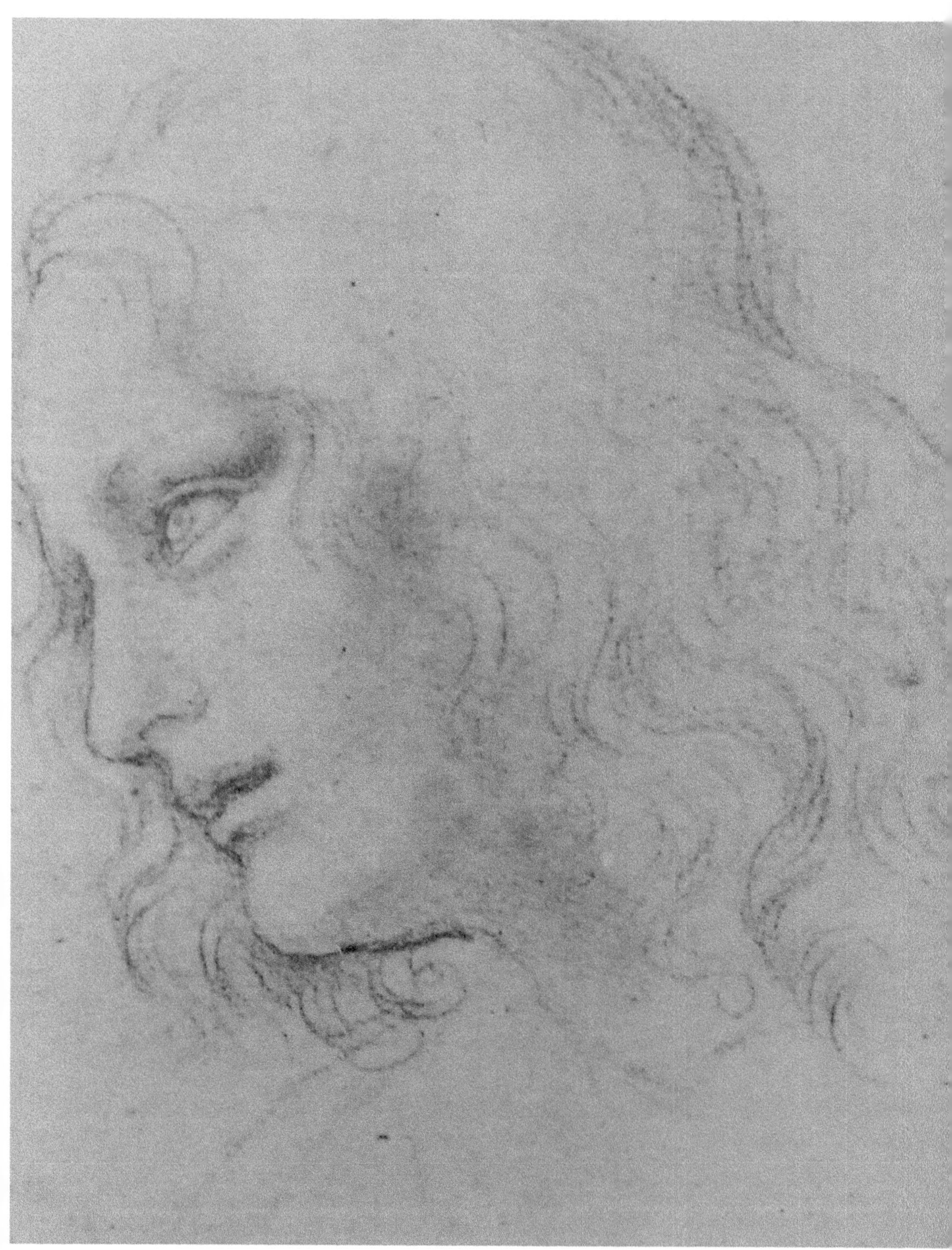

Leonardo, study for The Last Supper

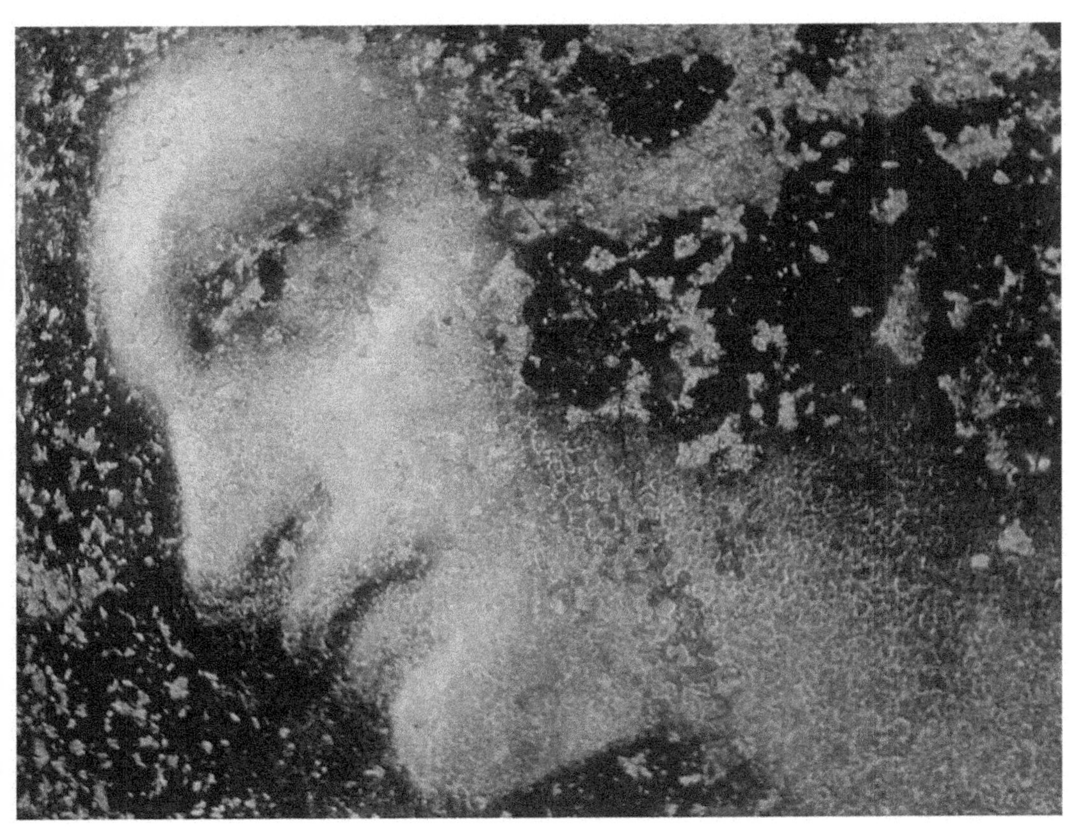

Leonardo da Vinci, The Last Supper, detail

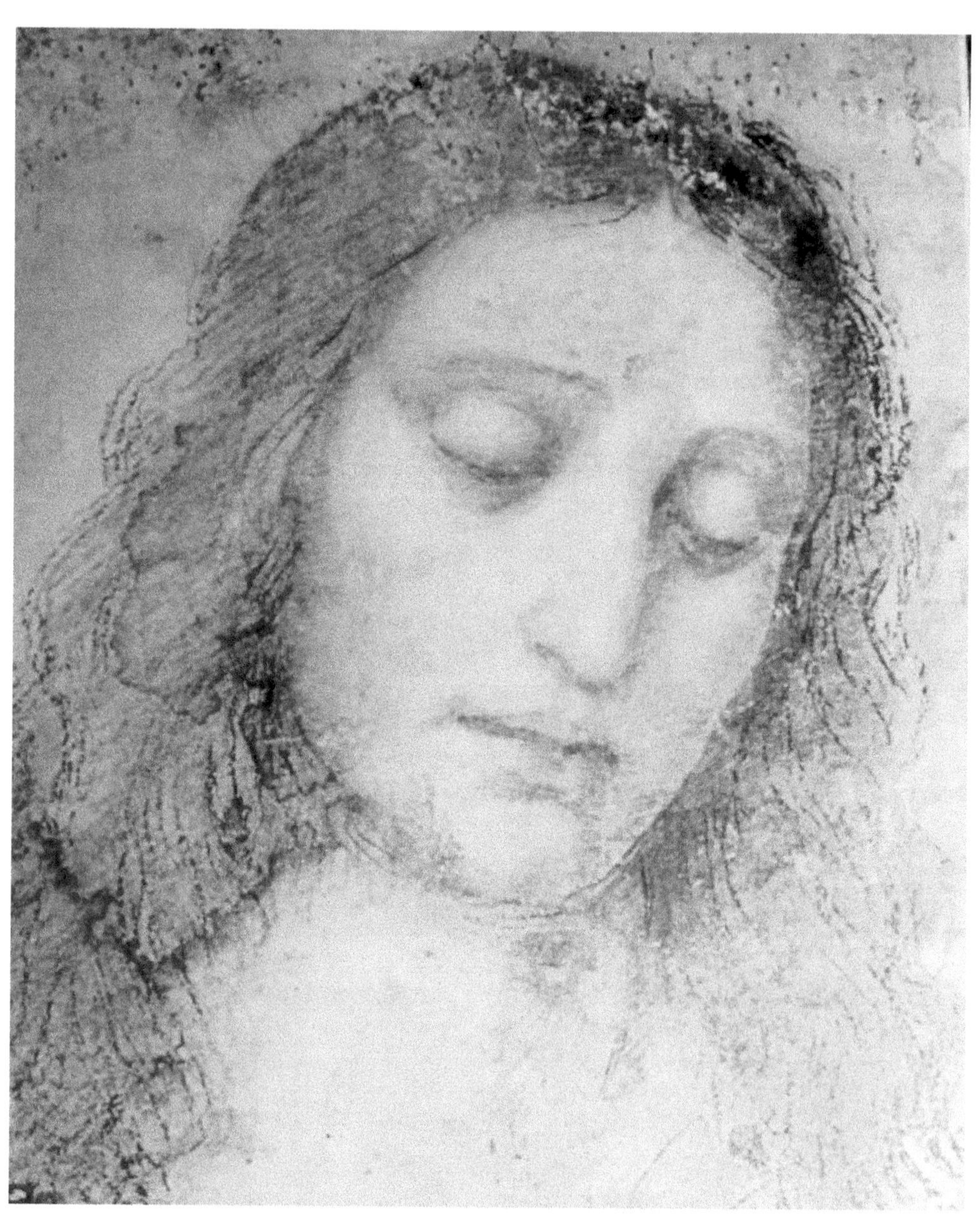

Leonardo da Vinci, Study For The Last Supper,

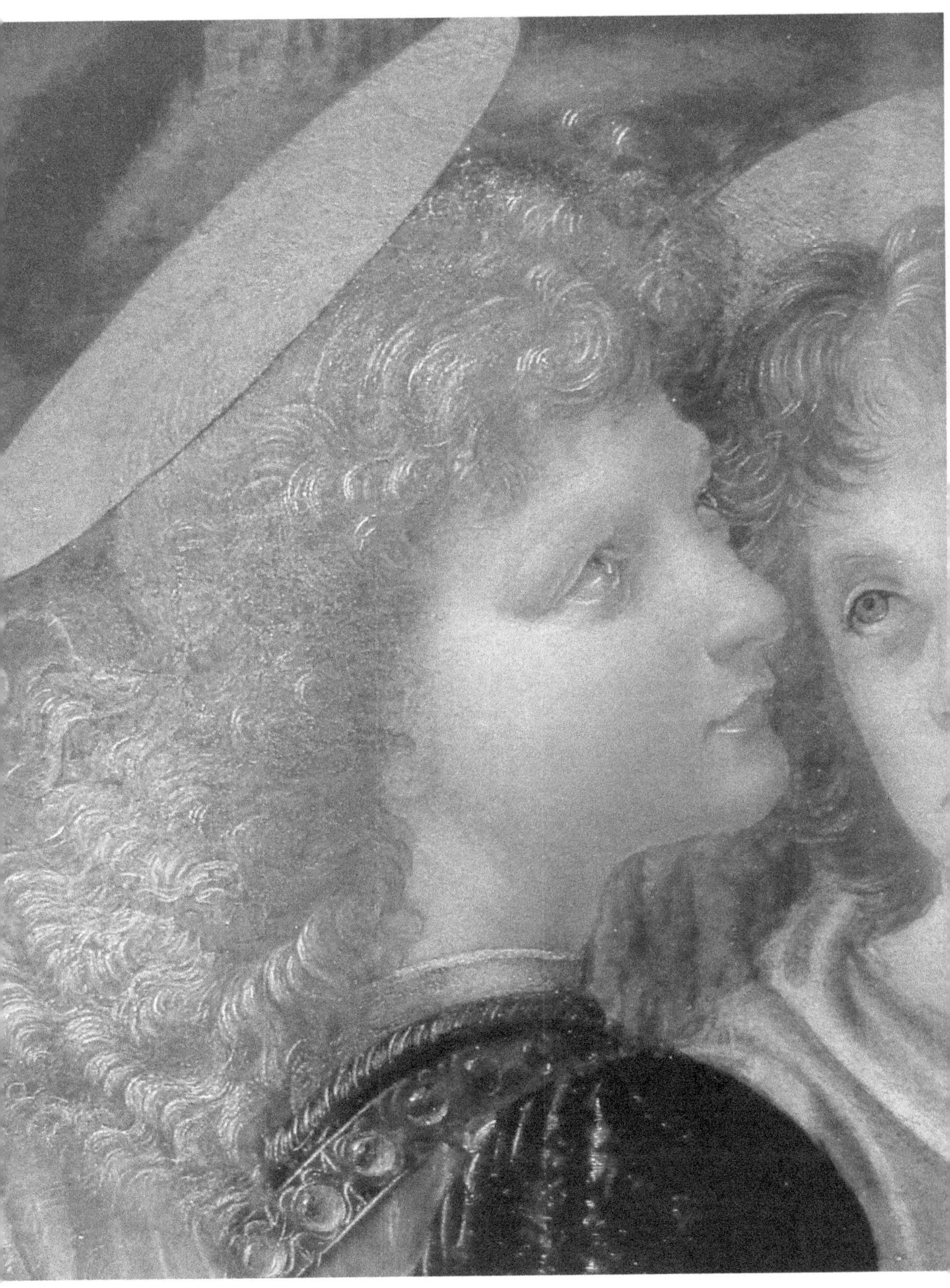

The angel in Andrea del Verrocchio's The Baptism of Christ, painted by Leonardo

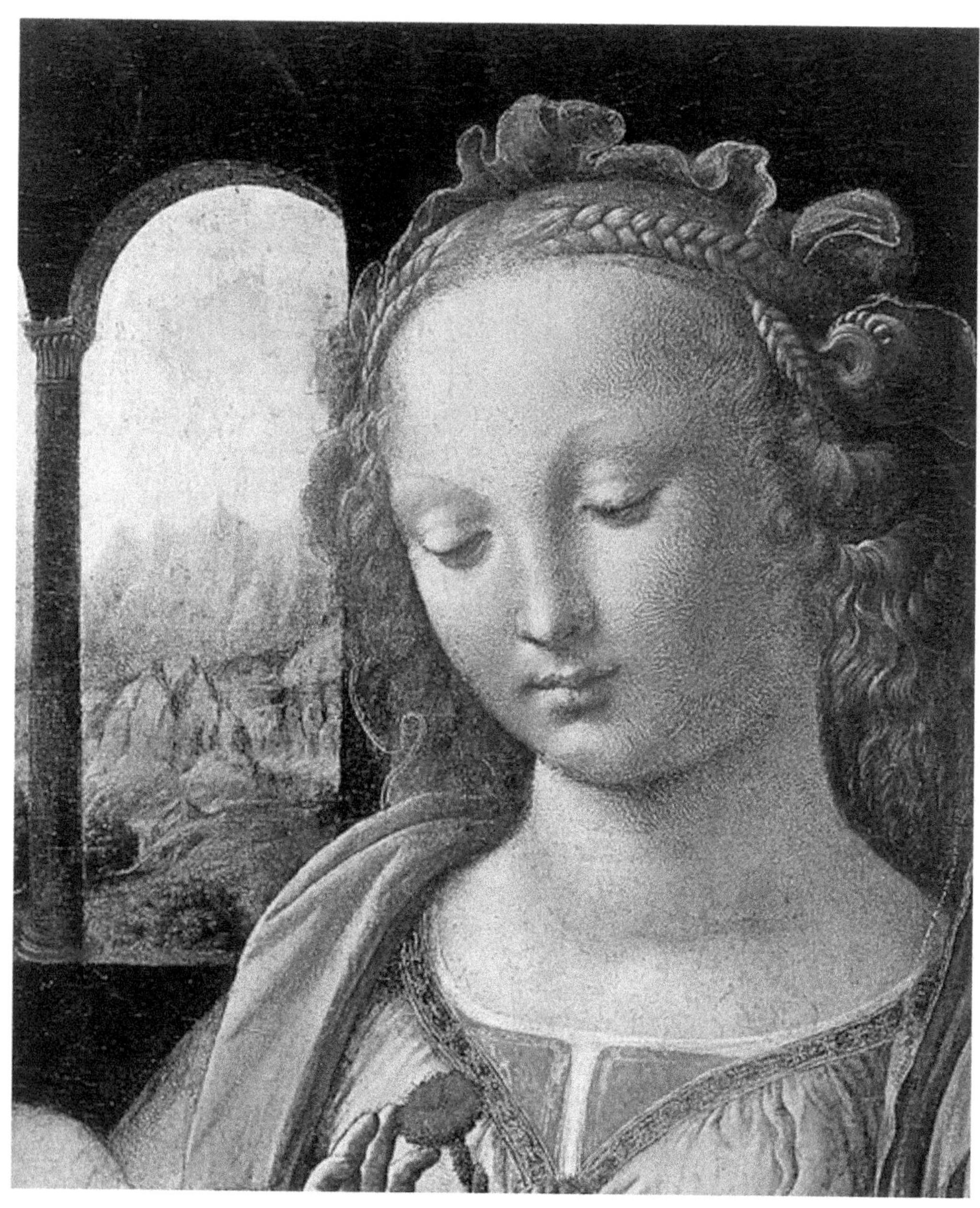

Leonardo da Vinci, Madonna of the Carnation, detail

8

Renaissance Sexuality

Imagine a nude painting of the Blessed Virgin Mary. The idea, to patrons, critics and consumers of Renaissance and mediæval art is shocking, as well as blasphemous. A naked Mother of God, it is unthinkable in terms of Renaissance and mediæval painting. There is a cult of the Virgin baring one breast, to suckle the baby Jesus, but the sexualization of the Madonna occurred in a different way. In Leonardo da Vinci's art, the Blessed Mother of God is heavily eroticized, but in a way that works within the strictures and structures of Renaissance art. His eroticization of women occurs within patriarchal discourse, and thus is protected, and glorified.

It is worth noting some of the elements of Neoplatonism in Renaissance art, because Neoplatonism is the magical and philosophical system that underlies the humanist renascence of Classical art. The hermetic doctrines of Neoplatonism come through Gnosticism, and are expounded by Renaissance figures such as Marsilio Ficino, Cornelius Agrippa and Pico della Mirandola. The basic tenet is that 'all is one', that what happens on earth is reflected by what happens in the heavens, and vice versa, that everything is related by a system of 'correspondences'. Humanity is at the centre of this new humanism, as the alchemist and philosopher Agrippa noted in his *De occulta philosophia* 'Man has in himself All that is contained in the greater world'.[1]

The Renaissance and Neoplatonic humanist worldview has remained the basis for art since the Renaissance, and the basis for much of philosophy – certainly the philosophy of the Romantic, religious, subjective, emotional kind, as found in Nietzsche, Kant, Freud, Jung, Shelley, and most of the 'great' art historians – Berenson, the Warburg school, Ruskin, Pater, Fry, etc. Renaissance Hellenic hermeticism was a philosophy created for and by the educated upper classes, and 'man', i.e., the white bourgeois male, the one depicted in Leonardo's famous drawing of *The Proportions of the Human Body*, was at the centre of the new world system.

The rise of the popularity of Greek and Classical mythologies in the Renaissance was both a cause and an effect of the new person-centred religion. God was displaced, though Catholic imagery lived side by side with 'pagan' images. The Renaissance, with its 'Neoplatonic mysticism and Aristotlean intellectualism'[2] paved the way for the movement into 'rationalism' and the 'age of reason' and 'enlightenment'. It allowed for an increasing prevalence in art of erotic imagery, so that high art could be more openly erotic in its treatment of 'high art' subject matter. Depictions of the Goddess Venus are thus an indicator or barometer of the increasing eroticization of the nude in Western 'high art', from Correggio, through Titian and Veronese to Manet, and beyond Manet to Rodin, Matisse, Picasso, and later, Allen Jones, Hans Bellmer and Tom Wesselman.

The erotic feelings the Virgin aroused were sublimated, or directed at different targets, in particular the Goddesses of the Classic world: Venus, Diana, Aphrodite, Circe. Here, in the depiction of the Classic goddesses, painters could focus on the female form, justified by the subject being one from mythology. Leonardo da Vinci painted a few mythological figures, the pleasure-loving figure of Bacchus, but the

1 Quoted in J. Ferguson: *An Illustrated Encyclopaedia of Mysticism*, 9.
2 E.H. Gombrich, *Symbolic Images*, 179.

most erotic was undoubtedly his *Leda*, now lost.

Greek mythology enabled Renaissance artists to use images and themes of a wilder, stranger and more erotic nature than the images, themes and codes of Christianity. While Catholicism suppressed sex at every opportunity, only allowing it to express itself in figures such as Mary Magdalene, who had to be portrayed as an eternal penitent, Greek mythology was fully human. The Greek gods and goddesses are playful, stupid, silly, deceitful, jealous, angry, wily, poetic, ignorant and erotic, quite unlike Jehovah or Jesus. Greek myths were subjects in which painters and sculptures could let themselves address erotic issues. Leonardo, however, painted many more images drawn from Christian and monotheic sources than from Classical mythology, unlike, say, Peter Rubens or Titian, who dove gladly into mythological and historical painting.

The myths, drawn from Ovid, Plato, Apuleius and others, contain many erotic moments, such as Zeus/Jupiter making love to Leda in the form of a swan, or Apollo pursuing Daphne – to escape him, she changed into a laurel tree (this was a favourite of Petrarch's), or Actaeon seeing Diana naked, or Pygmalion falling in love with his statue of Venus which comes alive, a subject one imagines who have attracted Leonardo da Vinci, with its vivid expression of the ambiguous relation between art and reality, or the god Zephyr chasing Chloris: when he embraces her, flowers spill from her mouth, as depicted in Botticelli's *Primavera*.

The New Testament stories do not allow for such wild eroticism as the Greek and Roman myths. Artists went back to the Old Testament to find erotic themes. Eroticism is found in many of the depictions of Adam and Eve, for instance, which is of course that paradisal state where sexual awareness was absent. In the Renaissance, Adam and Eve coyly cover their genitals. In depictions of Adam and Eve – in Cranach, Angelico, Dürer and others,[3] the genitals are covered or turned away from the viewer, yet that original Edenic state of pre-sexuality is the one state, surely, in which the body could be openly

3 A. Dürer: *Adam and Eve*, 1504, engraving, 25.2 x 19.4cm, Victoria & Albert Museum, London; and *Adam and Eve*, 1507, Prado, Madrid.

displayed. For the pre-sexual Paradise was where life was at its height, at its most holy, in the state God had planned. The myth of Paradise is tied up with notions of childhood, of the Golden Age, that time, *in illo tempore, ab origine*, when everything was wonderful. Paradise is a state of pure desire and pure gratification, where nothing stops the flow of desire, no responsibilities of any kind, the perfect state of childhood, free from social, familial, political, economic, racial and nationalist tensions. Interestingly, it is not usually Paradise that is depicted, as in Lucas Cranach's wonderful vision of Eden in his *The Golden Age*, where the couples dance, swim, eat and make love but the Fall, the moment when Adam and Eve eat the apple, as in Adriaen Isenbrandt's painting, or the moment when they are expelled from Paradise by the Archangel, as in the background of Fra Angelico's *Annunciations*, or as in Masaccio's famous fresco, where Adam and Eve sob and moan.[4]

Leonardo da Vinci does not portray nudity in his paintings. The only nudes in his *oeuvre* are the Baby Jesus, in *The Virgin of the Rocks* and in his drawings. What Leonardo's paintings offer us instead are teasing, tantalizing hints at nudity, in, for instance, *St John the Baptist*, where the androgynous saint hugs his robes to his chest, while exposing his shoulder and part of his chest, looking coy the while, like a Hollywood pin-up, the saint as movie starlet in a promo photo.

In other paintings, Leonardo da Vinci presents glimpses of skin, as in the *Ginevra Benci* portrait or the various *Madonna* paintings, where the slender, swan-like neck and alabaster skin of the chest is lovingly painted. The area of the neck and upper chest and shoulders are eroticized in Leonardo's painting, providing a focus for the viewer, as this part of the paintings glows with that pale phosphorescence Leonardo made his own.

St Jerome is nearly naked, which is befitting this image of a beleaguered saint. But the strangest nude (or nearly nude) figure in Leonardo da Vinci is the late work, *Bacchus*, which was originally a *St John the Baptist* in the wilderness image. Christian became pagan around 1683-95, when the jungle cat skin and the crown of vine leaves

4 Masaccio: *The Expulsion of Adam and Eve*, 1424-5, fresco, 208 x 88cm, S. Maria del Carmine, Cappella Branacci, Florence.

were added; the hair was changed, and the cross, feature of so many *St John the Baptist* paintings, became a thyrsus.

If he had painted nudes, one imagines they would be something like the *Adam and Eves* of Lucas Cranach and other Northern Renaissance painters, nudes that are not aware of their bodies being portrayed as spectacle. Yet Cranach's nudes, like the imaginary ones of Leonardo da Vinci, would surely be aware of their nudity too. Indeed, surely any Renaissance nude must be aware of its nakedness, otherwise it could not be a 'Renaissance' artwork. A mediæval nude might be able to display itself without erotic self-awareness, but not a Renaissance nude, for Renaissance art is always aware of itself *as art*. It knows what it is doing. And this is especially so with Leonardo's art. Leonardo's paintings are very self-aware texts, aware of being looked at much as the Virgin Mary casts her eyes downwards in humility and is acutely aware of being looked at. The Archangel Gabriel stares intently at the Virgin, but the Virgin does not return his gaze, as women are not supposed to return the male gaze in patriarchal cultures, and especially in Islamic countries. Indeed, women are not allowed to look at all, being veiled in some places. Men look, women are not allowed to look. In the meeting of two potential lovers in the movies, writes Richard Dyer:

> We have a closeup of him looking off camera, followed by one of her looking downwards (in a pose that has, from time immemorial, suggested maidenliness). Quite often, we move back and forth between these two close-ups, so that it is very definitely established that he looks at her and she is looked at.[5]

We see this downward glance of the woman throughout Western art, most especially in that moment of spiritual rape, where the 'handmaiden of the Lord', the Virgin Mary, conceives the Lord Jesus Christ in her womb, as depicted in Leonardo da Vinci's famous Louvre *Annunciation*, and in *Annunciations* by Botticelli, Fra Filippo Lippi, Fra Angelico, Andrea del Sarto, Roger van der Weyden and Gerard David, among others.

What the *Mona Lisa* does, then, on one level, is to break the law of

5 Richard Dyer: "Don't Look Now", *Screen*, vol. 23, 3/4, 1983.

being 'looked-at', and she looks at the viewer. Whereas the women in Leonardo da Vinci's *Portrait of a Woman with an Ermine* and *Portrait of Ginevra Benci* look away from the viewer, the *Mona Lisa* confronts the viewer head-on. Indeed, the very direct stare or look of the *Mona Lisa* has been one of the aspects of the painting that has most unnerved people down the years.

There is deep sexism in the Christianity, embedded at the core of this highly syncretic religion. At the heart of Christian theology is the Fall, where it is the woman who picks the apple and offers it to Adam. From the beginning, in the Judæo-Christian tradition, it is the woman who makes men 'fall'. In some depictions, the sexism is doubled, by having the serpent shown as a snake-woman – the torso of a woman, the legs, like those of a mermaid. The symbol of the half-woman half-fish, still in use today,[6] is another manifestation of patriarchal people's projection of their sexual fears onto women, so that what lies 'below the waist' is feared and objectified as something slimy and fishlike, something dark, from the depths of the unconscious, which is the sea. This is the kind of eroticism we find in Leonardo da Vinci's art, a 'dark' sexuality, as embodied by sprites, feys, sirens, Goddesses, serpents, spiders and panthers. The legs of the Virgin and St Anne fuse in Leonardo's two *Virgin and Child with St Anne* images, the Louvre painting and the London cartoon, becoming like a mermaid's tail. The mermaid appears sculpted on mediæval churches, some of the mermaids expose their genitals, like the *sheila-na-gig* figure, which again fuses sacred and profane, spiritual and sexual, desire and fear.[7]

The strangest image of Paradise is undoubtedly Hieronymous Bosch's *The Garden of Earthly Delights.* Bosch is one of the few artists who can be as fantastical as Leonardo da Vinci, although for pure strangeness, there is no one to touch Leonardo. Bosch's *Garden* is a veritable banquet of fantasy, power, racism, sexism, Freudianism, death, violence and outrageous juxtapositions. 'Art is never chaste' said

6 See the depiction of the Mary Magdalene in the wilderness sequence of *The Last Temptation of Christ* (Martin Scorsese, 1988, USA).
7 See Anthony Weir & James Jerman: Images of Lust: *Sexual Carvings on Mediaeval Churches*, B. T. Batsford, 1986, 48ff.

Picasso, 'if it's chaste it isn't art'.[8] In Bosch's case, as with Leonardo, this is certainly true.[9] There is nothing chaste about Bosch's vision of Paradise, no attempt at cloaking the explosion of desire. No wonder Bosch is a favourite of Surrealists, for they too allowed desire free rein. The Surrealists and their guru, Freud, also loved Leonardo for similar reasons, for his depictions, or rather, *suggestions*, of a dark eroticism that veers between fear and desire.

The Old Testament provides other opportunities among Renaissance artists for sensual scenes, among them Juliet, who decapitated Holofernes after making love with him, Samson and Delilah, Sodom and Gomorrah, etc. Like Salome with the head of John the Baptist, Judith and Holofernes was an opportunity for a bloody, sensual painting, as in Artemisa Gentileschi's brilliant painting.[10]

The image of Judith cutting off Holofernes' head is perhaps too gory a subject for Leonardo da Vinci, even though he was not shy of designing gore-inducing machines, the machines of war. Leonardo was horrified by war, even as he spent hours and hours designing those infernal machines. Serge Bramly writes:

> When one looks at his notebooks, one is obliged to admit that he spent a great part of his time pondering machines of destruction – bombards, bombs, explosive cannonballs (prefiguring shells), versions of a machine gun, giant catapults and crossbows, chariots carrying great scythes intended literally to cut the enemy to pieces. (341)

The head being cut off by Salome or Judith is clearly a castration metaphor. Indian Goddesses, such as Kali, used to decapitate their consorts as they made love to them on top.[11]

8 P. Picasso, in Dore Ashton, ed: *Picasso on Art: A Selection of Views*Viking Press, New York 1972, 15.

9 H. Bosch: *The Garden of Earthly Delights*, 1503-4, oil on canvas, centre panel: 220 x 195cm, Prado, Madrid.

10 Artemisa Gentileschi: *Judith*, 1615/20, Pitti Palace, Florence

11 Wendy O'Flaherty writes: 'The Goddess not only dominates her consort but kills him, cutting off his head. In this she resembles the female praying mantis, who bites off her consort's head... By eating his head, the mantis removes her consort's inhibitions and frees him to copulate more vigorously.' (*Women, Androgynes, and other Mythical Beasts*,University of Chicago Press, Chicago, 1980, 81.)

The anatomy of death and life greatly interested Leonardo da Vinci of course, even though his works sometimes display a fear of the body as well as a love. When Salome and Judith grasp the heads of the dead heroes, they grasp the site or foundation of male power. The head is where 'maleness' resides, where sperm and creative power are, where the essence of manhood is, as history shows. There have been many headhunting cults down the ages. Cortez saw 136,000 heads collected in Mexico's great Aztec temple, for instance, and Prescott estimated that 20,000-50,000 human sacrifices occurred in Mexico per year, while the Celts had their prophetic head of Bran, while the Greeks had the singing, oracular head of Orpheus. The symbolism of the skull is sexual.

When Leonardo da Vinci came to draw the sexual organs, as he did in a number of drawings, he connected the penis to the brain, in those famous drawings of copulation. 'Even as studious an anatomist as Leonardo in the high Renaissance was still drawing a supposed, but nonexistent, canal between the lower spine and the male genitals, as a result of this erroneous theory' writes Weston La Barre.[12]

Leonardo da Vinci's own views on sexuality are a mixture of love and loathing, as in Dante or Petrarch. Like Petrarch and Dante, Leonardo is a sensual character, but, at the same time, there is an Augustinian loathing of the body. On the one hand, Leonardo may be seen as a sensualist, though not as indulgent as, say, Boccaccio or Ovid; on the other hand, he recoils from sensuality as the Christian Fathers, St Augustine, Tertullian, Jerome, St Paul and Origen, did. In his *Notebooks*, Leonardo writes:

> The act of procreation and the members employed therein are so repulsive, that were it not for the beauty of the faces and the adornments of the action and the pent-up impulse, nature would lose the human species.[13]

And again, in another extract, Leonardo da Vinci makes clear his disbelief and loathing of sexual activity:

12 see Weston La Barre: *Muelos*,, 13-64; T.G.E. Powell: *The Celts*, Praeger, New York 1958; B. R. Ortiz: "Counting Skulls: Comment on the Aztec Cannibalism Theory of Harner-Harris", *American Anthropologist*, 1983, 82:2, 403-6.
13 Leonardo: *The Notebooks*, 24. See also B. Farrell, in Morris Philipson, 245.

For what motive do beasts who sow their seed sow it with pleasure, and why does she who awaits it receive it with pleasure and bring forth young in pain?[14]

Leonardo da Vinci's views on sexuality are typical of Western patriarchy: the connections made between sex and death, the simultaneous fear and desire, phallic identification, autoeroticism and narcissism, suppression, an insistence on the genitals rather than emotions, and so on. His own sexuality has been examined by various critics. He was, for Freud, the typical homosexual, with an ambivalent attitude to his mother. 'There is no record of any woman in his life – not even a female friendship' writes Serge Bramly (119). Indeed, Leonardo wrote biliously about women, speaking of 'fleeing the useless chatter of women'.[15] This sort of double-faced ethic is found also in the founder of Italian Renaissance humanism, Francesco Petrarch. In his exquisite, elegant, often ecstatic sonnets and *canzone*, Petrarch glorified his beloved Laura. Yet, in other writings, he spoke derisorily of women.[16] Instead, Leonardo had many male acquaintances, including a studio assistant, with whom he may have had an affair. One documented incident in Leonardo's sexual life was when he was 'accused, with three other youths, of having practiced sodomy on the person of one Jacopo Saltarelli, aged seventeen...a notorious prostitute.' (Bramly, 118)

Leonardo da Vinci knew about the relation between pornography and sexual desire, and between art and pornography. One statement in his *Treatise on Painting* sums up the whole of pornography: 'If the painter wants to see beautiful women to fall in love with, he has it in his power to bring them forth'.[17] This is the basic tenet of pornography: that, defrauded of real love, the artist or pornographer can make artificial love. S/he can make love objects, if s/he doesn't have real love objects. Instead of flesh-and-blood human beings, the artist or pornographer can make her/ his own, to her/ his own liking. 'If the painter', Leonardo says, 'wants a love object, s/he can make one.' It's

14 *Codex Atlanticus*, 320 v b.
15 Leonardo, quoted in K. Eissler, and in Bramly, 130.
16 See B.D. Barnacle: *Petrarch, Dante and the Troubadours*, Crescent Moon 1993.
17 Leonardo: *Treatise on Painting*, op.cit., fol. 35r.

an extraordinary concept, but it is in fact the basis of all art, really. Writers often say that no one wrote the books they wanted to read, so they wrote for themselves. Similarly, painters paint the paintings they want to see painted. Poets write the poems they want to read. If fantastic things don't exist in 'real life', the artist can make them: thus, Leonardo makes his Medusa head, his *Mona Lisa*, his Baptist, his St Anne and Madonna, his *Leda and the Swan.*

In his *Treatise on Painting*, Leonardo da Vinci again speaks of the pornographic qualities of art. Pictures can be so believable, he says, that they seem to come alive. It is the old shock of illusionism once again: to make paintings so 'lifelike' people think they're 'real'. Leonardo writes:

> It previously happened to me that I made a picture representing a holy subject, which was bought by someone who loved it and who wished to remove the attributes of its divinity in order that he might kiss it without guilt. But finally his conscience overcame his sighs and lust, and he was forced to banish it from his house. (*Leonardo on Painting*, 27-8)

This is another reworking of the myth of Pygmalion, where the sculptor's statue comes alive, and he makes love to the object he has created. This is art as the masculine mirror again, the artist creating his own love object. Leonardo knew about the problems of subjectivity. In his notebooks he writes: 'There is nothing that deceives us more than our own judgement when used to give an opinion on our own works.'[18] There are other famous occasions of the confusion of art and life, as when a youth was so obsessed with a statue of Aphrodite of Cnidos that he masturbated on it, leaving a stain, as recorded in Pliny's *Natural History*. Then there was Henry George Quinn who sneaked into the Uffizi to 'fervently kiss' the Medici Venus all over.[19]

Like so many male artists (Egon Schiele, Eric Gill, Jasper Johns, Hans Bellmer, Thomas Rowlandson, Robert Mapplethorpe, Tom of

18 Leonardo: *Codex Urbinus Latinus*, Vatican, 131 v, in *Leonardo on Painting*, 196.

19 Nicholas Penny: "Goddesses and Girls", in *London Review of Books*, 2-29, December 1982, 20; Simon Wilson: "Short History of Western Erotic Art", in Robert Melville: *Erotic Art of the West*, Weidenfeld & Nicholson 1973, 16.

Finland) Leonardo da Vinci made many studies of the penis. His drawings abound with studies of male nudes, while his only female nude seems to have been his *Leda*. He made two drawings of the vulva. One looks like a gaping hole, a cavern, with no clitoris or inner lips, verily the Gate of Hell of the Christian theologians ('woman is the gateway of hell' said the early Christian theologian Tertullian).[20] Martin Kemp writes of Leonardo's genital drawings:

> The notes accompanying the drawings reinforce this subjective response. He not only exhibits a sense of awe in the face of the mysteries of the origins of life, but also a more troubled reaction to the procedures and organs concerned with procreation. His remarks on various aspects of bodily functions, such as ingestion and egestion, suggest a distaste for man's 'animal powers', and his comments on the absurd and repellent aspects of the act of copulation indicate a response far from devoid of emotional tensions. (In M. Kemp, ed., 77)

His drawings of the penis are not accurate, either, but he was clearly more comfortable drawing the penis. He drew many male nudes, many of them excluding the head, concentrating on the thighs, buttocks, legs and genitals.[21] Leonardo da Vinci's drawings of men seen from the side recall the photographs of Robert Mapplethorpe, another controversial gay artist. Mapplethorpe shot black men side-on, emphasizing their genitals and sexuality.[22]

Even though copulation repulsed him, it also fascinated him. He could not resist drawing it. He was one of the most curious of all artists, so no area of life must be beyond his investigation. He studied the penis. Erect it was 'long, thick, and heavy', flaccid it was 'short, narrow, and soft' he wrote.[23] One of his funniest notebook entries is his

20 Leonardo: *The External Genitalia and Vagina*, drawing, Royal Library, Windsor

21 Leonardo: *Study of the Lower Half of a Man*, c. 1490, 19 x 14cm, pen and ink, Royal Library, Windsor; *Study of the Body and Leg of a Man*, c. 1504, red chalk, 25.2 x 19.8, British Museum, London.

22 See Mapplethorpe's *Michael*, 1983, photograph, and *Derrick Cross*, 1983, photograph; also: *Mapplethorpe: Fotografie*, text by Germano Celant, Idea Books Edizioni, Milan 1983; and see Dunne Dominick: 'Robert Mapplethorpe: Aestheticizing the Perverse", Artscribe International, Nov/ Dec 1988; Peter Schjeldhal: "The Mainstreaming of Mapplethorpe: Taste and Hunger", *7 Days*, 10 August 1988.

23 B 2v, quoted in S. Bramly, 124.

description of the penis as having a life of its own. This is a common male view, that the penis is 'uncontrollable', it does what it likes, ignoring its owner. In the 21st century, this view is seen in cartoons, such as those depicting the 'Wicked Willie', a man's alter ego, his dick, who talks to him, admonishes him, encourages him. The penis pops up and does its thing, in movies, in cartoons, in TV sitcoms, in magazines, in pornography. It's uncontrollable! men cry, after a rape. It wasn't me, they sob, it was my willy wot did it, your honour. Leonardo writes:

> It has dealings with human intelligence and sometimes an intelligence of its own; where a man may desire it to be stimulated, it remains obstinate and follows its own course; and sometimes it moves on its own without permission or any thought by its owner. Whether one is awake or asleep, it does what it pleases, often the man is asleep and it is awake; often the man is awake and it is asleep; or the man would like it to be in action but it refuses; often it desires action and the man forbids it. That is why it seems that this creature often has a life an an intelligence separate from that of the man, and it seems that man is wrong to be ashamed of giving it a name or showing it; that which he seeks to cover and hide he ought to expose solemnly like a priest at mass.' (B 13r, and *Notebooks*, 161)

Of course, Leonardo da Vinci's description of the wild willy is ridiculous. Men and their dicks! What a fuss about so small an appendage! D.H. Lawrence making a cult of out the phallus, Félicien Rops drawing penises crucified on a Cross, Eric Gill drawing his dick complete with measurements. The phallus is the divine mirror of the masculinist system. As Madeleine Gagnon writes: 'The phallus means everything sets itself up as a mirror. Everything that erects itself as perfection.'[24] When Renoir was asked how he painted when he hands were crippled by arthritis he replied '[w]ith my prick' (in J. Hobhouse, 135). In pornography, the eye becomes the phallus, and looking is equated with caressing the obscure object of desire with the phallus. Leonardo was regard as having a 'hand-eye' eroticism.[25]

Again and again in our discussion of Leonardo da Vinci's work and philosophy, we come back to notions of seeing, eyes, mirrors, desire and the phallus.

24 M. Gagnon: "Corps I", *La venue à l'écriture*, UGE, 10/18, Paris 1977; in E. Marks, 180.

25 K.R. Eissler: *Leonardo da Vinci*, 115-9, 213-4, 216.

Lacan, 'the French Freud' as he is sometimes described, created a post-Freud psychoanalysis based on desire, lack, the phallus and the mirror. The Lacanian Look emphasizes eroticism. Seeing is erotic, the eye becomes a kind of phallus, caressing the obscure object of desire, which it can never 'possess'. As the poet Rainer Maria Rilke wrote '[g]azing is a wonderful thing.'[26] The act of looking eroticizes the object. Jack Zipes explains:

> For him [Lacan], seeing is desire, and the eye functions as a kind of phallus. However, the eye cannot clearly see its object of desire, and in the case of male desire, the female object of desire is an illusion created by the male unconscious. Or, in other words, the male desire for woman expressed in the gaze is auto-erotic and involves the male's desire to have his own identity reconfirmed in a mirror image.[27]

This autoeroticism is found throughout Leonardo da Vinci's work. His eroticism is focused on himself. We don't need Freud to tell us that Leonardo's eroticism pivots around repression, masturbation and autoeroticism. Not only did he create many images of that obscure object of desire, the mother figure, who in the Lacanian system is a displaced phallus (the so-called 'phallic mother'), Leonardo also constructed many images around the mirror. There is the dopplegänger or 'Other', for instance, in his paintings – the second or double mother, the second or twin Jesus. And of course there is also the famous 'mirror writing'. In a famous passage in his notebooks, Leonardo speaks of the comparisons between mirrors and painting:

> You should take the mirror as your master, that is a flat mirror, because on its surface things in many ways bear a resemblance to a painting. That is to say, you see a picture which is painted on a flat surface showing things as if in relief: the mirror on a flat does the same. The picture is intangible inasmuch as something which appears round and detached cannot be braced by the hands, and the mirror does the same. And if you recognise that the mirror by means of outlines and shades and lights makes things appear to stand out, you, who have among your colours stronger light and shade than those in the mirror, will certainly, if you know how to put them together well, make your picture, also, look like something from nature seen in a

26 Rilke, letter to Clara Rilke, 8 March 1907, in *Gesammalte Briefe 1892-1926*, Insel Verlag, Leipzig 1940, II, 279.
27 Jack Zipes: *Don't Bet on the Prince: Contemporary Feminist Fairy Tales in North America and England,* Gower, Aldershot 1986, 258.

large mirror.[28]

The Look is an assertion of male power and sexuality. For the gaze is male, and feminists have grappled with the notion of a 'female' gaze,[29] Margaret Whitford writes of Luce Irigaray's work thus:

> Western systems of representation privilege *seeing*: what can be seen (presence) is privileged over what cannot be seen (absence) and guarantees Being, hence the privilege of the penis which is elevated to the status of the Phallus.[30]

Leonardo da Vinci's paintings, though, do not immediately site or position the viewer in a masculine viewpoint. Leonardo is one of the very few painters throughout history who created works which contain the self-evident possibility of a variety of viewpoints. Whereas the view of Boucher's female nude with her plump buttocks is sited by the painter as distinctly male and heterosexual, and Rubens' erotic paintings, like those of Titian, are, similarly, aimed at white bourgeois heterosexual males, Leonardo's androgynous, ambivalent people are not addressed necessarily to masculinist or feminist or lesbian or gay or whatever viewpoints. The ambiguity of gender is built into Leonardo's works, and this is rare among the 'Old Masters'.

In the Jungian system, Beatrice, Laura, Cleopatra, Isolde, Eurydice, Ariadne and all those women of myth, poetry and legend, are incarnations of the *anima*, which is, as Jung explains, something all males possess: '[e]very man carries with him the eternal image of woman, not the image of this or that particular woman, but a definitive feminine image.'[31] The *anima* is 'a personification of the unconscious in a man, which appears as a woman or a goddess in dreams, visions and

---

28 Leonardo: *Codex Urbinas Latinus*, Vatican, 32 r-v, in *Leonardo on Painting*, 202.

29 Maggie Humm: "Is the gaze feminist? Pornography, film and feminism", *Perspectives on Pornography*, eds G.Day & C. Bloom, Macmillan 1988; Lorraine Gamran & Margaret Marshment, eds: *The Female Gaze*, Women's Press 1988; E.D. Pribram, ed: *Female Spectators: looking at film and television*, Verso, 1988.

30 Marget Whitford: *Luce Irigaray: Philosophy in the Feminine*, 1991, 1990, 30.

31 Carl Jung: *The Development of Personality* vol. 17, Routledge, 1954, 198; Marie-Louise von Franz: *The Psychological Meaning of Redemption Motifs in Fairy Tales*, Inner City Books, Toronto 1980, 39f.

creative fantasies', write Emma Jung and Marie-Louise von Franz.[32] Male painters throughout history have depicted their version of the *anima*, it seems. Each (male) painter has a version of the 'inner feminine figure' as Jung calls her (1967, 210-1). For painters, this idealized *anima* figure seems to be another manifestation of that obscure object of desire, the eroticized woman, a mirror for male lust. The equation is: the more sublime and voluptuous the woman is painted, the more sublime and voluptuous is the artist's desire. The artist's model, then, can be seen as a Jungian *anima*, heavily eroticized, a Lacanian phallic mirror.

Leonardo da Vinci's *anima*-image veers from the 'innocent' joy of the young woman in the *Benois Madonna*, to the sombre otherness of the *Mona Lisa*. Leonardo's paintings, though they do seem to get darker, visually, retain their brightness to the end. The Leonardo Smile occurs right to the end of his artistic career. If the Madonna is the *anima*-image of Renaissance painters, then Leonardo's is often very bright, a shining, nay, radiant woman. The early *Madonnas* are luminous people, as is the softly smiling *Woman with the Ermine*. The early sketches, particularly drawings such as those for the lost *Madonna and Child and a Cat*, show a happy young Virgin, caught in a state of bliss with her child, oblivious of the outer world.[33] Or the *Benois Madonna*, where the Virgin and the child play with a flower, in a bliss of their own. 'The emotions of wonder and tenderness flow between the two figures, who are deeply aware of one another while at the same time immersed in the contemplation of the flower' writes Robert Payne (34). The painting exudes the wonder of love, where 'innocence' predominates: this very young mother and her offspring are not aware of their fatal future. Their heads are nearly identical: high, wide, smooth foreheads and small noses. The child here is 'abnormally large', writes Cecil Gould (42); rather, Virgin and child are depicted as equals, existing in a symbiotic relationship, both divine, both human, both in love with each

32 Emma Jung & Marie-Louise von Franz: *The Grail Legend*, tr Andrea Dykes, Sigo Press, Boston, Mass., 1980, 64.

33 Leonardo: *Madonna and Child with Cat*, 13.2 x 9.5cm, pen and ink, British Museum, London; *Madonna and Child with a Cat*, 12.5 x 10.5cm, pen and ink and wash, Uffizi, Florence.

other. This spiritual symbiosis (which has a sexual component, undoubtedly) reaches its climax in the Coronation of the Virgin, depicted many times in Renaissance painting.

Other images of familial or erotic symbiosis occur in the drawings made of the Virgin with a unicorn.[34] Leonardo da Vinci partook of the standard mediæval myth of the unicorn as the questing beast of purity and phallic wildness, only tameable by a virgin. The two together – the passive, nurturing virgin and the wild, untameable unicorn, fascinated Leonardo, as it fascinated many a Renaissance artist:

> The unicorn, through its intemperance and not knowing how to control itself, for the love it bears to fair maidens forgets its ferocity and wildness, and laying aside all fear it will go up to a seated damsel and go to sleep in her lap...[35]

The lady and unicorn is essentially the womb and phallus, meeting yet again: the unicorn lays its 'horn' in the 'lap' of the virgin. You don't need to be an expert on Shakespearean/ Renaissance bawdy to know that horn = phallus and lap = womb (as when Hamlet rests his head on Ophelia's lap and they discus 'country matters' – 'country' here being equated with cunt). Or a woman with an animal: the animal is the 'spirit familiar', like the animals of witches. The unicorn or cat is also the woman's lover, and Leonardo depicts women with animals as a meeting of equals. Again and again, Leonardo depicts bodies fusing with each other, limbs entwining, suggesting deep and complex relationships between people and animals. The early *Madonnas*, the *Madonna with Unicorns*, the *Madonnas with a Cat*, the late *Virgin, Child and St Anne*, all depict the symbiotic, incestuous entanglements of living forms.

The depth of these erotic and spiritual entanglements is exaggerated by Leonardo da Vinci's constant use of lines on top of lines. In the drawing of *The Madonna and Child with a Cat*, Leonardo experiments with many different poses, before deciding upon one, and tracing it through to the other side of the paper. Even when Leonardo employs a wash of brown ink to fill in some of the tones in his sketches, he is still

34 Leonardo: *Maiden with a Unicorn*, 27.4 x 19cm, pen and ink, British Museum; *Maiden with a Unicorn*, 9.3 x 7.1cm, pen and ink, Ashmolean Museum, Oxford.
35 Leonardo, quoted in McMullen, 63.

trying out different poses for his figures.[36] In Leonardo's art, faces and figures melt into one another. On one sheet of paper, he will draw the Virgin Mary in various poses – looking down, half-kneeling, with Christ on her knee, sucking at her breast; the Child or the Baptist looking up at her, twice; two lions and a wild beast are at the bottom of the sheet; profiles of young men and women are dotted around the paper; an old man, one of the figures art historians call a 'grotesque' is in the centre of the page.[37] All these sketches are set beside each other on one sheet of paper. Leonardo's an artist who buzzes with ideas, who moves from one idea to the next restlessly, coming back at times to develop a former idea further, but more often than not, he simply abandons them. His sketches of, say, the heart of an ox, or of the foetus in the womb, are detailed works in themselves, complex, with acres of his mirror handwriting describing the workings of his subjects, while other sketches will be half-finished, just bare outlines.[38] Clearly, Leonardo worked on many ideas at the same time. The nature of his drawings show that he must have been fired by many ideas at once. He had an associative mind, he was always making connections, so a number of seemingly different æsthetic projects were kept going simultaneously. One moment he might have been designing a war machine of some demonic complexity; the next moment, he's sketching, with extraordinary delicacy, a spray of cranberry or a lily.[39] The three studies for *Leda and the Swan* are placed on a sheet with a rearing horse.[40] Leonardo ponders at length how to pose his Leda, for that half-kneeling posture is extremely difficult to carry off convincingly. In the left hand of the three studies of Leda, Leonardo has overdrawn the figures again and again, trying to get the

36 Leonardo: *Madonna and Child with Cat* , pen and ink, British Museum, London.

37 Leonardo: *Sheet of Studies with the Virgin and Child and St John, c.* 1478-80, pen and ink, 40.4 x 29.1cm, Windsor.

38 Leonardo: *Five Views of a Foetus in the Womb, c*1510-2, pen & ink with red & black chalk, 30.4 x 21.3cm, Windsor; *The Heart of an Ox, c.* 1513, pen & ink on blue paper, 29 x 41.2cm, Windsor.

39 Leonardo: *A Lily (Lilium candidum), c.* 1472-5, pen and ink and wash over black chalk, 31.4 x 17.7cm, Windsor; *Spray of Cranberry (Vibernum pulus), c.* 1508, red chalk, 14.3 x 14.3, Windsor.

40 Leonardo: *A Rearing Horse and Studies for the Kneeling Leda, c*1505, black chalk and pen & ink, 29.3 x 41.3cm, Windsor. As well as many exquisite studies of horses, Leonardo also sketched mythical beasts, such as dragons and unicorns.

posture right.

It must be said that Leonardo da Vinci's drawing are really exquisite. Whether they are the result of a 'hand and eye eroticism' (Freud) or not doesn't matter. They are beautiful objects themselves, no matter how 'unfinished' the sketches are. When these sketches are surrounded by a rectangle in light pen – as with *Maiden and a Unicorn, The Madonna and Child with a Cat, Leda and the Swan* – the poetic effect is enhanced. With these tiny drawings, Leonardo encloses a world with an rectangle or an archway. The most overdrawn of Leonardo's drawings may be one of his studies for the painting *The Virgin and Child with St Anne and the Baptist* (National Gallery). In this drawing, Leonardo has used black chalk overworked with pen and ink, followed by a grey wash and heightening with white. One can make out the twinned heads of the two Mothers, and also their legs. But the centre of the two women, from their shoulders to their thighs, is a darkness of lines and tones. Somewhere here is the Christ Child – his face is vaguely discernible. The Baptist, on the right, is easier to spot. The drawing is an extreme form of Leonardo's multiple, layered, palimpsest technique, as Martin Kemp writes: 'The effect is more like the process of modelling a clay relief than an orthodox drawing. The relative illegibility, which permits new 'inventions' to rise by chance, as when he looked at patches on walls, is clearly an important aspect of the creative process for Leonardo.' (in M. Kemp, ed., 150) Yet the drawing has its own magic, a magic which is maybe not as potent as in the oil paintings, but which is nevertheless powerful.

The depictions of sexual union show that sexuality was not all horror for Leonardo da Vinci. He did, for instance, believe in love under certain circumstances. Like the Neoplatonists he believed in the bliss of ideal love. In his notebooks he wrote:

> If the lover is attuned to the object with whom he would be united, the result is delight, pleasure, and satisfaction. When the lover is united with the one he loves, he finds peace; relieved of his burden, he finds rest.[41]

This inner bliss has much to do with motherhood, and Leonardo da

41 Leonardo, quoted in Bramly, 127.

Vinci returned to it later with his *Virgin and Child with St Anne,* where the Madonna is again lost in bliss, playing with her son. The 'ideal woman' or *anima*-figure in Leonardo's *œuvre*, then, veers between the idealized Mother figure, who is feared and desired, and the dark side of the Mother figure, the Mona Lisa, with her smile and secrets.

The *Mona Lisa* is basically a *femme fatale* type. Or rather, she was regarded as a *femme fatale* during Pater and the 19th century æstheticians. Walter Pater wrote famously of the *Mona Lisa*, in a way which says more about Pater and late Victorian and Decadent art than it does about Leonardo:

> She is older than the rocks among which she sits... [she embodies] the animalism of Greece, the lust of Rome, the mysticism of the middle ages with its spiritual ambition and imaginative loves, the return of the pagan world, the sins of the Borgias. (123)

Pater reinvents the *femme fatale* image of the *Mona Lisa* for his own Decadent age.

The Leonardoan *femme fatale* type flourished in 19th century painting, especially in Gustave Moreau, Félicien Rops, Stuck and Munch. For 19th century æstheticians and artists, the *Mona Lisa* is an embodiment of mystery and evil, the woman as otherness and secrecy. But this reading of the *Mona Lisa* says more about the people propounding the theory, than about the painting itself. True, the *Mona Lisa* is a mysterious painting. But 'evil', 'sinful', 'sinister'? Not really. Dark, certainly, but Leonardo's darkness does not always connote evil and sin, as in usual Christian metaphysics. Critics have often stressed the frightening or disturbing or unsettling nature of Leonardo's art. There is always something of the head of the Medusa or Gorgon in Leonardo's art, critics claim, something of that Medusa head with its terrifying glare that Leonardo made to frighten his father. Michael Levey writes: 'he yet brings something of a Medusa touch to them [*The Virgin of the Rocks* and *Mona Lisa*], a disturbing and faintly disassociated air which makes the spectator draw back for a moment, as Leonardo's father had done.' (1967, 180) Leonardo's works attract strong responses: a Louvre attendant fell in love (or lust) with the *Mona Lisa*, and got jealous when other people came near it (or her). People have taken knives, stones and guns to Leonardo's paintings. Something about Leonardo's works inflames people. Leonardo's paintings exert a Medusa-like fascination of simultaneous fear and desire on people. Michelet wrote of the late work, *St John the Baptist*, '[t]he canvas attracts me, overwhelms me, absorbs me; I go toward it in spite of myself, like the bird toward the snake.'[42] What a vivid analogy this is: the Leonardo painting like a snake, eternal, chthonic, hypnotizing, devouring people like little birds.

What late 19th century art and æsthetics did was to create that Symbolist and Decadent fusion of women with sex, death, to make explicit the identification (that was always present in Western/ Christian theology and philosophy) of women with death, with decay, perversion, 'sin', 'evil', pain, violence, excess and terror. All the things usually associated with men are projected onto women. This sounds like simplistic Jungian psychology, but it applies in most cases. Such as Frank Kupka's fantastic winged deity, her breasts bare and her eyes ablaze, presiding over defeated armies of naked bodies: this is an archetypical Decadent image of women.[43]

The image of 'woman' is central to Renaissance, as it is to 19th century art, and particularly the naked woman, which we find in profusion in the work of Titian, Correggio, Piero di Cosimo, Moreau, Delville, Rops, Stuck, etc. In the manifesto of the revival of Rosicrucianism, the Salon de la Rose + Croix, Péladan wrote of '[t]he nude made *sublime*'.[44] This is what happens in Renaissance art: the nude is made sublime. Leonardo da Vinci, who avoided the nude in oil, made the nude sublime in pen and ink. There is, though, the so-called *'Nude' Gioconda*, which is by a 'follower' of Leonardo, though clearly not by Leonardo da Vinci himself.[45]

The *Mona Lisa* is an early version of the Symbolist/ Decadent vampire or sphinx. The *femme fatale* is one of the main types of 'women' in 19th century art: there are other incarnations or versions of the same

42 Quoted in S. Bramly, 396.
43 F. Kupka: *The Conqueror Worm*, print, Bibliothéque Nationale, Paris.
44 Joséphin Péladan: *L'Art idealistique et mystique*, Paris 1909, in Edward Lucie-Smith: *Symbolist Art*, 112.
45 Follower of Leonardo: *Nude Mona Lisa*, *c*. 1513, black chalk, 33 x 23cm, Musée Condé, Chantilly.

basic type; the woman as death, as a prostitute, as a dominatrix, a temptress, a queen, a warrior, an Amazon, etc. These are a few examples of 19th century *femme fatale* which may take Leonardo da Vinci's *Mona Lisa* as an influence. In Giulio Aristide Sartorio's *Gorgon and Fallen Heroes*, the woman stands triumphant literally on the broken heroes' heads: naked, of course, with her hair, ginger-red, of course, swirling about her, she is at once pin-up pornography and hated 'Woman', at once desired and loathed.[46] Another woman triumphant over the male occurs in Arnold Böcklin's *Calm Sea*, where a mermaid on a rock coils her tail around a drowning man, his eyes wide open in the throes of death. The mermaid, like the vampire of the sphinx, combines 'woman' and animality, 'woman' and otherness, woman and primæval, primitive, earthy/earthly instincts, below the belt, 'down there', the dark zones of sex.[47] Munch takes the domineering female figure to an extreme, in images such as his *Madonna*,[48] where the naked Goddess looks scornfully down on a shrivelled male figure, while sperm wriggle hopelessly around the frame. Munch's *Madonna* is an expression of male angst, male anxiety about (sexual) impotence, about the masochistic relation with women. We might see Munch's *Madonna* as a form of Leonardoan 'Woman', especially so with its emphasis on the mechanics of conception and birth.

The *femme fatale* type appears in Medusa, Salome, Delilah, Jezebel, Judith, Lilith, Ninue, the lover of Merlin, Venus, Helen of Troy, La Belle Dame Sans Merci, Cleopatra. These female 'types' combined beauty with death, immense power and all manner of sadistic, masochistic and fetishistic fantasies. These are the women who will whip you to death, if you wish, as in Sacher-Masoch's *Venus in Furs*. Figures such as Cleopatra provided the longed for combination of socio-political, religious sovereignty, wild eroticism, intrigue, magnificent settings and gory love-deaths. According to Vasari, Leonardo da Vinci had painted a gorgon's head on a shield and showed it to his father in a

46 Sartorio: *Gorgon and Fallen Heroes*, 1893-8, oil on canvas, 305 x 421cm, Galerie Nazionale d'Arte Moderna, Rome.
47 A. Böcklin: *Calm Sea*, 1887, wood, 200 x 100cm, Musée d'Art Moderne, Paris.
48 E. Munch: *Madonna*,1895-1902, lithograph, 60.7 x 44.3cm, Nasjonalgaleriet, Oslo.

darkened room with a ray of sunlight falling on it. His father was suitably taken aback.[49]

Other *Mona Lisa* types, who stare mysteriously at the viewer, with something of a death-dealing glance of the Medusa include the sphinxes of the Decadent era. These women-as-sphinxes, are eternally mysterious, simultaneously loathed and lusted after beings, as in Franz von Stuck's *The Sphinx*, where a nude woman is thoroughly eroticized, the emphasis being on her voluptuously painted body rather than her sphinx-like pose, raised on her elbows.[50] In Stuck's *The Kiss of the Sphinx*[51] sex and death are melted together in a *mors osculis*, the 'kiss of death' of occultism. In Lucien Levy-Dhurmer's *Salome*, the woman kisses the severed head of the Baptist on its platter, effortlessly creating that familiar fusion of sex and pain, castration and masochism, found in much of male art. (Marquis von Bayros drew John the Baptist sucking Salome's nipples).[52] This is a common them in patriarchal or male art: dying at orgasm, orgasm as the 'little death' (*petit mort*). For patriarchal people (mainly male artists), bliss is dying at orgasm. The Goddess Kali beheads her consorts during sex, and women in Decadent art, like Salome and Judith in Renaissance art, kiss their partners to death. The kiss is but a stylized and uncensorable way of depicting copulation. Women suck the life out of you, so patriarchal people say; the vagina is thus the 'gateway to hell', as Christian theologians put it, the vagina is the road to oblivion (think of Leonardo's two drawings of the vagina).

Another incarnation of the *Mona Lisa* is as a vampire. who gives that other kind of castrating 'kiss', sucking blood from the neck. Women are 'vamps' or 'nymphos' (familiar types in pornography – the 'unsatisfied' housewife', the woman who 'couldn't get enough', the familiar description of women who are raped).

Like the Madonna in *The Virgin of the Rocks* or the *Mona Lisa*, the vampire is a night creature, a Queen of the Night, who haunts the

49 See Serge Bramly, 97-8, 429.
50 F. Stuck: *The Sphinx*, Hessisches Landesmuseum, Darmstadt.
51 F. Stuck: *The Kiss of the Sphinx*, *c*.1895, oil on canvas, Museum of fine Arts, Budapest.
52 Marquis von Bayros: *Salome with the Head of John the Baptist*, *c*.1900, private collection.

nightworld. Much of Leonardo da Vinci is darkly Gothic. The vampire neatly summarizes the patriarchal love of the Gothic, of 'sin', blood mysteries, masochism (masochism in the 'voluptuousness' of the 'victim', who lays himself down for the vampire's attack).

9

The Cult of Venus

The common subject of the Renaissance nude was Venus. She is the divinity of the underbelly of Renaissance magic, which informs the Neoplatonic philosophy of Leonardo da Vinci and Botticelli. As the Goddess of Love in mediæval and courtly love poetry, Venus, with her phallic assistant, Cupid, as the cherub armed with bow and arrow, presided over erotic experiences. Venus was called upon to aid the lover in this pursuit of the Holy Grail, the mystic cauldron of Woman, her womb. Venus is both Holy Whore and chaste Mistress of 'Love'. She is Love personified. The Louvre birth plate, *c.* 1400, shows the Goddess Venus hovering over a Tuscan Garden of Love attended by two angels. Below are six 'famous warriors'. All of them are staring intently at the genitals of the floating Goddess.[53] The lines of sight are marked on the painted salver. The Goddess is depicted in a mandorla, just like the Virgin Mary in *Assumption* images. The centre of the picture is Venus' vulva. Leonardo was not as directly erotic as the Louvre birthplate. His eroticism is more subtle than that, deriving in part from that hidden aspect of the Renaissance, Neoplatonic philosophy and hermeticism.

53 *The Triumph of Venus*, anonymous, birth plate, School of Verona (?), *c.*1400, Louvre, Paris.

Countless female nudes depict Venus in various poses of shyness and abandonment. Leonardo da Vinci did not make female nudes in the 'high art' tradition, as Titian, Giorgione and others did. Giorgione's *Sleeping Venus* makes the looking at the body easier, because she is asleep.[54] Yet this depiction is created very definitely for the pleasures of eroticism, made for the *jouissance* of looking, just like Leonardo's *Madonna and Child* paintings, or his *Last Supper*, which he looked at for hours without moving. He would sit and stare at his painting, clearly enjoying the pleasure of looking. Examples of Renaissance eroticism range from Michelangelo Buonarroti's deliciously orgasmic *Dying Slave* to Botticelli's *Birth of Venus*, Titian's *Venus of Urbino*, and the Master of Flora's *Birth of Cupid*.[55] These are offered as gorgeous depictions of people, of mythical people painted sublimely, of people who expose their 'looked-at-ness' for all to see. Even in unexpected places, such as in Early Italian Renaissance art, such as Lorenzetti, we find erotic objectifications of women that look towards the 'high art' nude. And otherwise chaste and sober painters, such as Bellini, produced female nudes made to be looked at erotically.[56] Pisanello's drawing of the personification of 'Luxury' undoubtedly depicts a prostitute: his drawing is a form of Renaissance pornography, given 'high art' status because Pisanello was a 'major' artist.[57] Some images of the Renaissance and later nudes contain men in the picture, who modulate the viewer's gaze.[58] The man in the picture stands in for the viewer, and the gaze is distinctly erotic (and male, except in certain cases, such as Simon Vouet's image of Psyche and Amor, where the

54 Giorgione: *Sleeping Venus*, *c*.1508, oil on canvas, 108 x 175cm, Staatliche Kunstsammlungen, Gemäldegalerie, Dresden.
55 Titian: *Venus of Urbino*,1538, oil on canvas, 119.5 x 165cm, Uffizi, Florence; Sandro Botticelli: *The Birth of Venus*, *c*.1482, tempera on canvas, 173 x 279cm, Uffizi, Florence; Master of Flora: *Birth of Cupid*, *c*. 1540/60, oil on wood, 108 x 130.5cm, Metropolitan Museum of Art, New York; Michelangelo Buonarroti: *Dying Slave*, 1513, marble, 229cm high, Louvre, Paris.
56 Ambrogio Lorenzetti: *Peace, in Good Government*, *c* 1338-40, Palazzo Publico, Siena; Giovanni Bellini: *A Young Woman at Her Toilet*, 1515, Kunsthistorisches Museum, Vienna.
57 Pisanello: *Allegory of Luxury*, drawing, Albertina, Vienna.
58 Antonio Allegri de Correggio: *The Sleep of Antiope*, *c*.1525, oil on canvas, 189.8 x 124.1cm, Louvre, Paris; Peter Paul Rubens: *Angelica and the Hermit*, *c*. 1625-8, oil on wood, 43 x 66cm, Kunsthistoriches Museum, Vienna.

female contemplates the male body).[59]

In the representations of Venus, sacred and profane, private and public, fear and desire merge. On the one hand, Venus is depicted often with as much awe and slavish worship as the Virgin Mary. She is a Goddess, with her attendant cherubs, like the Madonna with her attendant angels. Cupid becomes Christ, echoing the tenet of Catholicism that *deus est caritas* ('God is Love'). But Cupid is often Venus' consort, not simply her messenger, much as Jesus and Mary were depicted as equals, if not lovers, crowned in a spiritual marriage in Heaven. The Goddess alone is not complete, if she is a Goddess of Love. A Goddess must have her consort, according to the male system. Women on their own bemuse and infuriate men. Surely, men think, there must be some companion in the set-up. Thus figures such as Salome, Joan of Arc, many saints (Hildegard of Bingen, Catherine of Siena, St Theresa, etc), Elizabeth I, and others are objects of fascination and ridicule for patriarchal people. Thus, the ancient deities, such as Ishtar, Isis and Venus had their male lovers; the same emphasis on heterosexual pairings occurs in Renaissance art. Thus, the Madonna is seen as Christ's lover in some Renaissance paintings, his equal, sitting beside him in Heaven. Christ crowns the Virgin, after her Assumption into heaven, as his consort. Mother and Son become lovers. Leonardo explored the notion of erotic pairing (discussed below).

Even those depictions where Venus seems to be alone, such as Botticelli's *Birth of Venus*, have a male element orchestrating the action.

In Botticelli's revered image, the god of the wind, Zephyr, blows Venus to the shore. The wind is symbolically masculine, associated with the creative breath of the Hindu *Upanishads*, with the Word of God, with male procreativity, etc. Behind Botticelli's Venus, then, with her (for men) ambiguous sexuality, lies male power.

Renaissance anthropomorphism, then, is supremely patriarchal, for it is always 'man' who is the measure of everything, not woman. This is true in Renaissance geometry and architecture as well as painting and

59 Simon Vouet: *Psyche Looking at the Sleeping Amor*, 1626, oil on canvas, 112 x 165cm, Musée des Beaux Arts, Lyons.

sculpture: men are very definitely at the centre of the Renaissance (and hence the modern) conception of art and artistic philosophy.[60] You see this everywhere in Renaissance, but most powerfully in Leonardo da Vinci's famous depiction of universal or Renaissance 'man' (*The Proportions of the Human Body*).[61] Here, as Lynda Nead writes, 'the male body is fantasized as pure form.' (18) It would be too subversive if a woman was at the centre of the universe; Leonardo's 'cosmic man' would not work; for 'woman' lacks the 'transcendent signifier', the phallus.

The eroticism of the Greek and Classical Goddess and figures, then, clashes at times violently with the passivity and meekness of the Virgin Mary in depictions of 'femininity' in Renaissance art. In the Vatican, for instance, which is the centre of world Christianity for many, there is a bathroom decorated with the *History of Venus* by Raphael. These rooms, however, are censored, left out of the Vatican guidebooks.

The myth of Venus is based on that of Aphrodite. According to Homer, Aphrodite, the 'foam-born', was birthed from the severed, castrated genitals of the god Uranus which were cast into the sea, creating white foam. The Goddess was blown ashore by the West wind, Zephyrus, to Cyprus, where she was greeted and covered by the Horae. This is the scene Botticelli depicts, and the sexual origin of Venus lies behind all those female nudes of the Renaissance.

60 see Robert Lawlor: *Sacred Geometry: Philosophy and Practice*, Thames & Hudson 1982, 90f; Marilyn A Lavin: *Piero della Francesca's Baptism of Christ*, Yale University Press 1981; Erwin Panofsky, 1972; Fred Gettings, 1978; Matilda Ghyka, 1946; Charles Bouleau: *The Painter's Secret Geometry: a Study of Composition in Art*, tr J. Griffin, Thames & Hudson 1963.
61 Leonardo: *The Proportions of the Human Body*, after Vitruvius, pen and ink, *c.* 1492, Accademia, Venice.

10

Venus Versus Virgin

Wonderful powers of the bodily appearance – the beautiful lineaments – the form – the voice – the complexion – the musculature and elasticity – the eyes, the senses of touch, of feeling – the outer nature – the angles – the closed-off spaces – the darkness – the veil. Through the selection of cloth-ing the body becomes yet more mystical.

Novalis, *Pollen and Fragments*

Venus and the Virgin thus represent the twin poles of patriarchal culture: the sexual and asexual, the naked and the clothed, the lover and the mother, etc. The two merge, confusedly and ambiguously, in many Renaissance artworks. The Virgin is both Mother and Lover of Christ, just as, according to psychoanalysis, the mother is the child's first lover. The cults of the milk and breasts of the Madonna only emphasize the erotic nature of the child-mother relation. The structure of the Madonna and Child image, which Leonardo da Vinci drew many times, with the child seated on the other's lap, echoes that of Osiris sitting on the 'throne' of his mother Isis, who is also his lover.

Even such seemingly gentle occasions such as the Annunciation are not free of sexist, patriarchal and erotic/ pornographic connotations. Leonardo da Vinci's first success with a complete painting (he had already painted the ethereal angel in Verrocchio's *Baptism*) was his *Annunciation* (Payne, 280). In Leonardo's *Annunciation*, as in *all* Renaissance *Annunciations,* from Simone Martini's exquisite Uffizi *Annunciation* to Konrad Witz's bizarre *Annunciation* in that misshapen room,[62] sexism is rife.

For a start, Mary is simply living her life when the Archangel Gabriel rushes in and tells her she is to bear the Son of God. Mary replies: 'how can this be, seeing I know not a man' (*Luke*). As soon as she accepts, in the very moment she assents, she conceives Christ in her womb. It is the Word become Flesh.

Renaissance painters, such as Leonardo da Vinci and Fra Angelico, depict it as a delicate, silent moment, the two figures, Gabriel and Mary, kneeling together in spiritual communion. Leonardo da Vinci's Virigins, like Angelico's, are shy, passive, sad creatures.[63] For Mary in the Gospels is a 'good wife'; she accepts the Word of God. Yet the Annunciation is clearly as a spiritual rape. She cannot refuse the Word of the Lord. So it is rape, because it is sex without consent.

Leonardo da Vinci's *Annunciation* is an awkward painting in some ways. It does not have the sophisticated spatial dynamism of Leonardo's later works. Both versions of the *The Virgin of the Rocks* have a dazzling sense of space, but the *Annunciation* is stiff and crude in places. The hands of Gabriel and the Madonna aim for delicacy, but their bodies are posed heavily and ungracefully. The familiar Leonardoan motifs are there – the distant, grey mountains, the tiny plants and flowers lovingly painted, as in Netherlandish *Madonnas*. If he had stopped painting at the point of *The Annunciation*, Leonardo would probably not be regarded as the greater painter than, say, Ghirlandaio, Perugino, Verrocchio, Signorelli or Flippino Lippi.

62 Konrad Witz: *The Annunciation*, *c*. 1445, oil and tempera on panel, 61.2 x 47.2in, Germanisches Nationalmuseum, Nuremburg.

63 Fra Angelico: *The Annunciation*, c. 1440, fresco, San Marco Museum, Florence; *The Annunciation*, late 1440s, 194 x 194cm, Prado, Madrid; The Annunciation, *c*. 1443, fresco, 187 x 157cm, cell three, San Marco Museum, Florence.

Some painters depict the movement of the power of the Word of God in their *Annunciations*. In Simone Martini's Uffizi *Annunciation*,[64] Mary bends away from the words issuing from Gabriel's mouth, embossed in gold. The string of Latin words are phallic, recalling the Lacanian link between language and sexuality. It is the very Word that changes itself into phallic power, into a spermatozoon, a seed.

One of the most violent representations of the Annunciation comes, surprisingly, from Botticelli. Leonardo da Vinci wrote of Botticelli's *Annunciation* thus:

> I recently saw an Annunciation in which the angel looked as if he wished to chase Our Lady out of Her room with a movement of such violence that She have been a hated enemy. And Our Lady seemed as if in despair She was about to throw Herself out of the window. Remember not to make such a mistake as this.[65]

As in Sandro Botticelli's fresco of the Annunciation at San Martino, the Guardi chapel *Annunciation* depicts Gabriel full of power, his clothes billowing about him on the breath of God, the Word of God. For all the refinement of Leonardo da Vinci's angels' robes, they are not as full of life as Botticelli's Gabriel's robes. Leonardo made many studies of how robes and drapes hang,[66] but somehow they come out a little lifeless in his *Annunciation.*

The *Annunciations* of painters such as Botticelli, Lippi, Angelico, Martini and Leonardo da Vinci illustrate that eternal paradox, the rape which is not a rape, that impregnation which is not an impregnation, that power over women which is denied by patriarchal people.

It's curious, but there is no major *Crucifixion* in Leonardo da Vinci's much-disputed *oeuvre.* The Crucifixion is the other main image of the Renaissance. All the major (and many of the minor) Renaissance painters made *Crucifixions* as well as *Madonna and Child* paintings. There are famous *Crucifixions* by Roger van der Weyden, Mantegna,

64 Simone Martini: *The Annunciation*, 1333, panel, 184 x 114cm, Uffizi, Florence
65 Leonardo, notebooks, quoted in McMullen, 75
66 Leonardo: *Cast of Drapery for the Legs of a Seated Figure*, 26.6 x 23.4cm, drawing, Louvre, Paris; *Cast of Drapery with a Figure Kneeling to the Right*, drawing, 18.2 x 23.3cm, Louvre, Paris.

Velasquez, Masaccio, Angelico and Raphael, but not Leonardo. (We have the two 'Baptist' paintings *St John the Baptist* and *Bacchus*)

One aspect of Christian and Renaissance imagery that most Christian thinkers would not acknowledge is the eroticism of the Saviour's naked body. Everyone else in the Crucifixion is clothed, but Christ is nearly nude. If we accept that *any* nude has erotic elements, as more commentators than Kenneth Clark have noted, then the eroticism of Christ's naked body must be addressed. Few art critics have acknowledged the eroticism of the naked Christ, yet it is certainly a significant element in the 'great' depictions of Christ on the Cross: by Rubens, Velasquez, and Mantegna.[67] Leonardo, as we have said, produced many drawings of male nudes, emphasizing the buttocks, thighs, legs and genitals, but not a full-blown Christ Crucified. More to his taste were the depictions of Christ with his Mother, a young Christ not yet embarked upon the hell of his time on Earth. Leonardo's Christ is essentially an innocent, a deity for sure, but more of a baby, a young child, happy to be with his Mother in childhood bliss. Even the depictions of the Baptist in the wilderness, the *Bacchus* painting, does not depict hardship and despair, as it might well do. The Louvre *Baptist* is a holy, holy, holy image, having nothing to do whatsoever with the wild Baptist in the wilderness, in his painful time before he was beheaded at Salome's order. Only the fur the John the Baptist hugs so delicately to his naked chest hints at his former life in Leonardo's Louvre painting. In *St Jerome*, though, Leonardo painted despair and doubt.

Christ's nakedness sends conflicting signals. Clearly, nudity has a religious or mythic aspect, connoting nature/naturalness, purity, birth, creation, renunciation, unveiled reality, truth.[68] In art, however, nudity is ambiguous: in religious contexts it is both spiritual and sexual,[69] a duality which Leonardo da Vinci exploits in his *Madonnas*, which are both erotic and mystical. Christ's body in Renaissance painting is often

67 Mantegna: *Calvary*, 1459, 67 x 93cm, Paris, Louvre; Rubens: *Christ between the Two Thieves (Coup de Lance)* 1620, 429 x 311cm, Musée des Beaux Arts, Antwerp; Velasquez: *Christ Crucified*, 1630, 248 x 169cm, Prado, Madrid
68 See J.C. Cooper: *An illustrated Encyclopaedia of Symbols*, 112-3
69 See Marina Warner: *Monuments and Maidens*, 304

sexless, or androgynous, or feminized.[70] Christianity is an ambivalent cult; it has a clothed, virginal woman as the object of worship on the one hand, and a naked, equally virginal and chaste man on the other. In the most holy of churches, nudity is sanctified by the statues, icons and paintings of Christ on the Cross.

The dying or dead Christ, naked but for a slip of cloth and sometimes depicted entirely naked but with his legs bent to one side, hiding the 'transcendent signifier', the phallus, is an image of homoeroticism. Theologians and art historians down the ages did not or would not admit that Christ was or could have been an object of lust. Yet this is clearly the case in some depictions of the naked Saviour, such as paintings by Giovanni Battista Rosso, Caravaggio, or da Messina.[71] These nude figures send a mass of signals, from the pathetic to the narcissistic, from the erotic to the spiritual.

Patriarchal people (mostly male) protect their own interests. So homosexual art is OK, because many male critics and artists appreciate homosexual representations or issues. The reality of lesbian art becoming part of the establishment in the arts is far off. Two of the greatest artists of the High Renaissance (and therefore of all Western culture, according to patriarchal critics) were homosexual (Leonardo da Vinci and Michelangelo Buonarroti). Leonardo's homosexuality, like Michelangelo's, does not tarnish his image, standing, status or 'genius' at all.

---

70 See William Thompson: *The Time Falling Bodies Take to Light*, 109.
71 Antonello da Messina: *Crucifixion*, 1475, 52.5 x 42.5cm, Musée des Beaux Arts, Antwerp; Caravaggio: *Entombment*, 1604, 300 x 203cm, Vatican, Rome; Rosso: *Dead Christ Supported by Angels*, c.1524-7. Oil on wood, 133.6 x 104.4cm, Museum of Fine Arts, Boston

11

Michelangelo Buonarroti

When we compare Leonardo da Vinci with Michelangelo Buonarroti, we see how alike they are, in their eroticization of the male form, and yet how unlike they are in aspects of their art. Michelangelo's art is large-scale, bombastic, agile, distinctly public and out-in-the-open. Leonardo's art is equally vigorous, but is introspective, unfinished, always in a state of flux.

Michelangelo Buonarroti's art is 'masculine', celebrating the male form – in his *Ignudi* in the Sistine Chapel,[72] for instance, while his *Dying Slave* is one of the most voluptuous images of eroticism combined with death in Western art.[73] Michelangelo's slave dies utterly voluptuously, his arms pulled up to expose his body. Unlike Leonardo da Vinci's figures, who seem to recede into themselves, or into the darkness in the background, Michelangelo's figures are confident in their nudity and their sexuality. They exude confidence – too much, it

72 Michelangelo Buonarroti: *Ignudi*, 1508-10, fresco, Sistine Chapel, Vatican, Rome
73 Michelangelo Buonarroti: *Dying Slave*, 1513, marble, 229cm high, Louvre, Paris

seems, for the owners of the Sistine Chapel: figures in Michelangelo's *Last Judgement* had to have drapes painted over their genitals during the Counter-Reformation.[74] Leonardo's art, though, has been much more altered by people in later years. In fact, as the critics say, Leonardo's art is the most vandalized art in history.

Beside Michelangelo Buonarroti, the precocious, religious, obsessive hero of the era, other Renaissance sculptors often seem lightweight, insubstantial or hackneyed. Michelangelo's sculptures are full of the spirit of life which is expressed with an assurance of touch and modelling that is in itself erotic. His sculptures assert their eroticism, whatever the subject, from the superb *Dawn* and *Dusk* of the Medici tomb, to the late *Pietà*.[75] Leonardo da Vinci's sculpture, on the other hand, is extremely disappointing. Well, there hardly is any. There are drawings, plans, would-be projects, but, finally, as Serge Bramly writes:

> Leonardo is among the least well represented by his works; not a single sculpture survives, and the fewer than fifteen paintings that remain include several that are unfinished and some in which his is not the only hand. (13)

The story of Leonardo da Vinci's equestrian statues is a sad one: the endless plans and sketches, the restarts and set-backs, the joy of possibility and the melancholy of actuality. The great bronze statue of a horse came to nothing. Leonardo adores horses, and there are many sketches of them, and of course they form a large part of the *Adoration of the Magi*. The model of the horse was displayed in November 1493, and was probably very impressive, being over seven metres high. Poets praised the horse statue, but it was not cast in bronze. The project remained just that – a project. It remained plans on paper, and letters, hints, thoughts, but not the finished artwork.

Michelangelo Buonarroti's sculptures, on the other hand, are very definitely *there*. They exist in churches and museums dotted around Europe and the world. Michelangelo took the anonymous, often

74 Michelangelo Buonarroti: *The Last Judgement*, 1536-41, fresco, Sistine Chapel, Vatican, Rome

75 Michelangelo Buonarroti: *Tomb of Lorenzo de' Medici* h. 173cm, Medici Chapel, Florence; *Pietà*, late 1550s, marble,226cm high, Florence

indifference eroticism of Greek statues and turned into something 'modern' or Renaissance, something decidedly individual and subjective. The anguish of (some of) Michelangelo's figures is that of a 'great' artist striving to achieve the Holy Grail or Philosopher's Stone of sculpture, the perfect form, that Neoplatonic impossibility. Leonardo too searched and searched. His artistic life was a religious quest which took in mathematics, philosophy, anatomy, botany, geography, geology, biology and science. It was a quest for knowledge, for *knowing* about things and about the world around him. Michelangelo pursued the perfect work of art; whereas Leonardo was not so concerned with the artwork as a *finished* thing. For Leonardo, the quest or process was just as important as the artwork. The *thinking* about the artwork was just as important as the actual *doing* of it. Here Leonardo is in tune with the Minimalist and Conceptual artist of 1960s North America, such as Sol Le Witt or Donald Judd, where notions of 'process', 'seriality' and planing are the basis for their art.[76]

'Beautiful' as they are ('beauty' is precisely the right term for Renaissance's notions of perfection), Michelangelo Buonarroti's statues are not final, finished forms. Like Leonardo da Vinci's works, they are fluid, aching for the touch of completion which nobody can give them. Besides Michelangelo, other Renaissance sculptors' works seem indistinct, weak, dispassionate or inconsequential – Lucia della Robbia, Benvenuto Cellini, Baccio Bandinelli, Giambologna, Bartolommeo Ammanati and Donatello, just as, set beside Leonardo most Renaissance painters seem indistinct, weak, dispassionate or inconsequential.

76 Frances Colpitt: *Minimal Art: The Critical Perspective*, University of Washington Press, Seattle, 1990; Gregory Battock, ed: *Minimal Art: A Critical Anthology*, Studio Vista 1969

12

Leda and the Swan

Like Michelangelo Buonarroti, Leonardo da Vinci produced an erotic version of *Leda and the Swan.* Both Michelangelo's and Leonardo's images are lost. How the art world would love to find them, and any other of Leonardo's lost works. We know both, though, because they were copied.[77] Leonardo's *Leda* was burned by Madame de Maintenon around 1700, or was destroyed by one of Louis XIII's henchmen. Michelangelo's picture is explicitly erotic: the huge swan lies between the deity's legs, the feathers of his wing over her vulva, a touch that expresses male 'possession' of the woman's sexuality.

Leonardo da Vinci made his *Leda and the Swan* as pornography is made; at the request of a (male) client: 'I executed the painting...for a lover. He wished to see the features of his goddess mirrored so that he might kiss them without arousing suspicion: Leonardo wrote.[78]

77 After Michelangelo Buonarroti: *Leda and the Swan*, 16th century, Royal Academy, London.
78 Quoted in Peter Webb, 112.

From the drawings,[79] we can see that the lost painting was a female nude, rare in Leonardo da Vinci's *oeuvre*, seen standing or 'half-kneeling' beside a huge swan. In the drawings, she caresses the swan's neck or beak. This is extraordinary: a young, voluptuous goddess stroking the neck of a giant swan *painted by Leonardo da Vinci, the world's most extraordinary painter*. And if this wasn't amazing enough, to Leda's right, are the two sets of divine twins, hatched out of enormous eggs. The children are in the act of climbing out of the broken egg shells. In the drawings and the copies by various artists[80] it is a powerful image by any standards. How much more powerful it must have been in the flesh, so to speak. The preparatory drawings for the head of Leda, with that familiar hairstyle that Leonardo made his own, are particularly beautiful.[81] Frustratingly, we have to rely on the accounts of Leonardo's lost works, unable to see them for ourselves. And I, for one, would like to see his *Leda and the Swan*. Cassiano del Pozzo saw Leonardo's *Leda* in 1623 and wrote:

> A Leda standing, almost completely nude, with at her feet the swan and two eggs, from which four babies have come out (Castor and Pollux, Helen and Clytemnestra). It is somewhat dry in style, but exquisitely finished, particularly the woman's breast. The landscape and foliage are represented with great diligence. But it is in a bad state since it is made up of three panels which have split apart and the painted surface has been broken.[82]

Serge Bramly writes that the elements in the painting 'are in no way evocative of desire or amorous ecstasy' (378). He is wrong, Leda, a female nude, is supremely erotic, as is the way she strokes the swan's neck. The swan, after all, is the supreme phallic deity of the Classical world. He is Zeus or Jupiter, the father-god and godfather of all the

79 Leonardo: *Leda and the Swan*, c. 1504, pen and ink over black chalk, 12.5 x 11cm, Boymans Museum, Rotterdam; *Study for Leda*, pen, 15.5 x 14cm, Chatsworth.
80 Anonymous, the 'ex-Spiridon version', *Leda and the Swan*, wood, 132 x 78cm, Rome; anonymous: *Leda and the Swan*, 112 x 86cm, Galleria Borghese, Rome.
81 Leonardo: *Study of a Woman's Head, c.* 1504-6, pen and ink over black chalk, 17.7 x 14.7cm, Royal Library, Windsor; *Study of a Woman's Head and Coiffure, c.* 1504-6, 20 x 16.2cm, Royal Library, Windsor.
82 Pozzo, quoted in *The Complete Paintings*, 107.

gods, who was pure phallus, a phallus gone wild. Zeus is astonishing in his wildly phallic, wildly sexual exploits. He seems to have fucked every Goddess in Greek mythology. He thunders about the sky, raging like the most macho instinct gone wild. He slept with Mnemosyne over nine nights and she later gave birth to nine daughters, the Muses; he raped Demeter in the form of a bull, and she bore Kore; he married Hera; he 'pursued' (raped) Electra, Taygete, Callisto (in the form of Artemis), Aegina, Antiope, Niobe, Mera, Leto, Danæ, Semele, Europa, Leda, Hesione, Elara, Naerea, Protgenia, Thalia, and many others. Zeus had everybody, it seems. He appeared to Semele in all his thunderous majesty, but the sight killed her. Nevertheless, he took the child in her womb, put it in his thigh, and later it became Dionysus, the wild god of wine.

It is this ithyphallic god that Michelangelo Buonarroti painted, lying between Leda's legs. Leonardo da Vinci's Leda is more in control, for she stands above the swan, putting her arm around it. She is at the centre of the picture, as the Madonna always is in *Madonna and Child* paintings. She stands above the swan and the children; she orchestrates the passions evoked in the picture; she is the link between the relationships in the picture, between herself and the swan, between herself and the divine children, and, importantly, between the viewer and the whole scene.

Leonardo da Vinci's *Leda* is also a meditation on biology, on birth and the mysterious process of Nature. Leonardo brings his usual scientific precision to bear on the images of birth, plants and animals. The egg shells, the plants, the swan and the woman are portrayed with that naturalism and accuracy which is so peculiar to Leonardo. For, at the same time, *Leda and the Swan* is a bizarre image. On their own, the three basic elements – children in egg shells, the nude woman, and the swan – would have made a compelling painting, coming from Leonardo da Vinci. Put together, they make for a very strange image. Something about this image is frightening, though it is not because of the horror at Nature that some critics have felt when regarding Leonardo. Art critics, it seems, recoil from depictions of biology and birth. Images of pregnancy and birth have been ruthlessly censored throughout history.

The horror that the Christian theologians felt when they considered the mysteries of life is amazing. We are born, said Tertullian, between urine and fæces. Nice. And St Paul's hatred of the body is well-known. Of *Leda and the Swan*, Serge Bramly writes:

> The large broken eggs shock our sensibility [no they don't]: we think of their being laid and wonder what suffering they were brought into the world [not necessarily]. This Leda no more appeals to the delirium of the senses than the *Mona Lisa* does [?]; it speaks of the obscure mechanisms of childbirth, of genetic aberration, of the imperious and primitive surge of life in the depths of the body and the entrails of the earth [typical male body-fear]. Some critics admit to finding the contents of this work terrifying. Looking at it, one senses only too well the transcendence of science: one feels how the painter in conceiving his picture, had studied the relentless growth of plants, whirlpools of water, and abdomens dissected by flickering candlelight: One grasps above all the fascination, unease, and irrational anguish aroused by the "hideous" idea of procreation and the "great mystery" of woman. (378-9)

No, Serge Bramly's reading of *Leda* is wrong, or only partly right. The repulsion comes from the critic, not the artist. Though some aspects of biology repulsed Leonardo da Vinci, they also fascinated him.

13

The Leonardo Smile

Many pages have been written about the enigmatic Leonardo Smile, which is at once inviting and repelling, at once mysterious and joyful, complex and simple, timeless and evanescent, so transient yet always fixed. The Leonardo Smile is the apotheosis of ambivalent emotion. It is comparable too with the smile of so many Buddhist and Oriental statues, those Buddhas and deities which are found throughout the East, and in Western shrines and museums. The Oriental smile speaks of a quiet inner harmony, a religious unity and tranquillity. Leonardo's Smile is not, for some, as tranquil as Eastern statues.

For European intellectuals, the Gioconda Smile is the cruel smile of the Medusa, the Fatal Woman, the eulogized Black Venus (S. Freud, 162). In fact, the Leonardo Smile is the most transparent of all images, for it reflects the emotions of whoever is looking at it. This is clear from much of Leonardo criticism, where the critics seem to be talking about themselves, not Leonardo. Leonardo's art is more like a mirror than most other painter's works, except perhaps Andy Warhol. Warhol, like Leonardo, is one of those artists who create a myriad of responses, from disbelief through jealousy to admiration. As Nico in Warhol's Velvet Underground music group sang, 'I'll be your mirror'. Warhol's art is a mirror, as is Leonardo's, a carefully controlled, stylish reflector. The Gioconda Smile of the *Mona Lisa* is at the heart of the Leonardo cult (and the screenprints of Marilyn Monroe are at the heart of the Warhol cult).

The Leonardo Smile appears in *The Adoration of the Magi*, the two *Virgin of the Rocks*, the *Mona Lisa*, *Lady with the Ermine*, *St John the Baptist* and, most powerfully, perhaps, in *The Virgin and Child with St Anne*. Freud has his opinions on the Leonardo Smile: for him, Leonardo da Vinci was recapturing his mother's smile. In his art, Freud suggests, Leonardo triumphed over 'the unhappiness of his erotic life' (S. Freud, 163). Julia Kristeva sums up Freud's treatment of Leonardo thus, in her essay on Giovanni Bellini, "Motherhood According to Bellini":

> Relying on biographical evidence and on paintings as *narrative* such as *Virgin and Child with St Anne* and the *Mona Lisa*, Freud could maintain that Leonardo's "artistic personality" was formed, first, by the precocious seduction he was supposed to have experienced at the hands of his mother (the vampire tail of his dreams would represent the tongue of his mother, passionately kissing the illegitimate child); second, by a double motherhood (taken from his mother, Leonardo was raised in his father's family by his stepmother, who had no children of her own); and finally, by the impressive authority of an office-holding father. The father finally triumphed over the drawing power of the mother, which determined the young man's interest in art, and near the end of his life, Leonardo turned toward the sciences. Thus, we have the typical homosexual configuration of a homosexual structure. Persuaded by precocious seduction and double motherhood of the existence of a maternal phallus, the painter never stopped looking for fetish equivalents in the bodies of young people, in his friendships with them, in his miserly worship of objects and money, and in his avoidance of all contact with and access to the feminine body. His was a forbidden mother because she was the primordial seducer, the limit of an archaic, infantile jouissance that must never be reproduced. She established the child's diffident narcissism and cult of the masculine body which he ceaselessly painted, even when a mother figures at the centre of the painting. Take for example Leonardo's Virgins: *Madonna with the Carnation* and *Virgin and Child with St Anne*. There we find the enigmatic smile, identical with that of the Mona Lisa, herself furtively masculine; with naive tenderness, face and torso impulsively female infant, who remains the real focus of pictorial space and narrative interest. The maternal figure is completely absorbed with her baby; it is he that makes her exist. (244-5)

The source of the Leonardo Smile may not be in Freudian conflict and taboo: instead, it may be an attempt on Leonardo's part to express an inexplicable joy, the kind of joy one feels sometimes at simply being alive. Like the joy of suddenly feeling a ray from the sun on one's face after hours of cloud. Whether such joys are erotic in motive, cause or nature is debatable. What is certain is that Leonardo's smiling people are mesmerizing. As Rudolf Otto writes of the experience of the Numinous, what he terms the *mysterium tremendum* 'may become the hushed, trembling, and speechless humility of the creature in the presence of – whom or what? In the presence of that which is a *mystery* inexpressible and above all creatures.' (13)

The Leonardo Smile is thus the record of something ineffable, ungraspable, a partially visible manifestation of something that remains resolutely invisible. In his quest of the representation of the invisible, Leonardo da Vinci was doomed to fail. He knew it. All artists know it. The failure of the quest is built-in to the art-making process. The journey must end in disappointment. Julia Kristeva writes:

> It is no accident that the major segments of this economy, which was to determine Western man's vision for four centuries to come, are fitted into place by virtue of the themes of motherhood, the woman's body, or the mother (Mona Lisa or the virgin). The artist, as servant of the maternal phallus, displays this always and everywhere unaccomplished art of reproducing bodies and spaces as graspable, masterable *objects*, within reach of his eye and hand. (in ib., 246)

14

The Black Goddess

The divine presence in Leonardo da Vinci is distinctly female and feminine. For him, the 'mystery' of life is embodied best in women, in Goddess figures. Leonardo's women are simultaneous objects of awe and veneration, as paintings, and producers of awe and veneration, as Goddesses. Many elements in Leonardo are feminized or feminine: not only the androgynous or feminized males, such as the Baptist or St Jerome, but also the profusion of flowers, for instance, in the two *Virgin of the Rocks* These flowers symbolize the Virgin Mary (carnation, iris, lily, etc) but also they point towards 'woman' as the Goddess of Flowers and Plants, as the Earth Mother, the fertile Mother of all. The Madonnas are depicted in caves, again an explicit female symbol ('the Great Earth Mother is the mother of stones' writes a Jungian, Erich Neumann [261-2]). Leonardo's Madonnas are Queens of the Underworld, presiding over the unconscious, unborn underworld states of being. The Louvre *Virgin of the Rocks* is particularly rich in floral imagery. At Christ's feet, for instance, is *cyclamen purpurascens* which symbolizes love and devotion.[83] Exquisite indeed are Leonardo's depictions of

83 William A. Emboden, 1987, 116.

plants, from the finely detailed vegetation in the two *Virgin of the Rocks* paintings to the many drawings. Every painter of the Madonna had to be skilled at drawing flowers – in particular the lily, the central flower of *Annunciations*, as well as violets, carnations, columbines, irises and, of course, roses. Leonardo da Vinci made many drawings and studies of flowers: the clump of star of Bethlehem, a twig of oak leaves and acorns, a spray of blackberry, a stem of lilies.[84]

All the signifiers in Leonardo da Vinci's portrayals of the Madonna are of an abundant world, of flowers and plants, in which life is thriving. Leonardo's vision of a vegetative, organic Goddess emphasizes that the authentic *participation mystique* with the Earth is feminine. The cave in *The Virgin of the Rocks* is so clearly a creative womb, a world-womb, with the Madonna at the centre of it. 'Womb and phallus are everywhere, and power is expressed through them' writes Robert Payne (74).

In *The Virgin of the Rocks* there is the suggestion of an immense, holy touch, a miraculous touch which heals, like the 'laying on of hands' in Jesus' life. The Madonna raises her hand, which is stretched out, foreshortened, towards the viewer, at once blessing the Christ child and encouraging him. In the two *Virgin of the Rocks*, Leonardo makes the hand central; in all of Leonardo's art, the hand is prominent.[85] It is the 'organ of organs', as Aristotle says.[86] The Virgin enacts the ancient ritual of the 'laying-on of hands'. The hand gesture is the mechanism of divine power. Leonardo takes the Hand of God, as featured in Gothic art, and changes the sex of the divinity who hands out magic.

This gesture of the Virgin's appears in other Renaissance paintings (in Antonello de Messina's *San Cassiano Altarpiece*, Mantegna's *Madonna della Vittoria*, and Correggio's *Madonna and Child*) though Leonardo da Vinci's is unquestionably the most powerful. The upraised hand of the Virgin is a gesture of power, for at the heart of Leonardo's world is not the Judæo-Christian male God or Jehovah, but a Goddess

84 Leonardo: *A Lily*, 31.4 x 17.7cm, pen and ink; *Star of Bethlehem*, 19.8 x 16cm, red chalk & pen & ink; *A Branch of Blackberry*, 15.5 x 16.2cm, red chalk; *Oak Leaves with Acorns*, 18.8 x 15.4cm, red chalk, all Royal Library, Windsor

85 Leonardo has made some beautiful studies of hands, as in *Study of a Woman's Hands*, Royal Library, Windsor.

86 Aristotle, quoted in Benjamin Walker, 167-8.

who has more in common with ancient deities such as Isis or Inanna than with the relatively recent phenomena of the Virgin Mary.

Indeed, Leonardo da Vinci can be seen to be obsessed with the ideas of female power and motherhood. Two works depict the trinity of matriarchy, the powerful bonding of child, mother and grandmother, embodied in the Louvre *Virgin and Child with St Anne* and in the London or Burlington 'cartoon', *St Anne with the Virgin, Child and Baptist.* It is St Anne who is the power behind Leonardo's Goddess figures. She is the crone, the wise old woman, later depicted as a 'witch' in mediæval culture. She is an incarnation of the Black Goddess, the occult deity of secret energies and mysteries.

The 'Black Goddess' is a product of masculine desire and fear. Leonardo da Vinci's women are types of Black Goddesses, though modulated by the strictures and structures of Renaissance holy art. The fiercest Black Goddess is undoubtedly the Indian Goddess of Hinduism and Tantrism, Kali. In depictions of Kali when she is in her devouring, deathly aspect, male fear of women reaches a peak. Kali is a Black Goddess who dances on top of men; she copulates with them and slays them at the same time. Statues of Kali show her sucking the life or essence (sperm or *soma*) out of the male, while she brandishes swords, fire, skulls and snakes in her many arms.[87] Kali is the 'dark one', the Queen of Blood, who presides over extraordinary blood sacrifices. She is the ultimate manifestation of the 'monstrous feminine', the Freudian 'Terrible Mother', the castrating, devouring, corpse-eating Goddess.[88] The connections between Kali and Leonardo's Goddesses are obvious: the Medusa, with her castrating stare, has affinities with Kali, while the Mona Lisa, at least in Walter Pater's description, as the ultimate *femme fatale* or vampire, is like Kali.

Kali is the manifestation of excessive anxiety about sexuality and relations with women amongst patriarchal religions. What Western religionists did in the Judæo-Christian era was to suppress what Robert Briffault calls 'the chthonic aspects of the Queen of heaven' (III, 183),

87 Kali the Devourer, copper casting, northern India, modern, Victoria & Albert Museum, London.

88 Heinrich Zimmer: "The Indian World Mother", in *The Mystic Vision, Eranos Yearbooks*,6, Bollingen Series XXX, 1968.

all of that wild sexuality, producing the Devil, notions of 'sin' and 'evil', witches, and any scapegoats they could muster. What patriarchal people prefer is the homely, passive, nurturing 'woman', embodied in the personality of the Blessed Virgin Mary. Even here, though, in the cult of the Madonna, there are many vestiges of ancient Goddess worship. Beliefs, for instance, that somehow 'woman' or the 'eternal feminine' encompasses everything. Whatever there is in the male world, it is enfolded in the female world, like the child is enfolded by the other in the womb, and, later, in her arms, sitting on her lap. In times of anxiety, people often return ('regress', Freudians would say) to 'primæval' feelings and situations. The key image of a *regressus ad uterum* or return to the Mother, is the Madonna and Child, found throughout the history of world art, and everywhere: in Peru, in Sumer, Africa, Greece, in Aztec art, everywhere there are images of mothers and babies. In Western art, we find the *Madonna and Child* everywhere.

The artworks show just how much patriarchal religion still regards 'Woman' or the 'eternal feminine' or the Goddess as central and crucial to life are those sculptures of the seated Virgin which open up to reveal the Christian figures inside: God, crucified Christ and various saints.[89] Here, the Madonna envelops not only all of humanity, as in the *Madonna della Misericordia* paintings, where the Virgin shelters everyone under her cloak,[90] but also all the protagonists of Christian religion. All the mysteries of religion, including the Creator Himself, God, are contained within the body of the Madonna. Here, Mary is the Mother not only of Christ but of God, the Mother behind everything. She is also the church, the very building of the church. You enter her body when you enter a church. The cathedrals of the mediæval era were called 'Notre Dame', Our Lady, and they are explicitly wombs of the Goddess (inside they are hot and dark, and blood mysteries, such as the Mass or Eucharist, occur there, as in wombs). The entrances to cathedrals, those Gothic arches, can be seen as vulvas. The entrances

89 "Vierge Ouvrante", 15th century, painted wood, France, Musée de Cluny, Paris; *Virgin, c.* 14th century, wood covered with linen, gesso and gilt, Germany, Metropolitan Museum of Art, New York.
90 Piero della Francesca: *Madonna della Misericordia*, centre of a polyptych, *c.* 1460?, 134 x 91cm, Town hall, Sansepulcro, Italy

to churches are often narrow slits, shaped like vulvas. The ribbed shapes around the pointed doorways echo the labia. The cave in *The Virgin of the Rocks* is vaginal, an opening that echoes the interior of the church, suggesting perfumes with its flowers, and a powerful sense of ritual with its complex hand gestures. As Robert Payne writes of *The Virgin of the Rocks* 'in the very shape of the grotto, sexual symbols are consciously or unconsciously displayed to advance the theme of absolute purity. Womb and phallus images are everywhere, and power is expressed through them' (74).

The Christian view, then, echoes that of antiquity and prehistory; that, behind everything that male gods may create, is the Goddess. She is the primordial darkness of the universe behind everything, or, in ecological terms, she is the primal sea out of which life grew. We see this clearly in Leonardo da Vinci's two *St Anne and Virgin* images, where St Anne stands behind everything, cradling, nurturing.

Black Goddesses include the Gnostic Sophia, Diana and Isis (later Goddesses of witches), Hecate, Medusa, Circe, Lilith, Adam's first partner, and the Indian Kali.[91] The Black Goddess appears in Tantrism, Taoism, Catharism, alchemy, witchcraft, Neoplatonism and other 'occultisms'. The *Tao Te Ching* speaks of 'knowing the male, but keeping to the role of the female': '[k]now the white, but keep to the role of the black'.[92] For some, the black Mother is the origin of humanity; we are all descended from one African woman (Sjoo, 32). Peter Redgrove writes that the Black Goddess is the deity of the invisible, of the unconscious, of second sight and 'supersensible' eroticism (137). This is Leonardo's world, this dark, hypersensitive, erotic environment.

Leonardo da Vinci's Goddesses are dark, fecund, mythic types, figures of mystery and power. His St Anne trades in the mediæval and Renaissance cult of St Anne, especially prevalent in Northern European art.[93] A popular image was the Virgin and Child surrounded by various virgins and this Holy Family was presided over not by Joseph but by St Anne (although Joseph is the apex of the pyramidal structure of figures

91 See Monica Sjöo, 210; Peter Redgrove; Ean Begg; Robert Graves: *Mammon and the Black Goddess*, Cassell 1965
92 *Tao Te Ching*, tr D.C. Lau, Penguin, 1963, 85.
93 See L. Dresen-Coenders, 101, 123-4

in Raphael's *The Holy Family with St Elisabeth and St John Baptist*).[94] Quentin Massys' *St Anne Altarpiece*, Jan Baegert's *The Holy Family* and the Master of the Magdalen Legend's *Holy Family* are images of tranquil domesticity, a vivid portrayal of home life and motherhood, emphasizing the holy lineage of Jesus, set amongst a group of women.[95] Feminine solidarity is the theme of these St Anne paintings: the extended family sometimes includes various saints (Jude, Mary Cleophas, James, Simon, Joachim).[96]

St Anne becomes another representation of primæval Nature, of the Goddess as Earth Mother. Leonardo's Dark Moon or Negative Goddess is a Renaissance version of 'woman' as origin of life, of 'woman' as nurturer and carer. In one sense, the St Anne pictures are nostalgic, looking back on the happy unity of childhood. Indeed, Leonardo's Marys are – rarely in Renaissance art – shown smiling. Probably the most inscrutable smile in Western art is not that of the *Mona Lisa*, but of St Anne in the Louvre *Virgin, Child and St Anne*. St Anne's smile is so many things: it is impossible to pin *one* reading on it. It is not a smile with only one cause. She smiles softly, wistfully, joyously, magically, spectrally – any number of adjectives might describe St Anne's smile. In the study of St Anne's head, at Windsor, is one Leonardo's most ravishing drawings.[97] Kenneth Clark raved about it – and rightly: 'The drawing has human mystery'. Certainly, the drawing is full of mystery. It is text so soft and delicate – it seems as if the Goddess's face is dissolving before our eyes. She melts. The chalk is powdery, as if the slightest breeze would dislodge this drawing, and blow it all away. The drawing is unmistakably a Leonardo artwork: no one else makes art quite like this. Indeed, you might say that the *Study for the Head of St Anne* is one of the great works of the Renaissance (and therefore of all

94 Raphael: *The Holy Family with St Elisabeth and the Young St John Baptist*, 1505-7, panel, 51.5 x 42in.

95 Quentin Massys: *St Anne Altarpiece*,1509, Musée Royal des beaux-Art, Brussels; Jan Baegert: *The Holy Family*, panel, Landesmuseum fur Kunste, Munster; Master of Magdalen Legend (d. 1527), *The Holy Family*, Koninklijk Museum, Antwerp.

96 See Margaret Whitney, 126.

97 Leonardo: *Study for the Head of St Anne*, c.1510, black chalk and ink, with red chalk, 18.7. x 12.9cm, Windsor.

Western art). Like Leonardo's drawing *Study for the Head of an Angel*, the one used in *The Virgin of the Rocks*, the *St Anne* sketch is, on one level, without compare, a drawing as sublime as drawing – as art – can become. Who else can achieve such transcendence and phosphorescence in drawing? Raphael? Andrea del Sarto? Michelangelo? Botticelli? Rembrandt? Ingres? Klee? Klimt? Hockney? No one really comes close to this sort of luminosity in drawing. In terms of figurative, three dimensional illusion and representation, Leonardo really is the master, towering above all other figurative artists.

Here, St Anne is the rock, the roots, the pivot, the foundation of life. She smiles softly at the Virgin pulling the child away from the lamb. The two Mothers, St Anne and the Madonna, merge together, physically. Their limbs entwine. Michelangelo Buonarroti painted a *Holy Family*, where the Virgin takes Jesus from Joseph over her shoulder, a typical example of brash, dynamic Michelangeloan art.[98]

St Anne is at the back of everything. From her body grows the Madonna, and then the child. St Anne melts into the darkening blue of the landscape, while the Madonna stands out in vermilion. The pyramidal structure of Leonardo da Vinci's *St Anne, Virgin and Child* is surmounted by St Anne's face. Fra Pietro da Novellara described to Isabella d'Este a cartoon (now lost) depicting St Anne, the Virgin, the Child and the lamb:

> Since he has been in Florence, he has worked on one cartoon, which represents an infant Christ of about one year, freeing himself almost out of his mother's arms and seizing a lamb and apparently about to embrace it. The mother half-rising from the lap of St Anne is catching the Christ to draw it away from the lamb...St Anne, just rising from her seat, as if she would wish to hinder her daughter from parting the Christ from the lamb... The figures are life-size, but they fill only a small cartoon, because all art seated or bent, and each one is placed before the other, to the left.[99]

Leonardo da Vinci's *Holy Families* do not pivot around the so-called 'nuclear family': father, mother and children; they centre on the grandmother, mother and child. The figures are eroticized. The Goddess

98 Michelangelo Buonarroti: *The Holy Family ('Doni Madonna')*, 1504-05, panel, 47.3in diameter, Uffizi, Florence.
99 Pietro da Novellara, in April 1501, quoted in Martin Kemp, ed, 69.

is sexualized, even in motherhood. As psychologists note, the mother-child relation is the first sexual relation in one's life, and, for Freud, Leonardo's Madonnas explore this primal, primæval mother-child relation.

Psychologists see in Leonardo da Vinci's images the tensions of incest, of childhood sexuality, of emotional traumas and the complications surrounding mother-child relationships. Fred Gettings sees Leonardo's *Burlington Cartoon* as a depiction of *two* Jesuses, a fusion of the celestial and earthly bloodlines (1978, 54-55). In mythology, twins are common – Osiris and Set, Castor and Pollux (whom Leonardo had depicted in his lost *Leda and the Swan*). The idea of the two Jesuses, also put forward by Freud, expresses the ancient conflicts between the god and his rival for the Goddess's love. In ancient mythology, there is a god of the waxing year who is usurped by the god of the waning year. There is always, it seems, a rival in the heterosexual relations of gods and goddesses. The theme of the rival is taken up by Shakespeare in many plays: in *The Tempest*, for example, where Prospero, the banished Duke, has a political rival and a magical/spiritual one, Caliban. Again, the 'feminine' mysteries dominate Shakespeare's last play; Caliban, Prospero's rival, takes his magical power, as Prospero does, from the Witch Sycorax.[100] The world of *The Tempest*, then, like that of Leonardo, is pervaded by feminine mysteries.[101] (There are many other similarities between Leonardo and Shakespeare; not just that both artists are regarded as 'geniuses', the very apotheosis of their artform, but also in their use of sexually ambivalent, androgynous figures. Shakespeare wrote parts of 'women' characters that were played by men. Characters such as Rosalind, Viola, Portia and Julia have ambiguous sexual identities, creating confusion amongst critic and audience alike,

100 See Ted Hughes: *Shakespeare and the Goddess of Complete Being*, Faber 1992.
101 See B.D. Barnacle: *Shakespeare: Love, Magic and Poetry in Shakespeare's Sonnets and Plays*, Crescent Moon 1993.

just as in Leonardo's Madonnas, angels, Baptists and Jesuses.)[102]

In Leonardo da Vinci's paintings, the myths and conflicts of matriarchal incest are questioned, the mother-son paradox in which, symbolically, the son is simultaneously father, husband and child. The religious dimension of incest is noted by some in Egyptian religion, for instance. C.G. Jung wrote that 'usually incest has a highly religious aspect' (1967, 152, 191).

Leonardo da Vinci's art allows for a multiplicity of readings. It is distinctly non-didactic, non-monoscopic. Freud, for instance, analyzed the Louvre *St Anne, Virgin and Child* as an expression of childhood emotional conflicts: the smile in both figures, says Freud, is 'the blissful smile of the joy of motherhood' (*Leonardo*, 157). But Leonardo's Two Mothers defy a final, standard analysis. They remain a mystery. For in Leonardo's art, as in so much of art, the opposite is also true. As Tom Chetwynd writes: 'in symbolism, as in life, everything is continuously changing into its opposite' (268-272). Leonardo's figures, like the statues of Michelangelo Buonarroti or the nude Christs of Velasquez, Rubens, van der Weyden or Ribera, might be seen as expressions of conflicts between sexuality and spirituality, or culture and nature, or the visible and the invisible, or any manner of dichotomies.

102 Marjorie Garber: "The Transvestite's Progress", in Jean L. Marsden, ed: *The Appropriation of Shakespeare: Post-Renaissance Reconstructions of the Works and the Myth,* Harvester Wheatsheaf 1991, 145-6; Alan Bray: *Homosexuality in Renaissance England,* Gay Men's Press, 1982; Jean Howard: "Crossdressing, the theatre and gender struggle in early *modern* England", *Shakespeare* Quarterly (39), 1988, 432; Stephen Orgel: "Nobody's perfect: or why did the English stage take boys for women?", *South Atlantic Quarterly,* (88), Winter 1989, 7-28.

15

After Leonardo da Vinci

After Leonardo da Vinci and Michelangelo Buonarroti, Renaissance art lost some of its passion, although it became increasingly openly erotic. Images such as Peter Lely's *Nymphs by a Fountain*, anything by Rubens, Fragonard's *Bathers*, Jacques-Louis David's *Cupid and Psyche*, and Ingres' study for *Ruggiero and Angelica* are openly erotic, displaying the body as a sensual object.[103] Myths such as that of the Judgement of Paris and the Three Graces allow ample opportunity for painting acres of quivering female flesh, something Leonardo did not indulge in, as in paintings by Rubens, Cranach and Baldung Grien.[104] Artists such as Tintoretto, Veronese, Boucher, Tiepolo, Watteau, Reni, Rembrandt, Guercino, Correggio, Gros, Girodet, Géricault, and

116 Peter Lely: Nymphs by a Fountain, c. 1650-5, canvas, 129 x 144.8cm, Dulwich Picture Gallery, London; David: Cupid and Psyche, 1817, canvas, 184.1 x 241.6cm, Cleveland Museum of Art; Jean-Honoré Fragonard: Bathers, canvas, 64 x 80, Louvre, Paris; Jean-Auguste-Dominique Ingres: Study for Ruggiero and Angelica, c.1819, canvas, 84.5 x 42.5cm, Musée Ingres, Montauban.
104 Rubens: *The Judgement of Paris, c.* 1638-9, Prado, Madrid; Lucas Cranach: *The Judgement of Paris,* 1530, Staatliche Kunsthalle, Karlsruhe; Hans Baldung Grien: *The Three Graces, c* 1540, Prado, Madrid; Raphael: *The Three Graces,* panel, 6.6 x 6.6in, Condé Museum, Chantilly.

Delacroix do not hide their depictions of erotic bodies behind mythological narratives, as Renaissance artists did.[105] Unlike Leonardo, their images often put eroticism in the foreground: the pretence at mythological or historical painting is not longer upheld, and the nude form becomes primary.

The Romantic and Decadent *femme fatale* is nothing new in the 19th century: they improvize on depictions of the vampiric woman Leonardo da Vinci had brought to fulfilment in the *Mona Lisa.* Paintings such as Guido Cagnacci's *Lucretia* is explicitly erotic; Lucretia stabbing herself sublimely merges sex and death in a single image of 'woman', in a way more in keeping with post-Renaissance times than Leonardo da Vinci's *Leda.*[106]

One mythic image allowed artists to paint a scene that depicted nudity and eroticism, magic and heterosexual love, the myth of Danæ. Leonardo da Vinci did not paint a *Danæ*. She was not really a subject suited to Leonardo's tastes. She was emprisoned in a tower by her father, who was warned by an oracle that she would bear a son that would murder him. The god Jupiter saw her, lusted after her, and descended to her in a shower of gold, which she caught between her legs; the result was Perseus. Painters depict the moment when the golden semen of the phallic deity falls on the nude Danæ, as in the versions by Correggio, Titian, Rembrandt and Mabuse.[107]

The sexploits of phallic deities such as Jupiter, whether he's chasing Leda as a swan or impregnating Danæ as a golden shower, provide many opportunities for artists to make erotic art which is justifiably 'noble' because it comes from Classic mythology. Thus, we find Giulio Romano depicting Jupiter with an erect penis about to have 'intercourse' with (i.e. rape) Olympia,[108] while in Antoine Coypel's (?)

105 Tintoretto: *Susannah and the Elders*, c. 1560, oil on canvas, 76 x 95.6in, Kunsthistorisches Museum, Vienna, *The Three Graces*, 1578, oil on canvas, 57.5 x 61in, Ducal Palace, Venice; Correggio: *Jupiter and Antiope*, c. 1525, oil on canvas, 74.8 x 48.8in, Louvre, Paris.
106 Guido Cagnacci: *Death of Lucretia*, canvas, 87 x 66cm, Musée des Beaux Arts, Lyons.
107 M. Levey: *Early Renaissance*, 180.
108 Guilio Romano: *Jupiter and Olympia*, 1525-35, Mansell Collection, London.

picture of *Leda and the Swan*,[109] Jupiter's genitals are again the focus of the image, as the woman sits astride his legs. But although he did not show nude bodies cavorting in lust, Leonardo remains one of the most erotic of artists. He *suggests* more than most painters; his art evokes a powerful presence, even in the absence of his unfinished, abandoned or lost projects; the very invisibility of certain aspects of his art add to his magic.

109 Antoine Coypel (?): *Jupiter with Leda and the Swan*, from *Histoire Universelle*, c.1750, British Museum.

Illustrations

Art by Leonardo da Vinci, followed by some of his contemporaries, and some artists who were influenced by Leonardo.

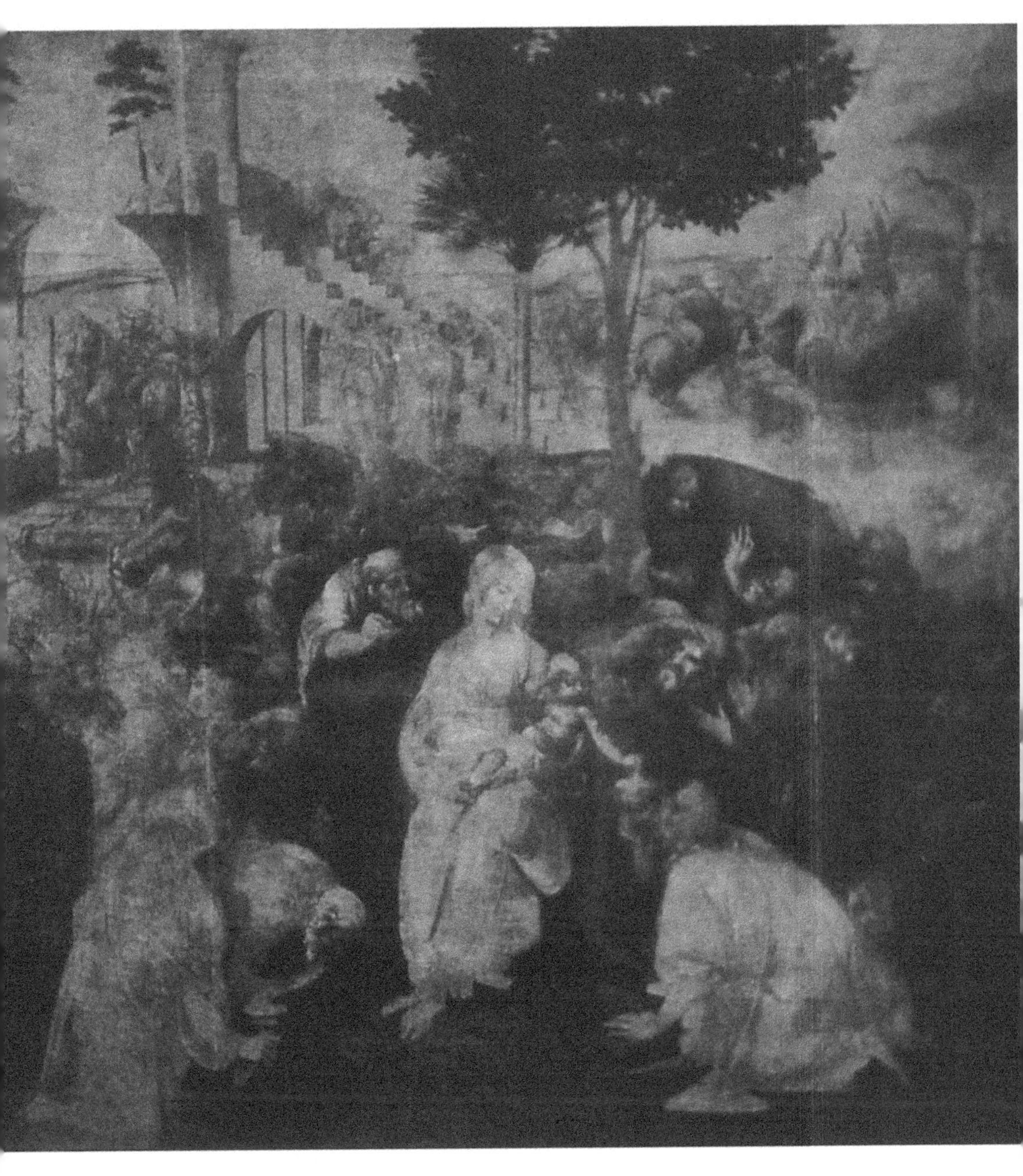

Leonardo da Vinci's beyond beautiful *Adoration of the Magi*

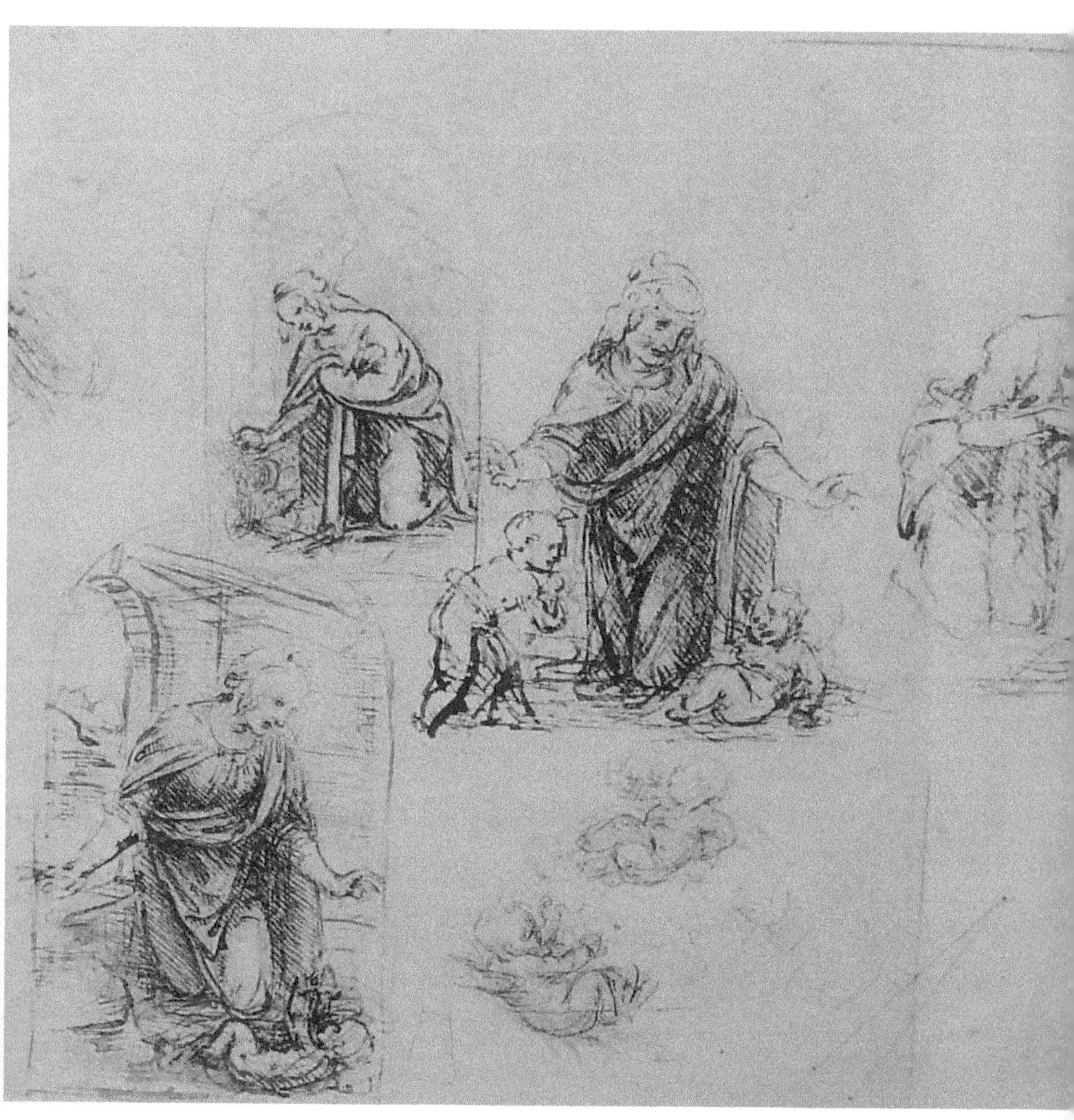

Leonardo, studies for Adoration paintings

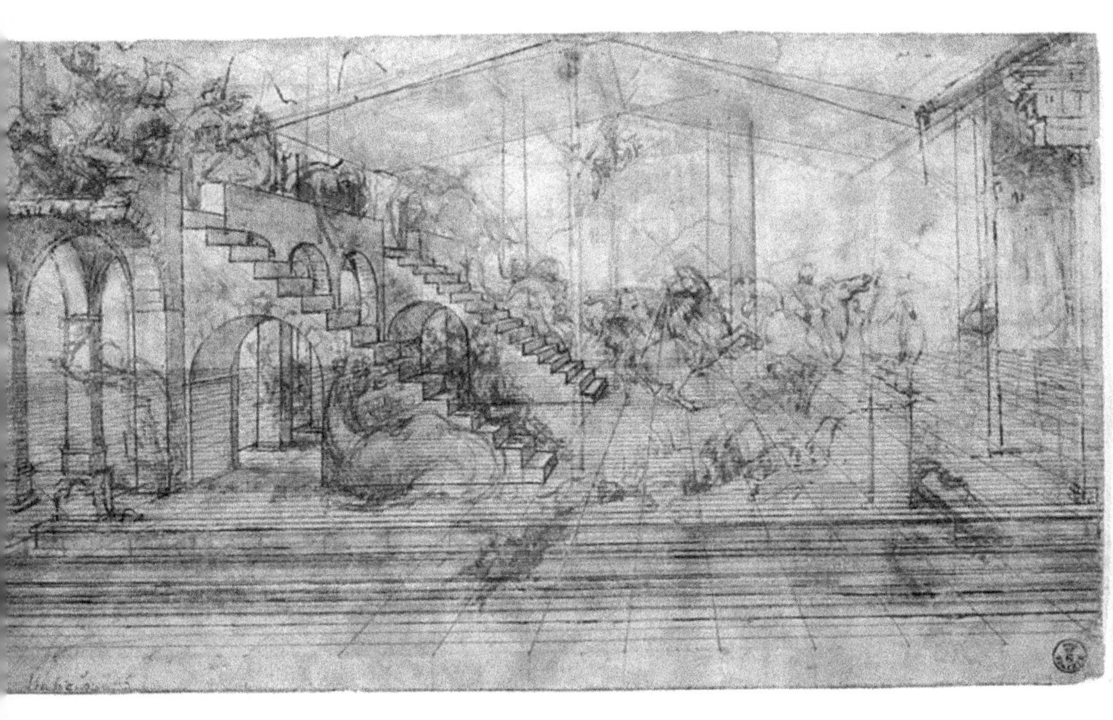

Leonardo da Vinci, Study for the Adoration, Uffizi Gallery

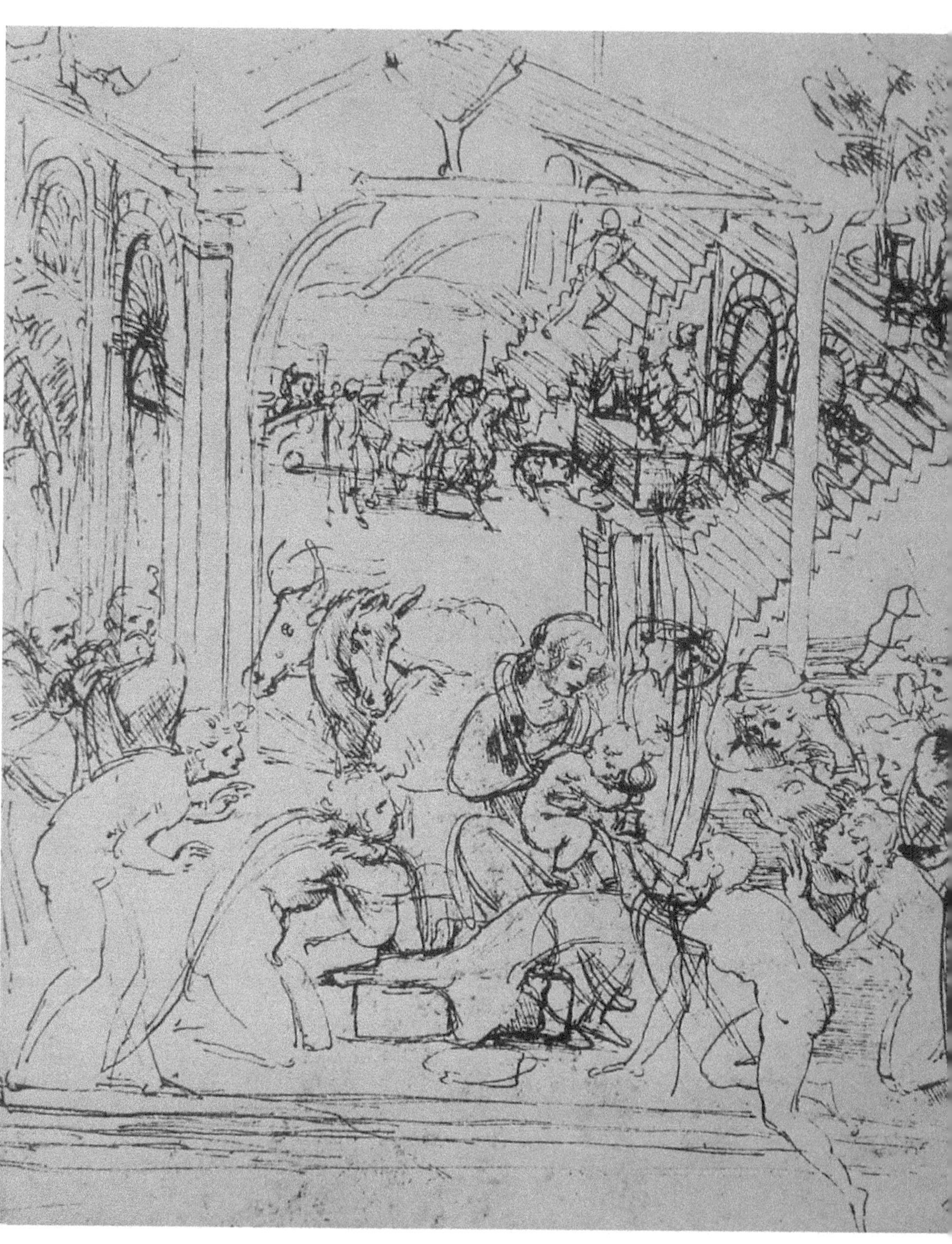

Leonardo, Study For the Adoration of the Magi

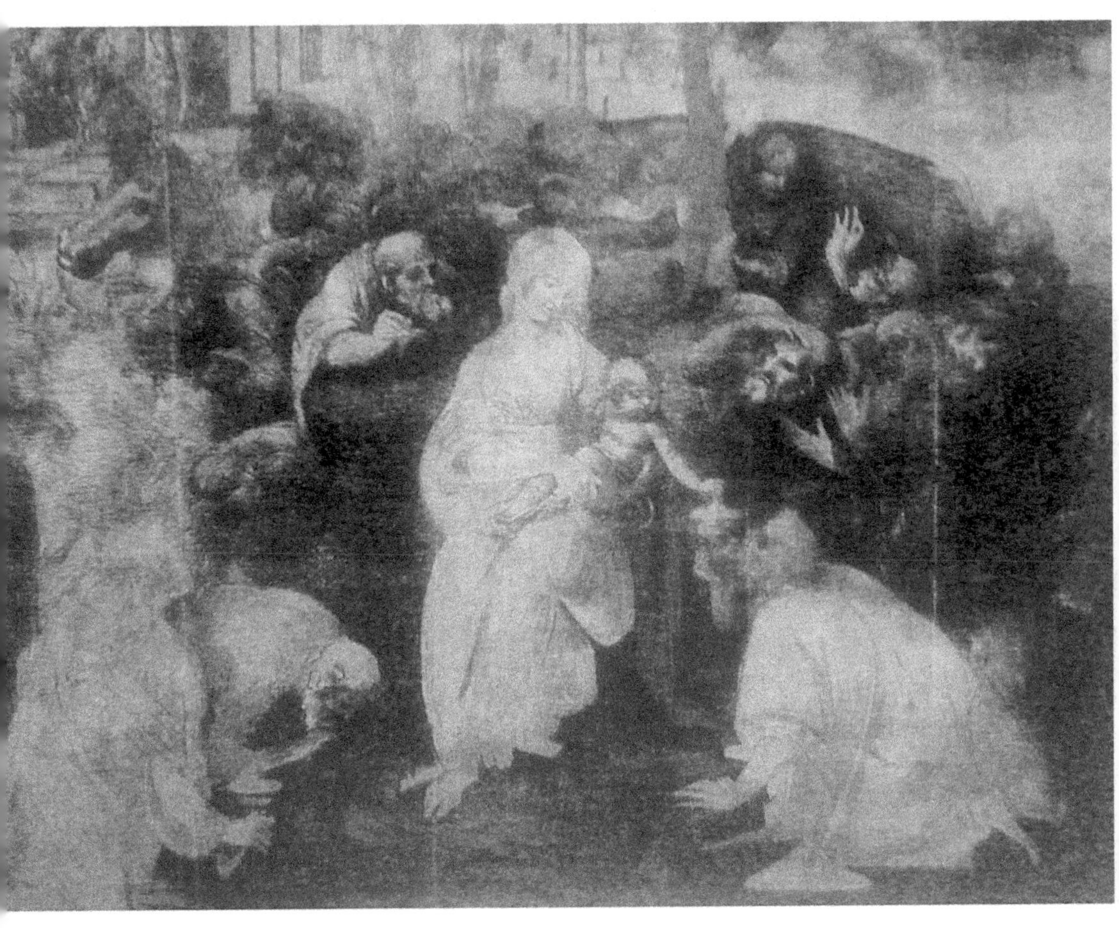

Leonardo, Adoration of the Magi, detail

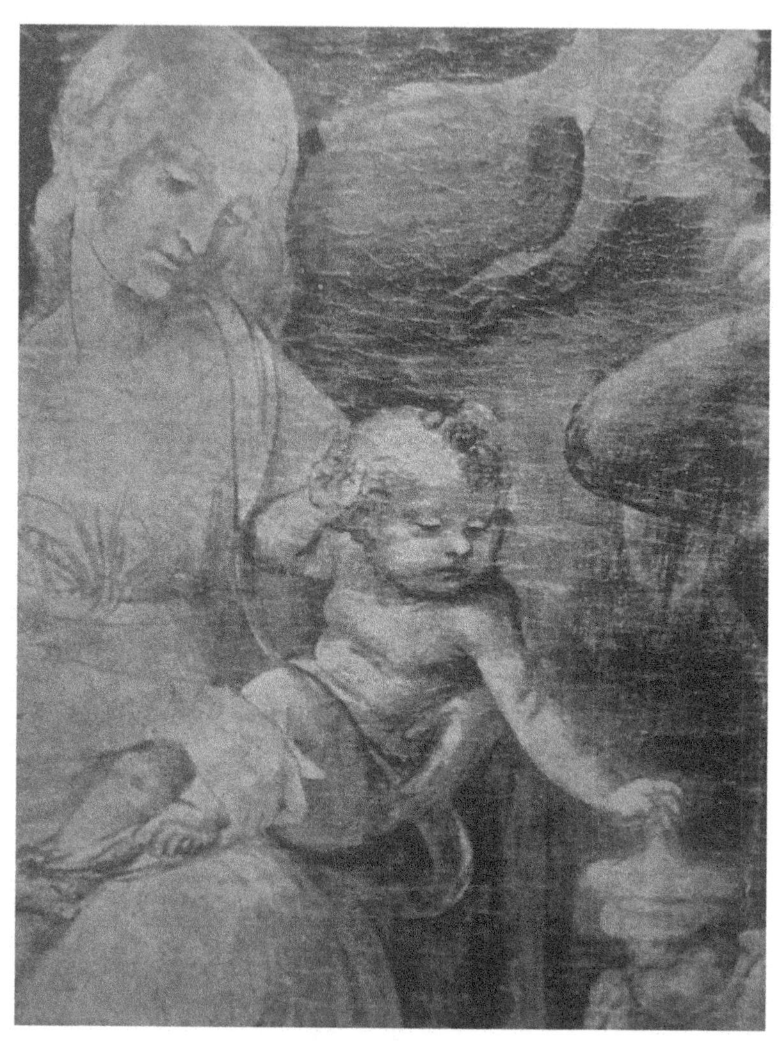

Leonardo da Vinci, *Adoration of the Magi*, detail.

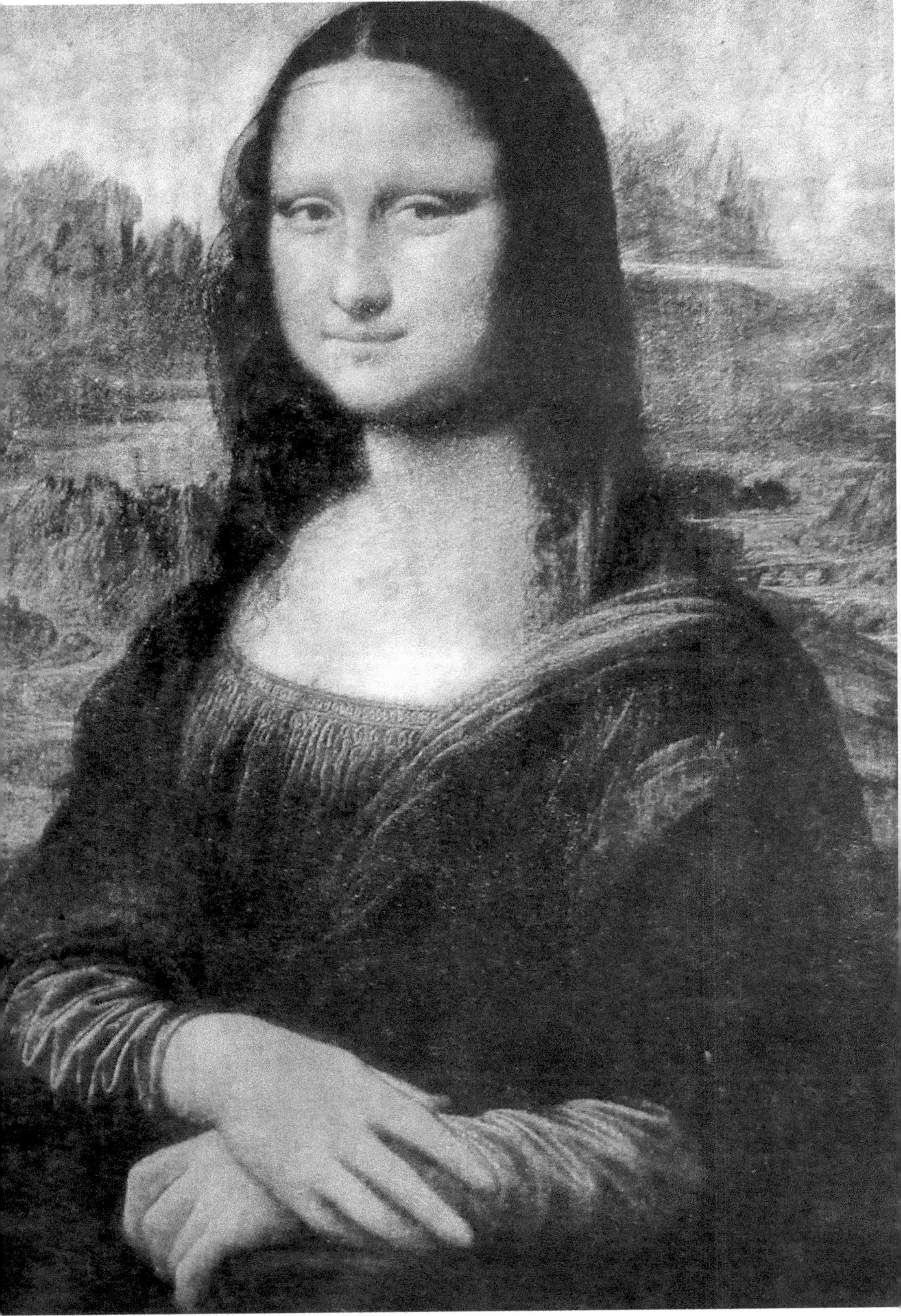

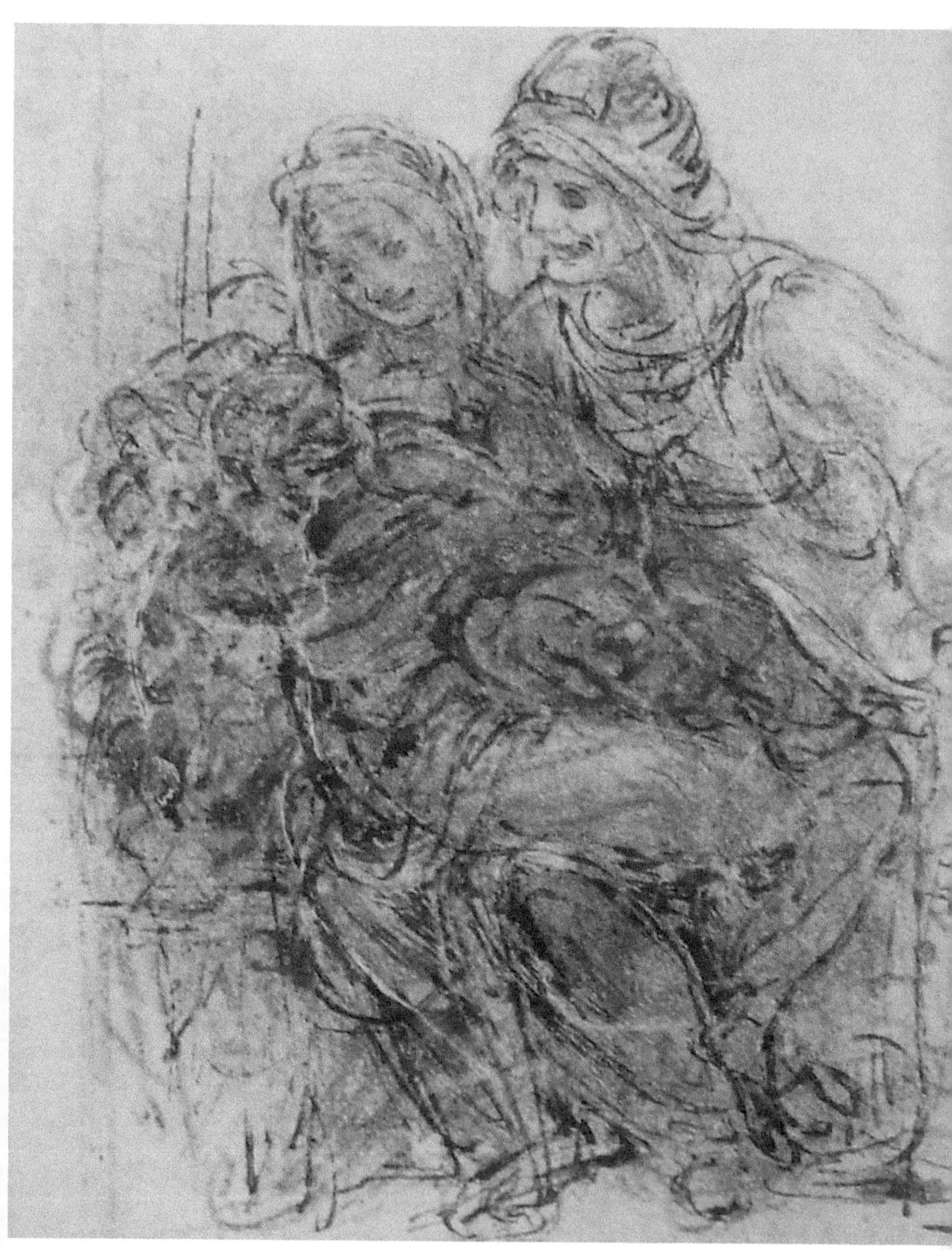

Leonardo, Study for The Virgin and Child With St Anne

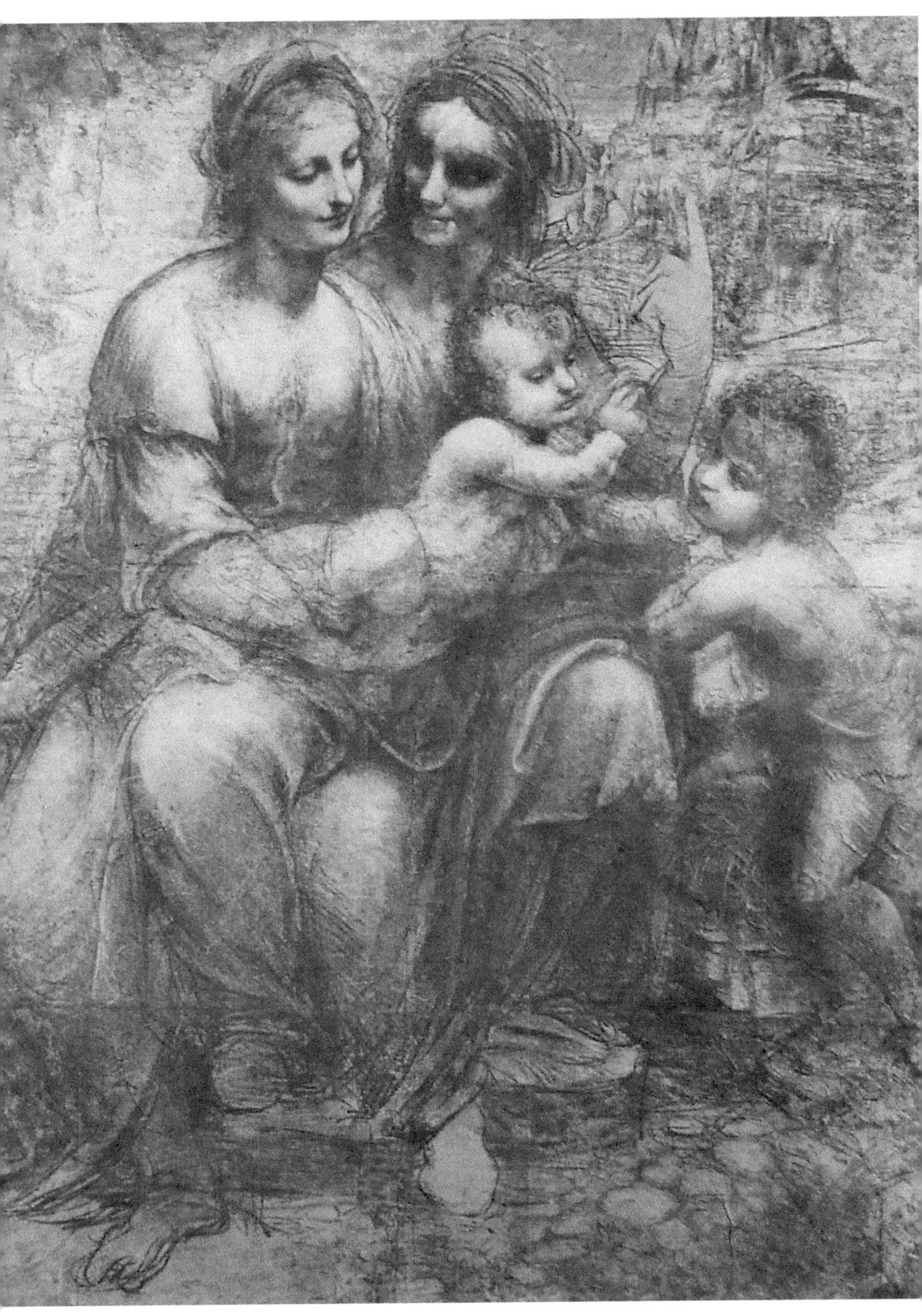

Leonardo, The Virgin and Child With St Anne, National Gallery, London

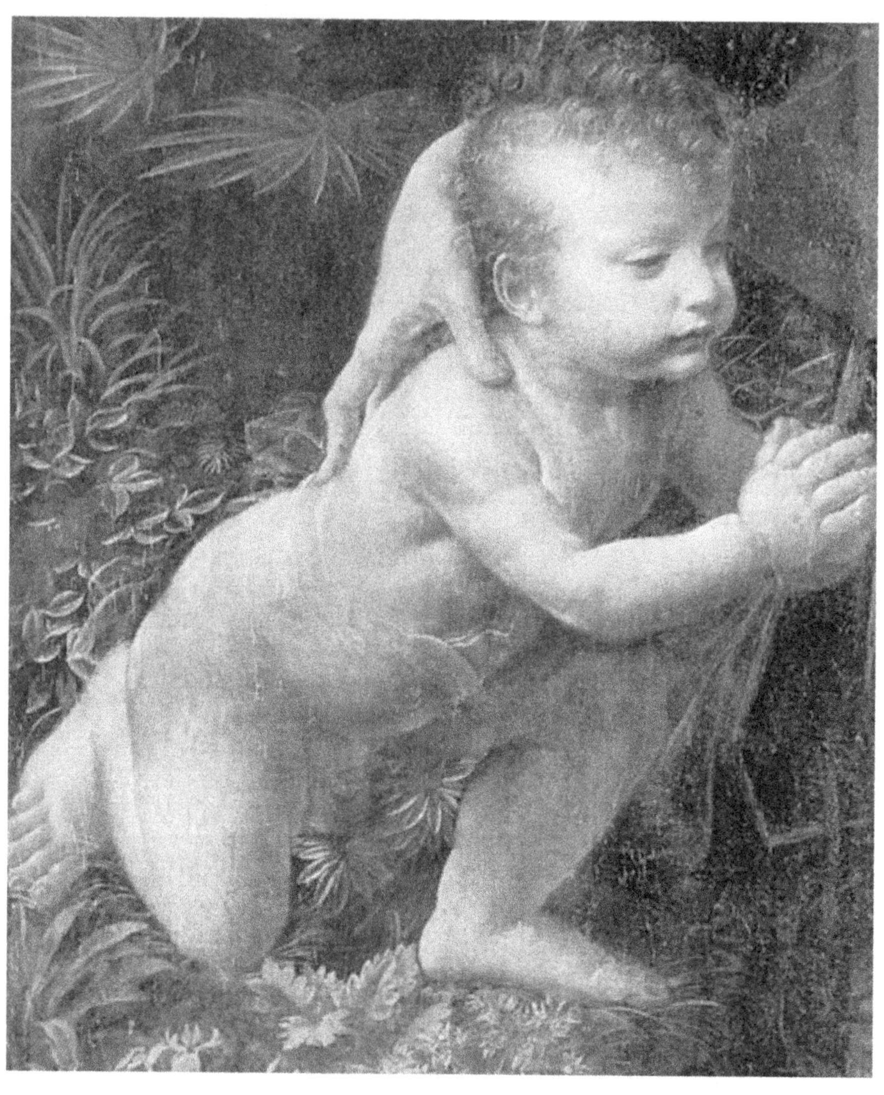

Leonardo da Vinci, detail from the Louvre Virgin of the Rocks,

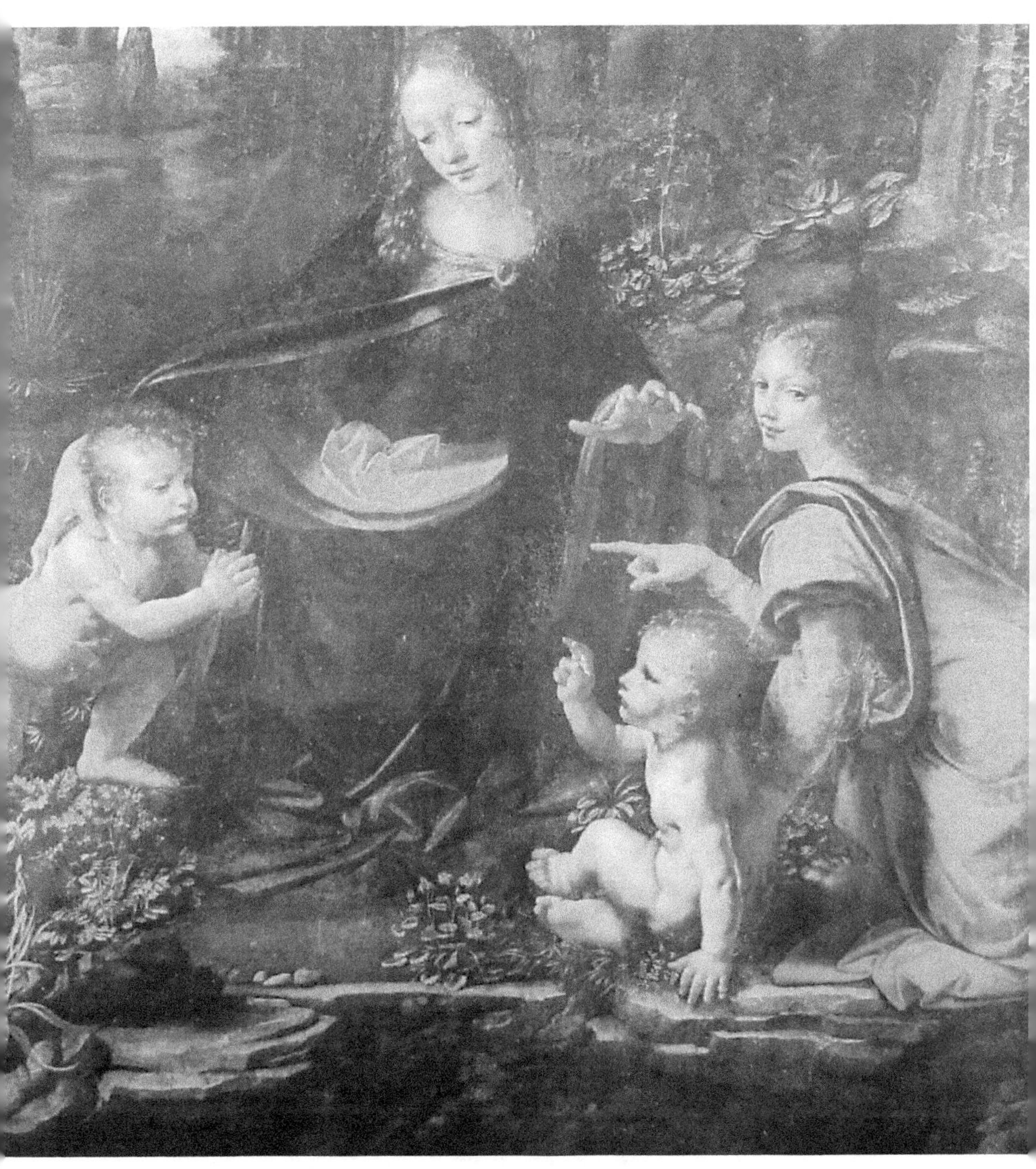

Leonardo, The Virgin of the Rocks, detail, Louvre, Paris

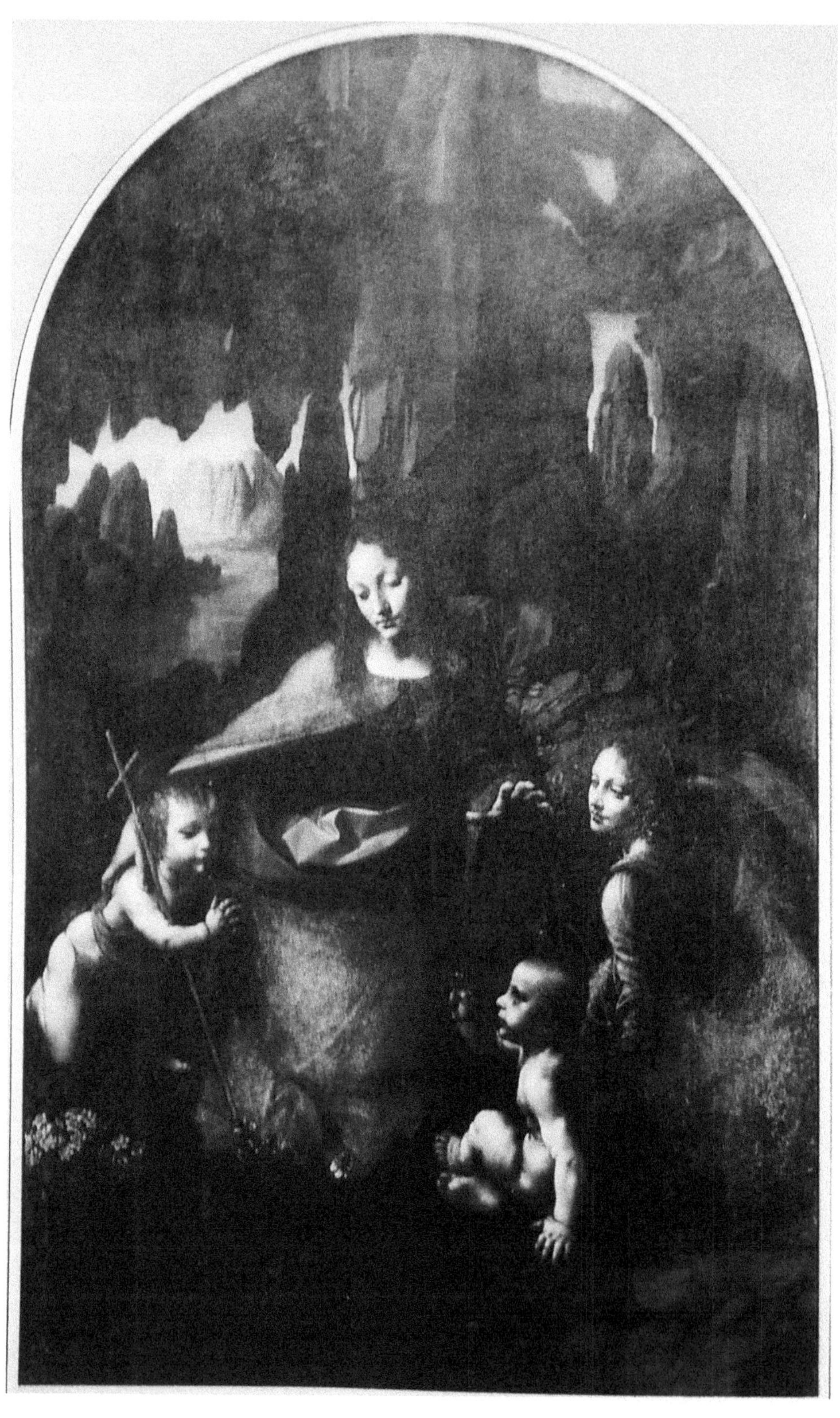

Leonardo da Vinci, *The Virgin of the Rocks*, National Gallery, London

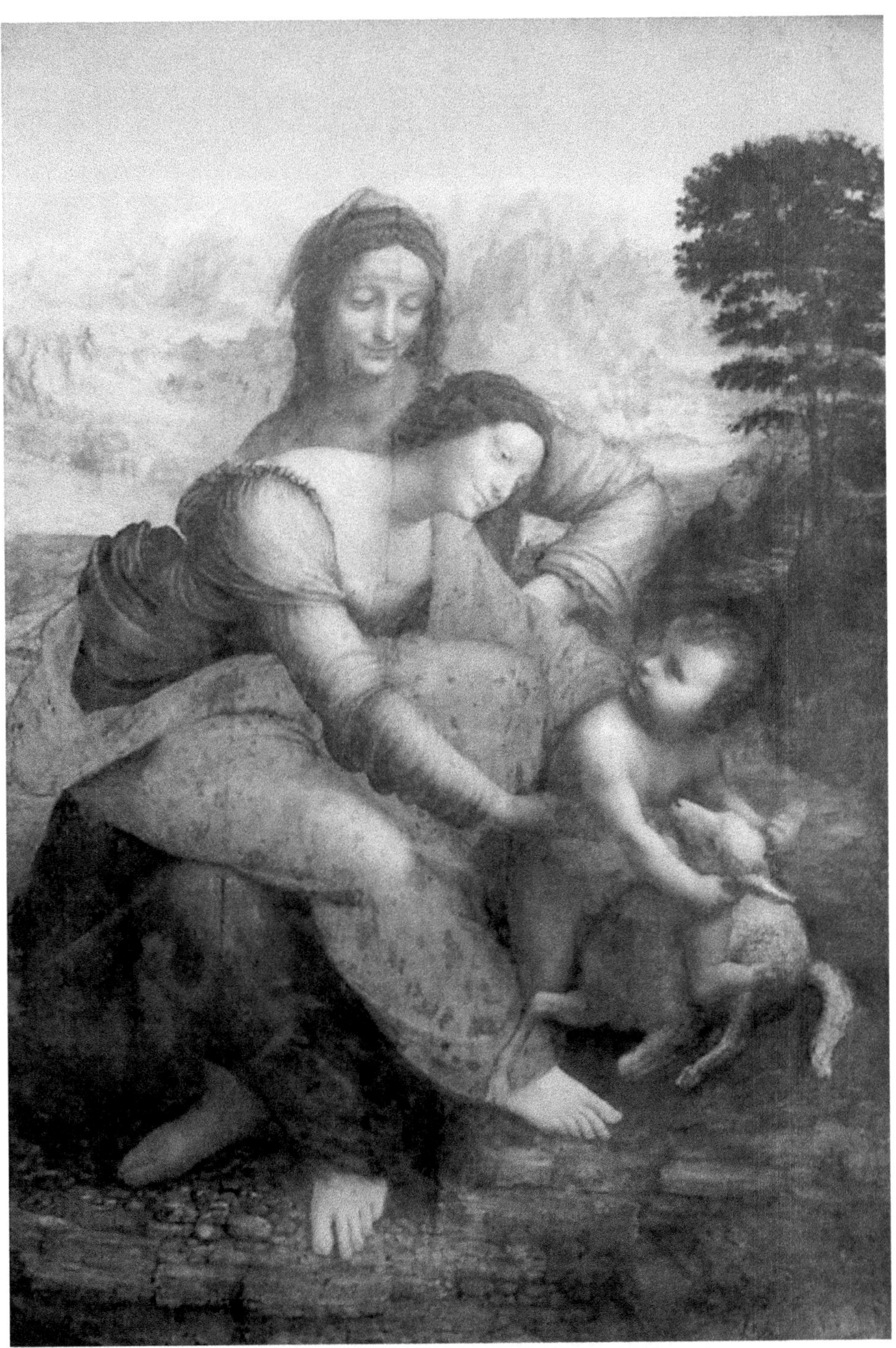

Leonardo da Vinci, The VIrgin and Child With St Anne,
Louvre, Paris

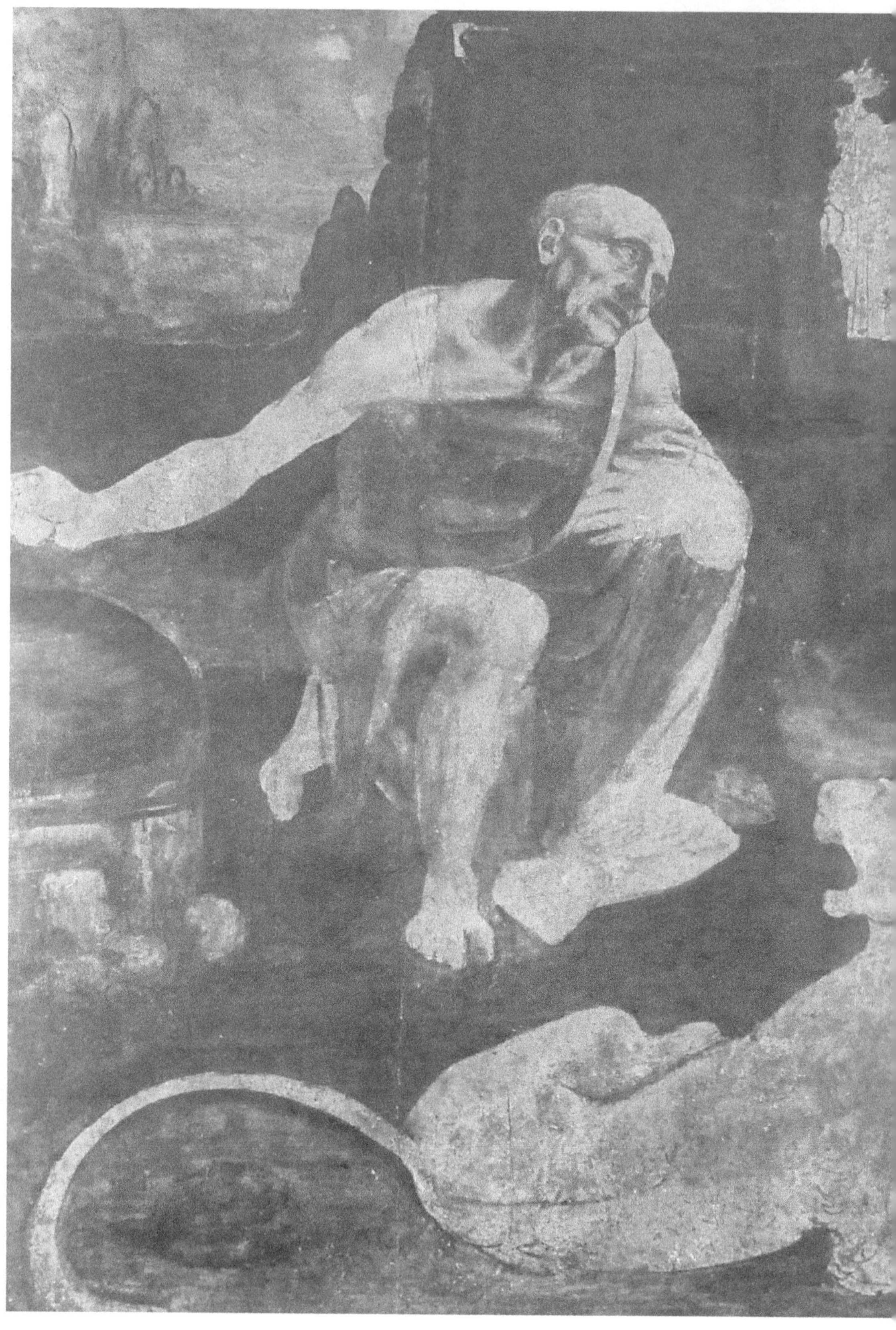

Leonardo, St Jerome, Vatican Museum, Rome

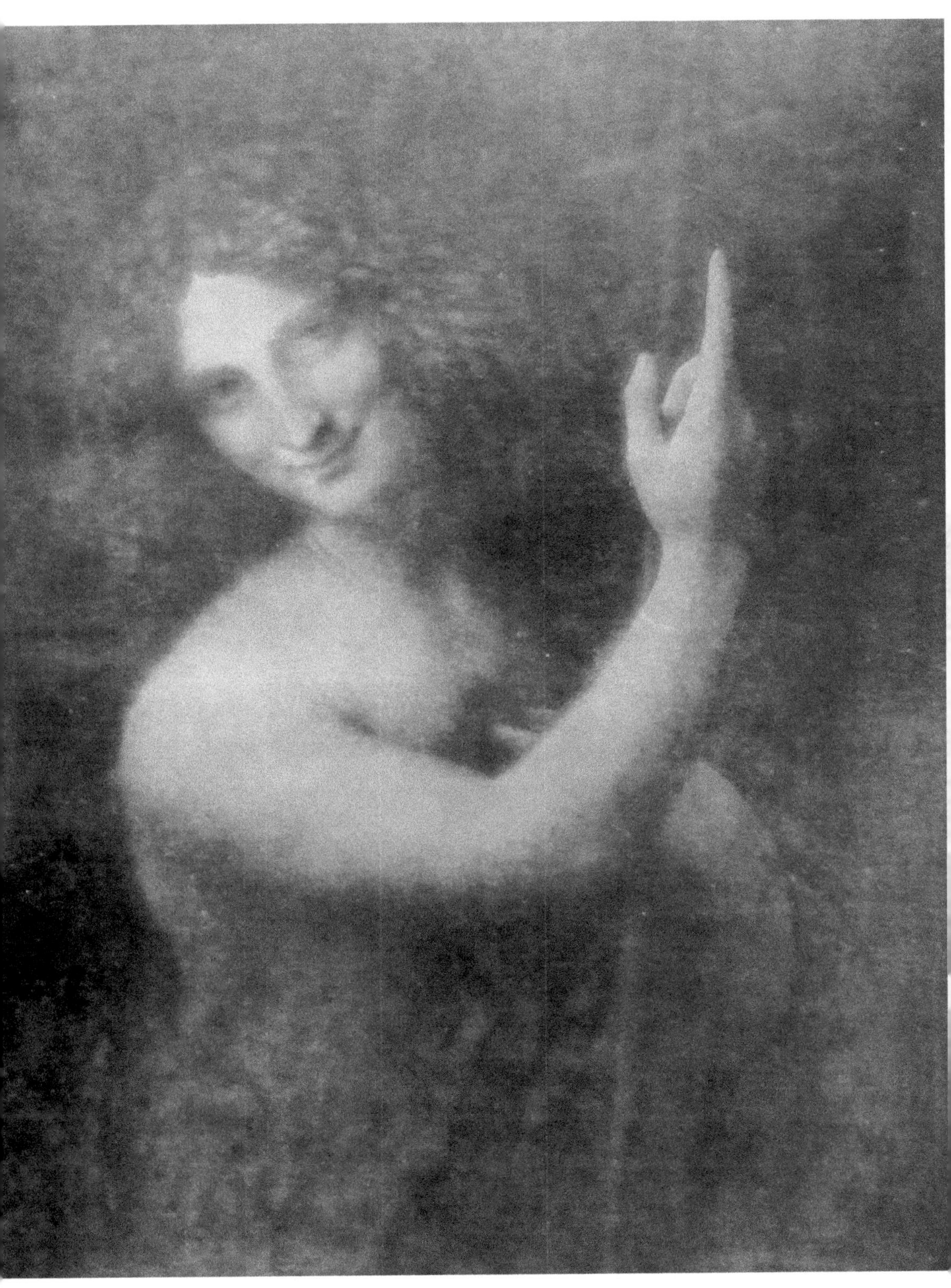

Leonardo da Vinci, St John the Baptist, Louvre Museum

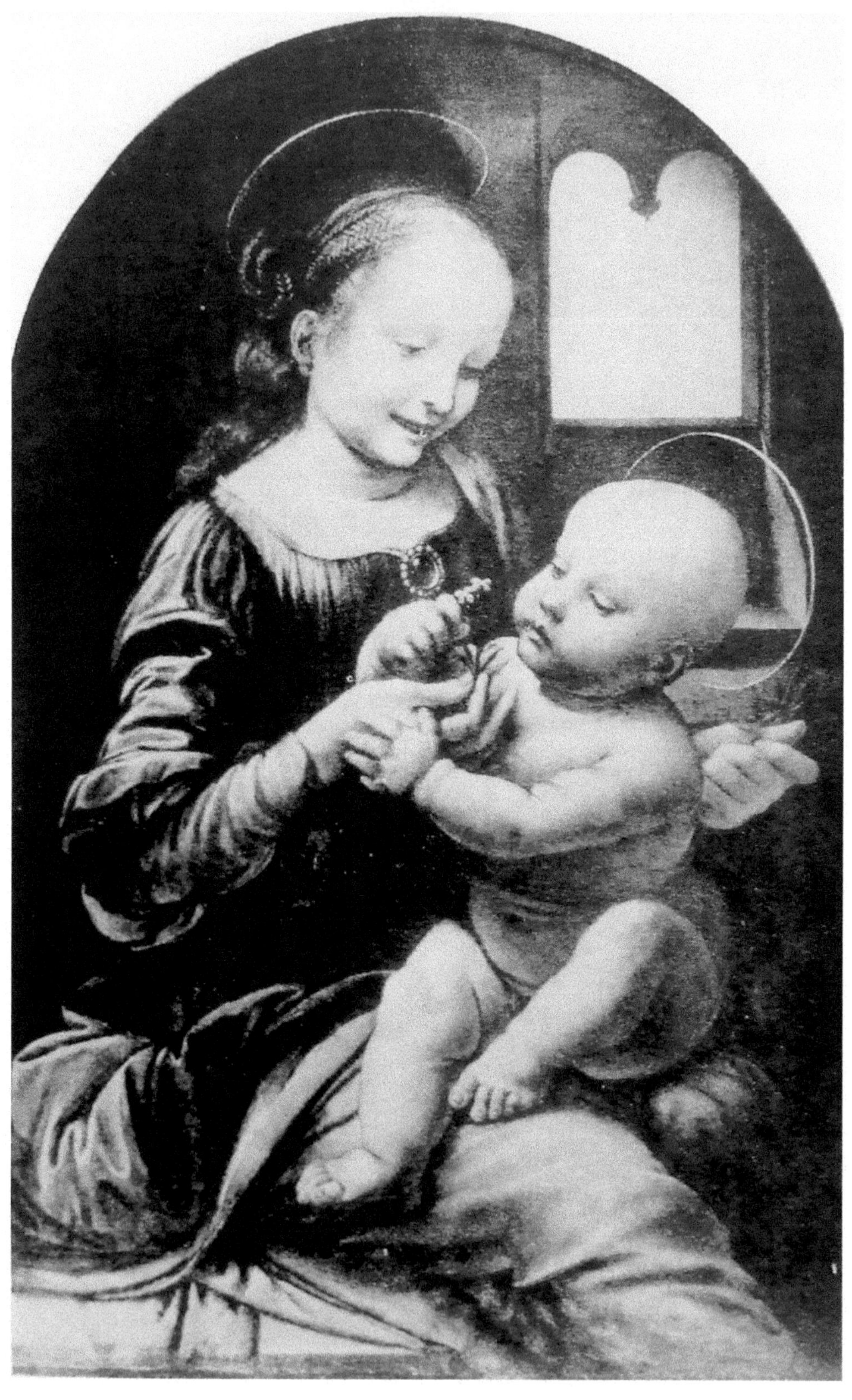

Leonardo da Vinci, The Virgin and Child, Hermitage Museum

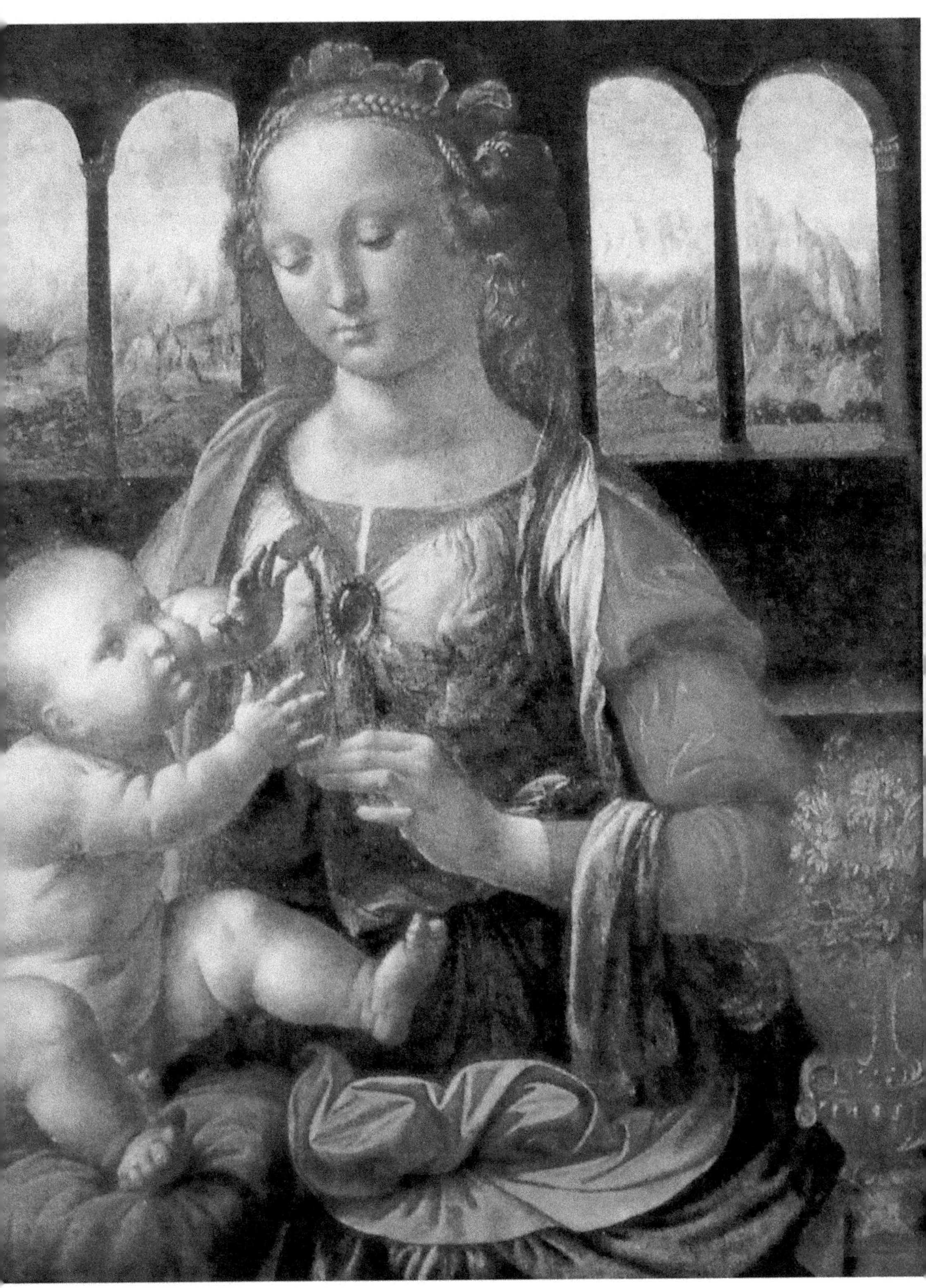

Leonardo da Vinci, The Madonna and Child, Munich

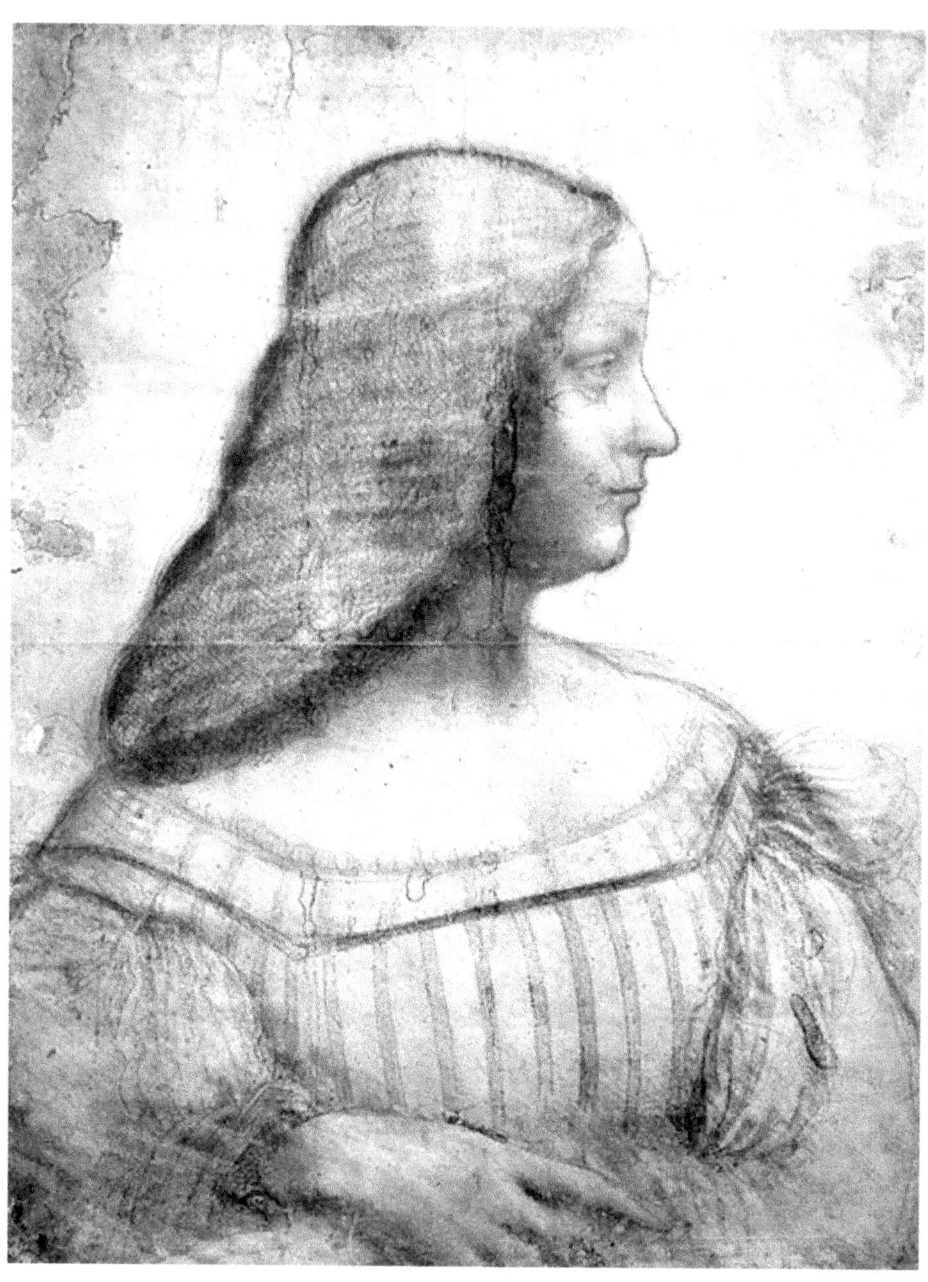

Leonardo da Vinci, Isabella d'Este, 1500, Louvre, Paris

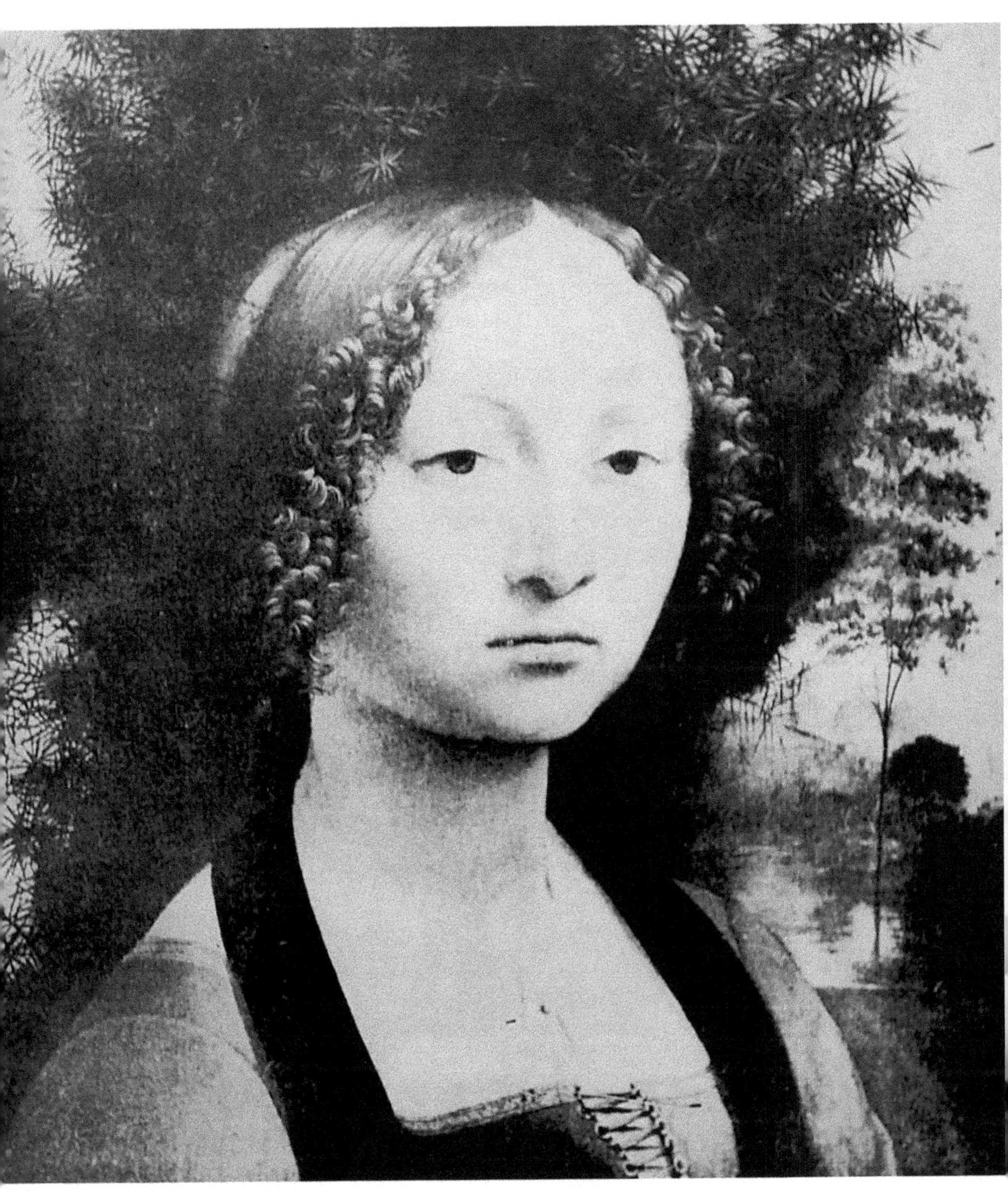

Leonardo da Vinci, Portrait of a Woman (Ginerva Benci?), c. 1474-76, National Gallery of Art, Washington

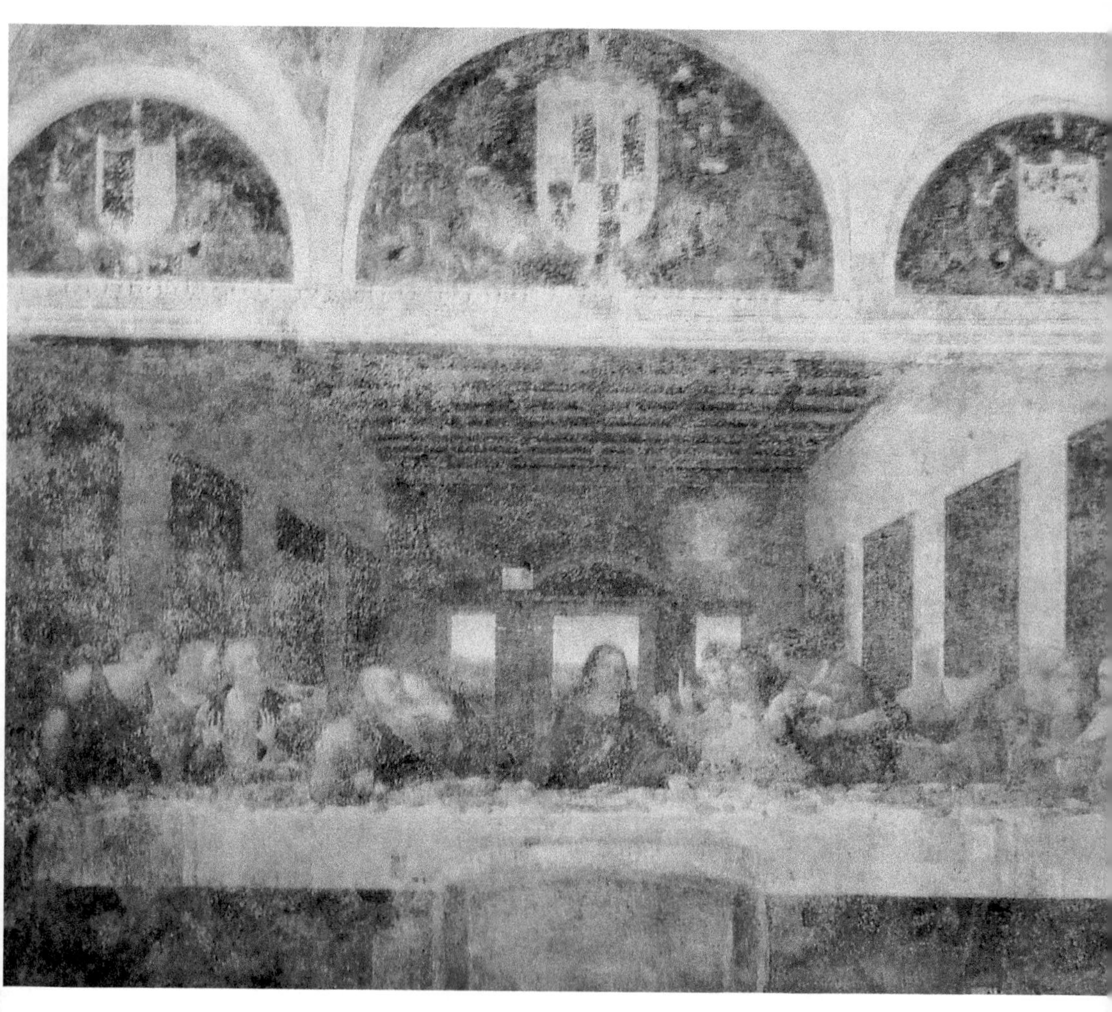

Leonardo da Vinci, The Last Supper, Milan

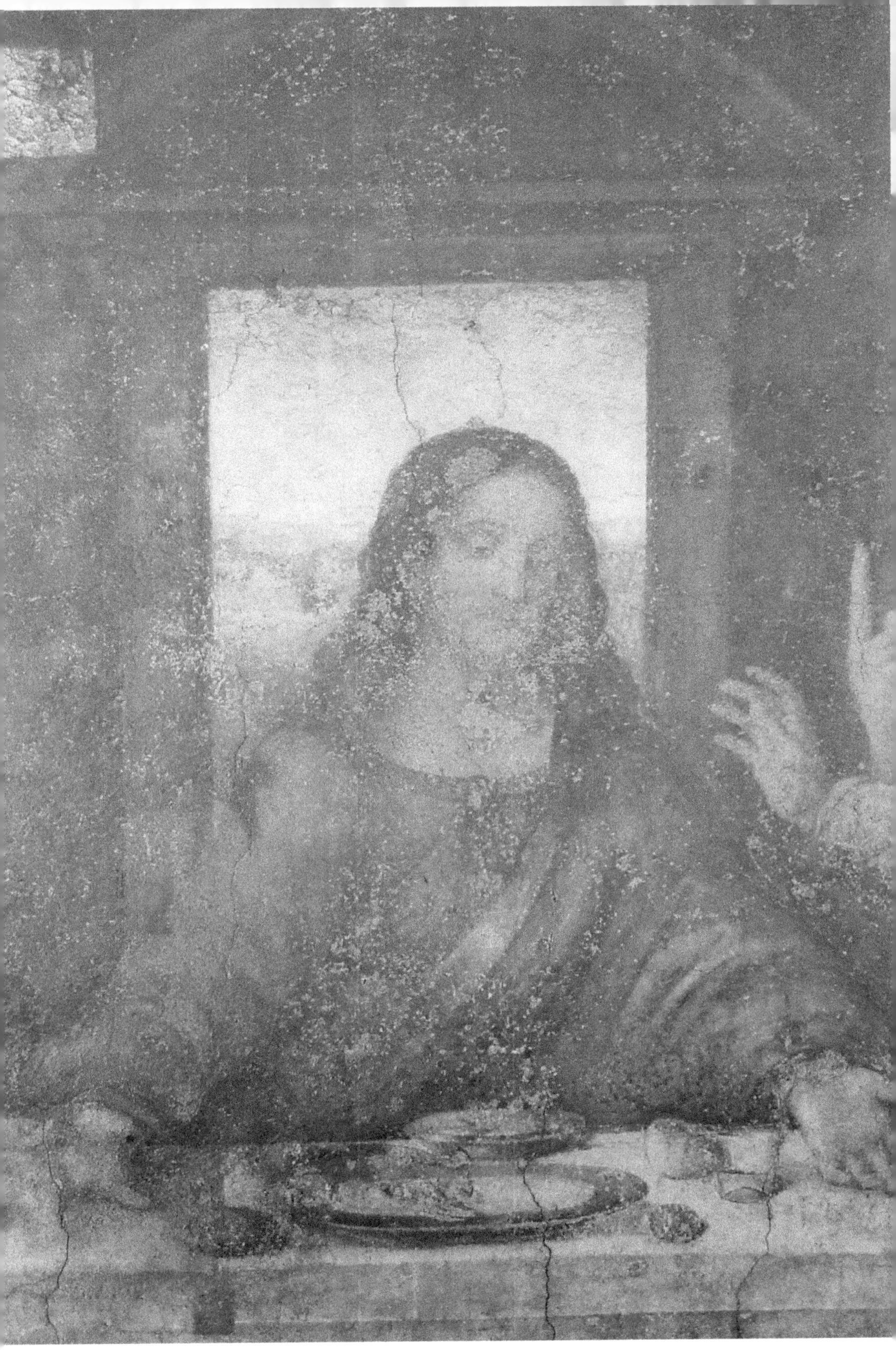

Leonardo, Jesus in The Last Supper, Milan

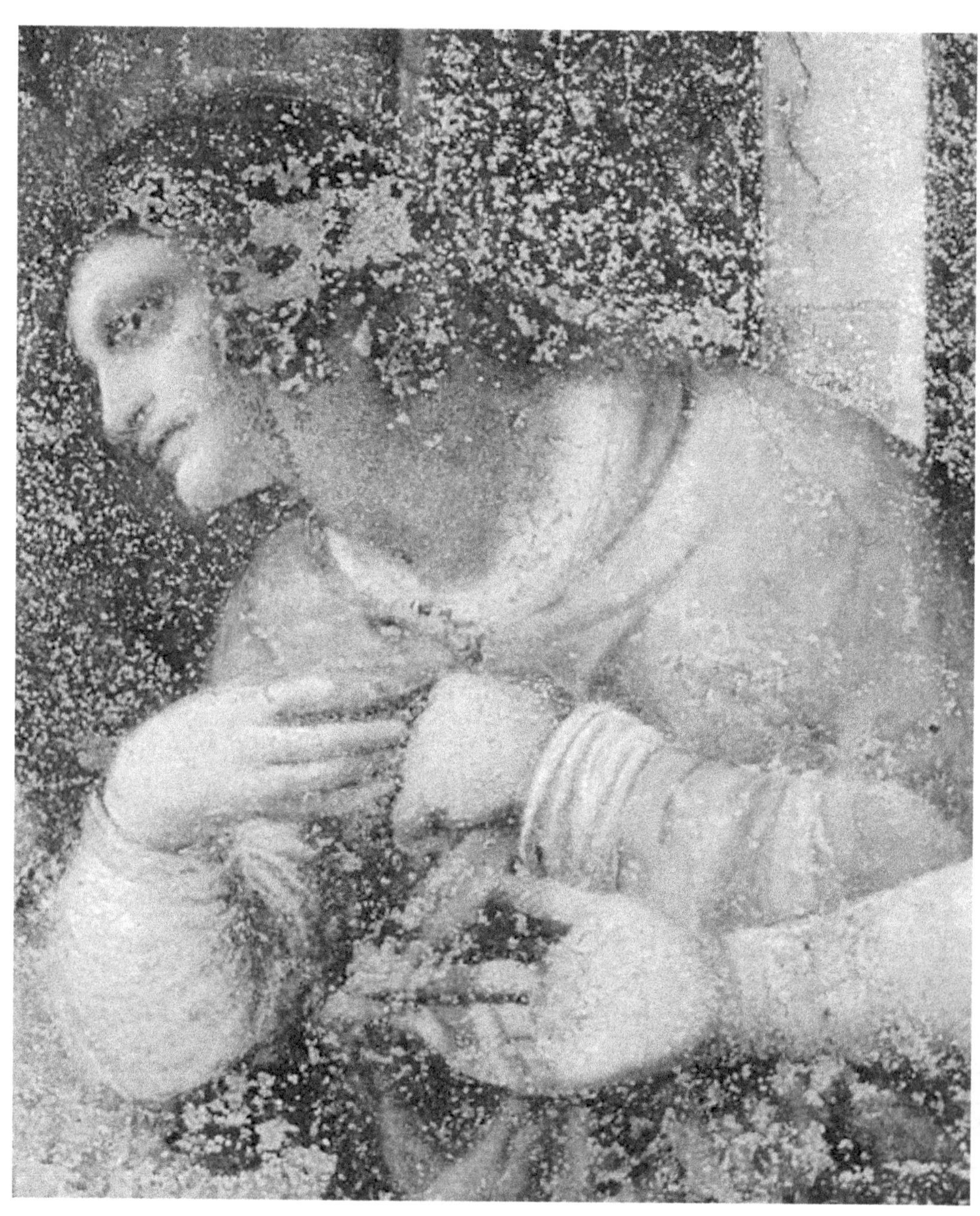

Leonardo da Vinci, The Last Supper, detail

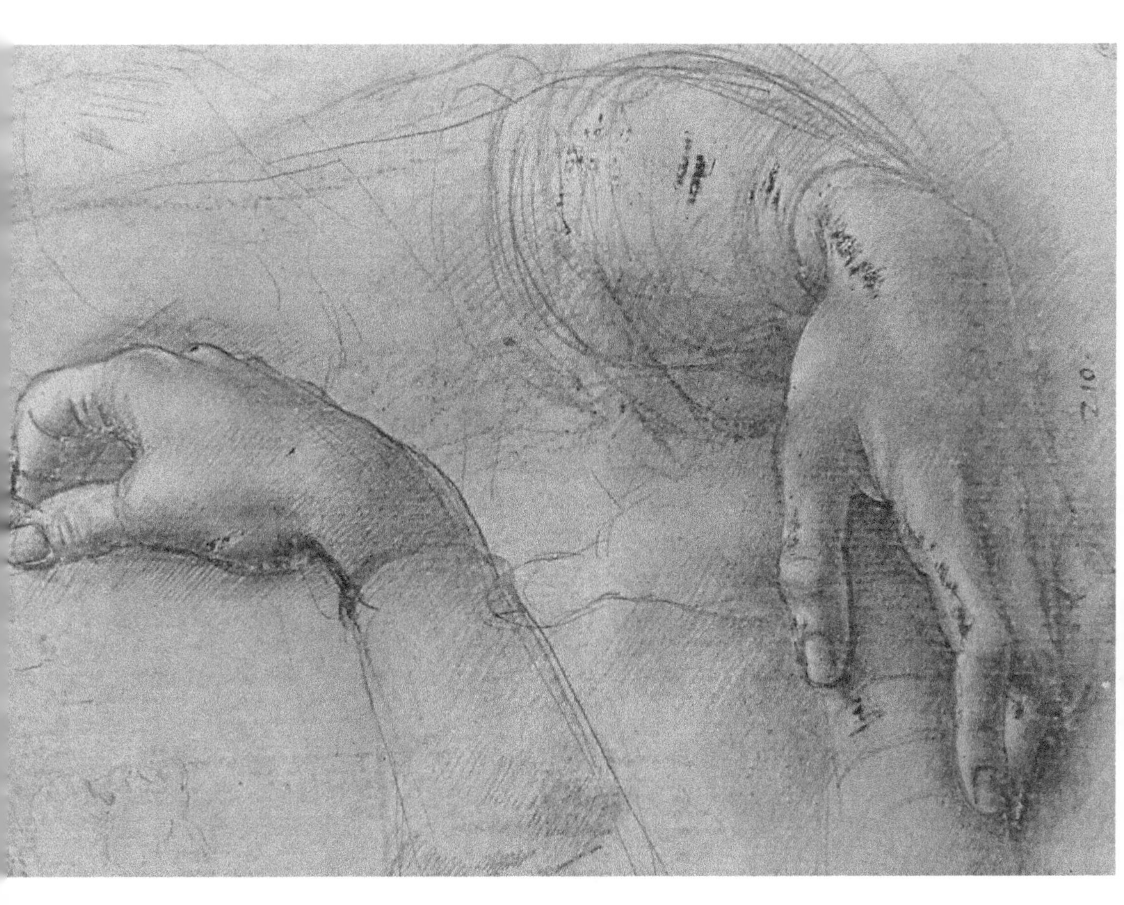

Leonardo, study of hands, Royal Collection, Windsor

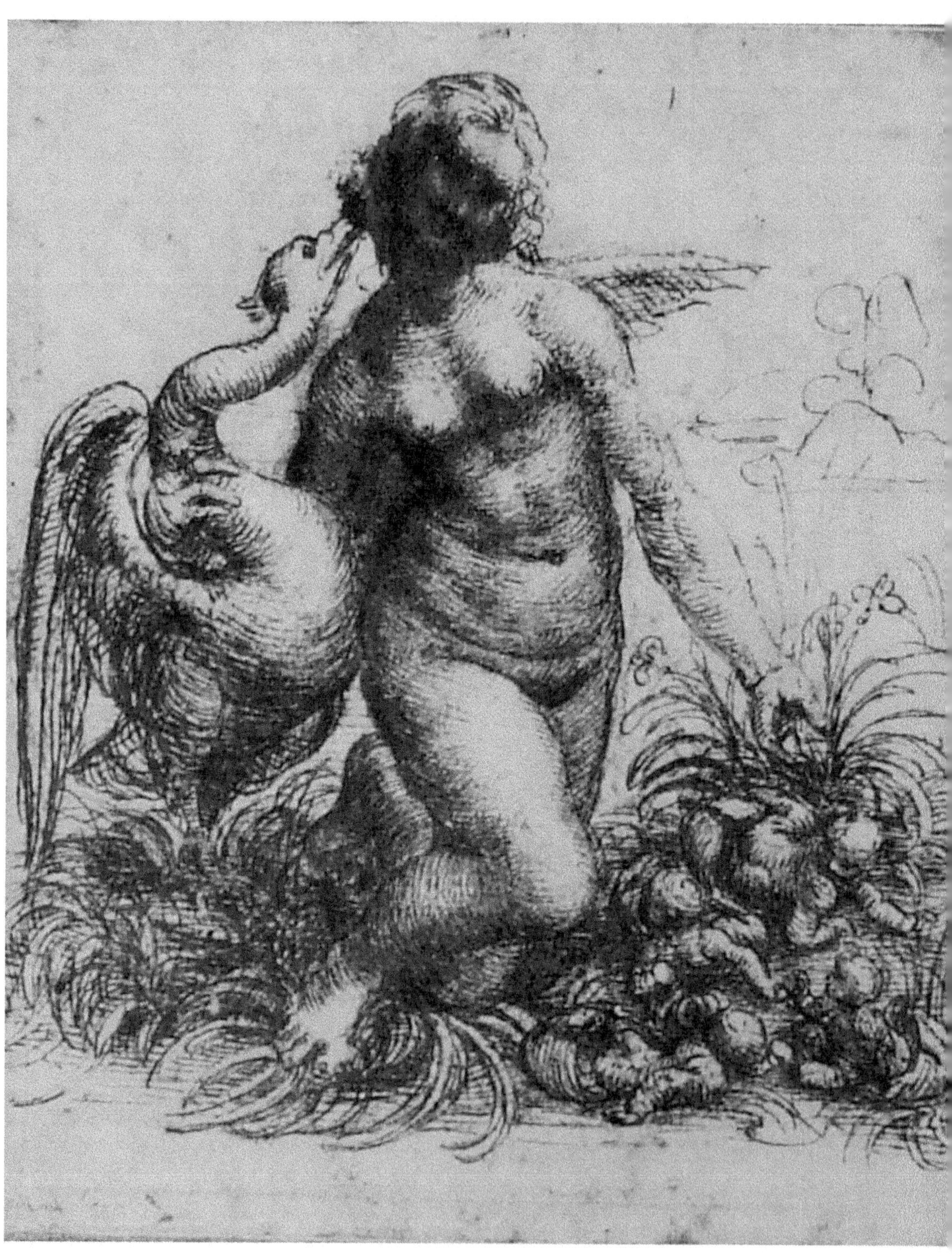

Leonardo da Vinci, Study for Leda and the Swan

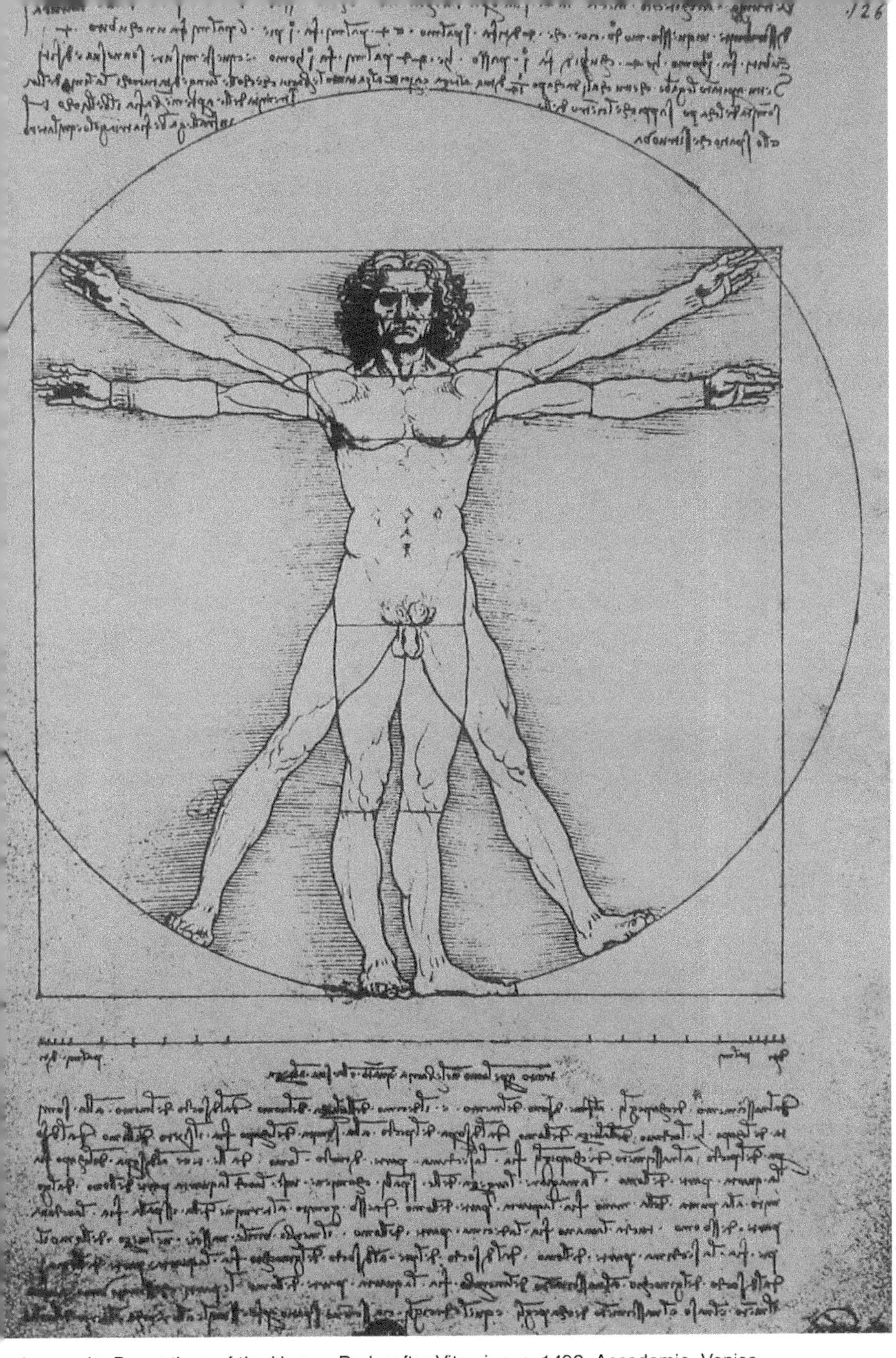

Leonardo, Proportions of the Human Body, after Vitruvius, c. 1492, Accademia, Venice.

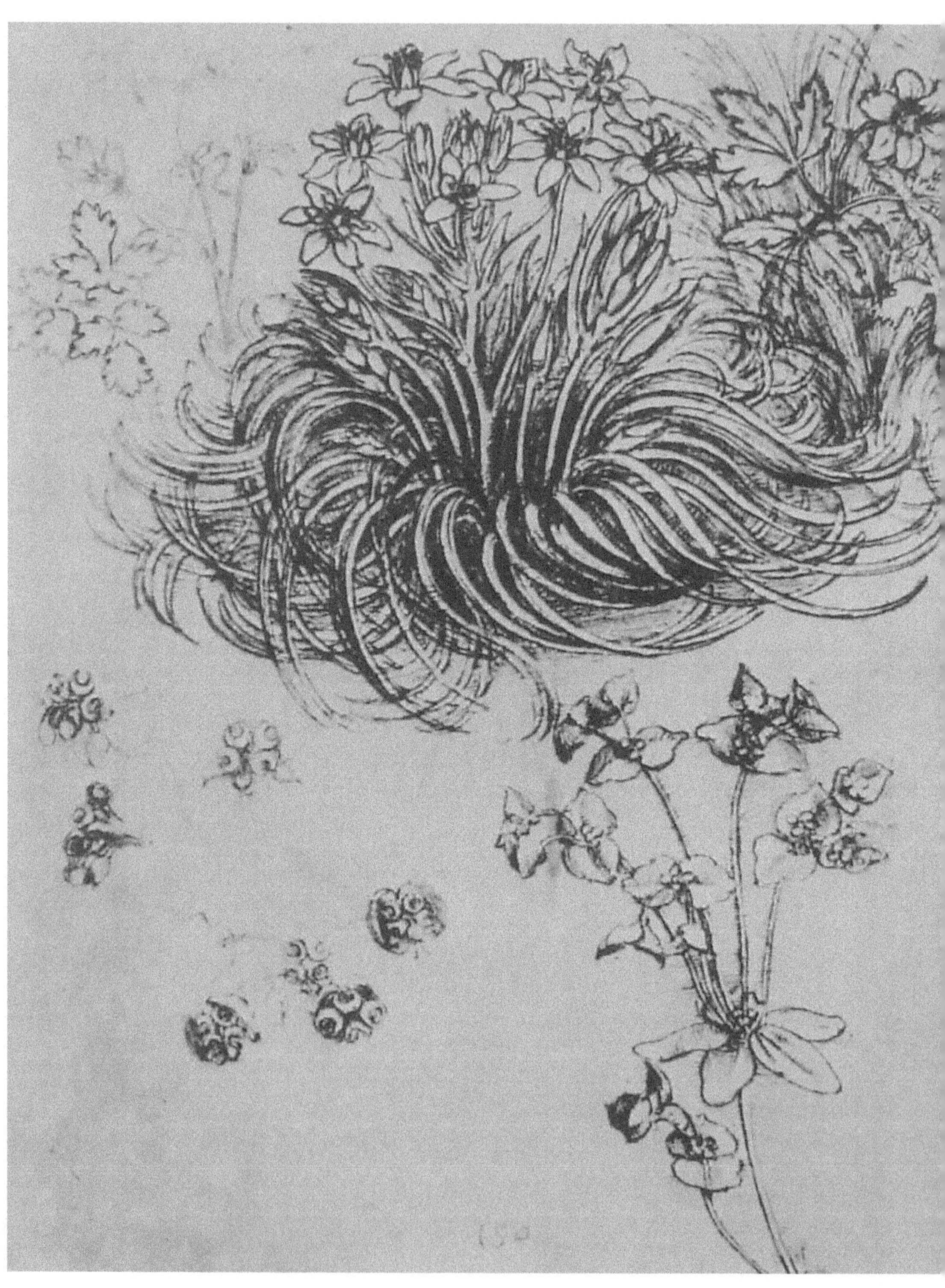

Leonardo, drawing of Ornithogalum Umbellatum and a Euphorbia, Royal Collection, Windsor

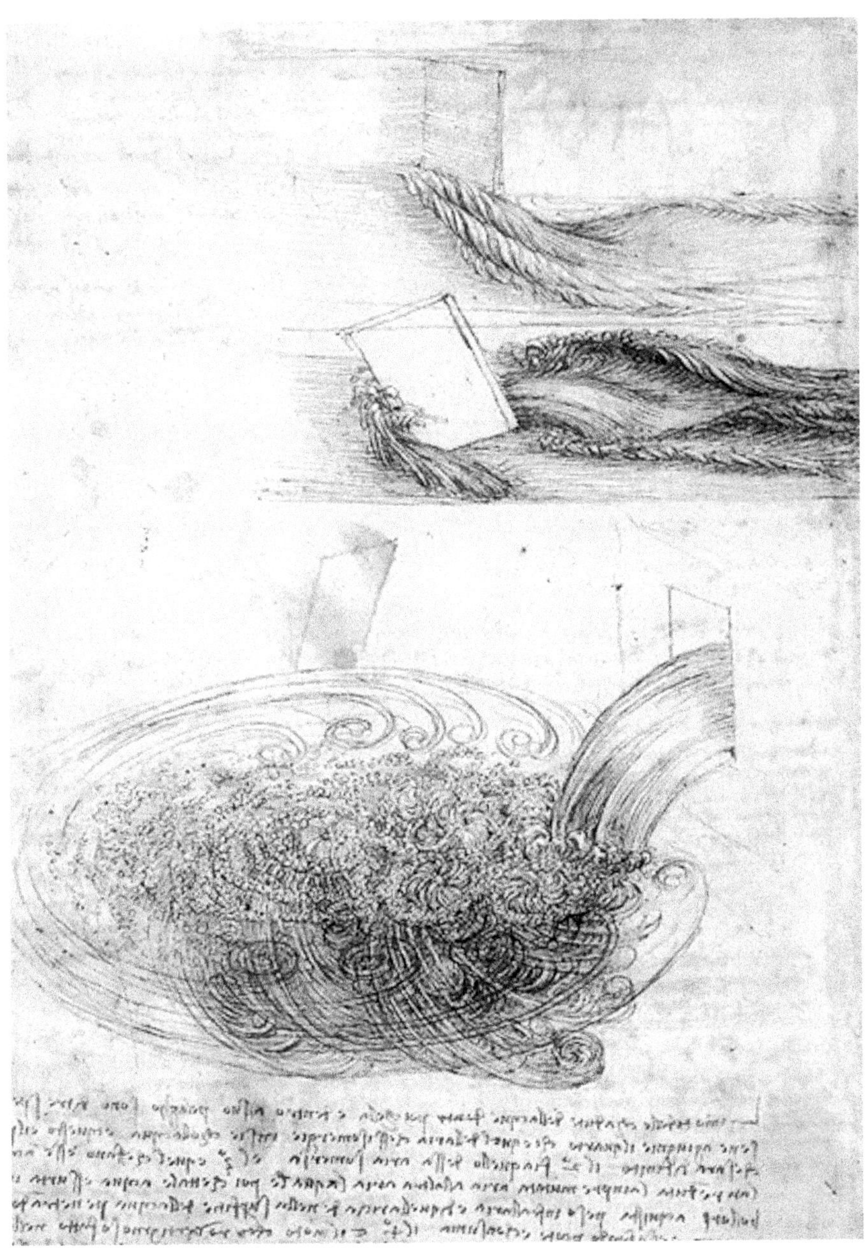

Leonardo da Vinci, Studies of water passing obstacles and falling

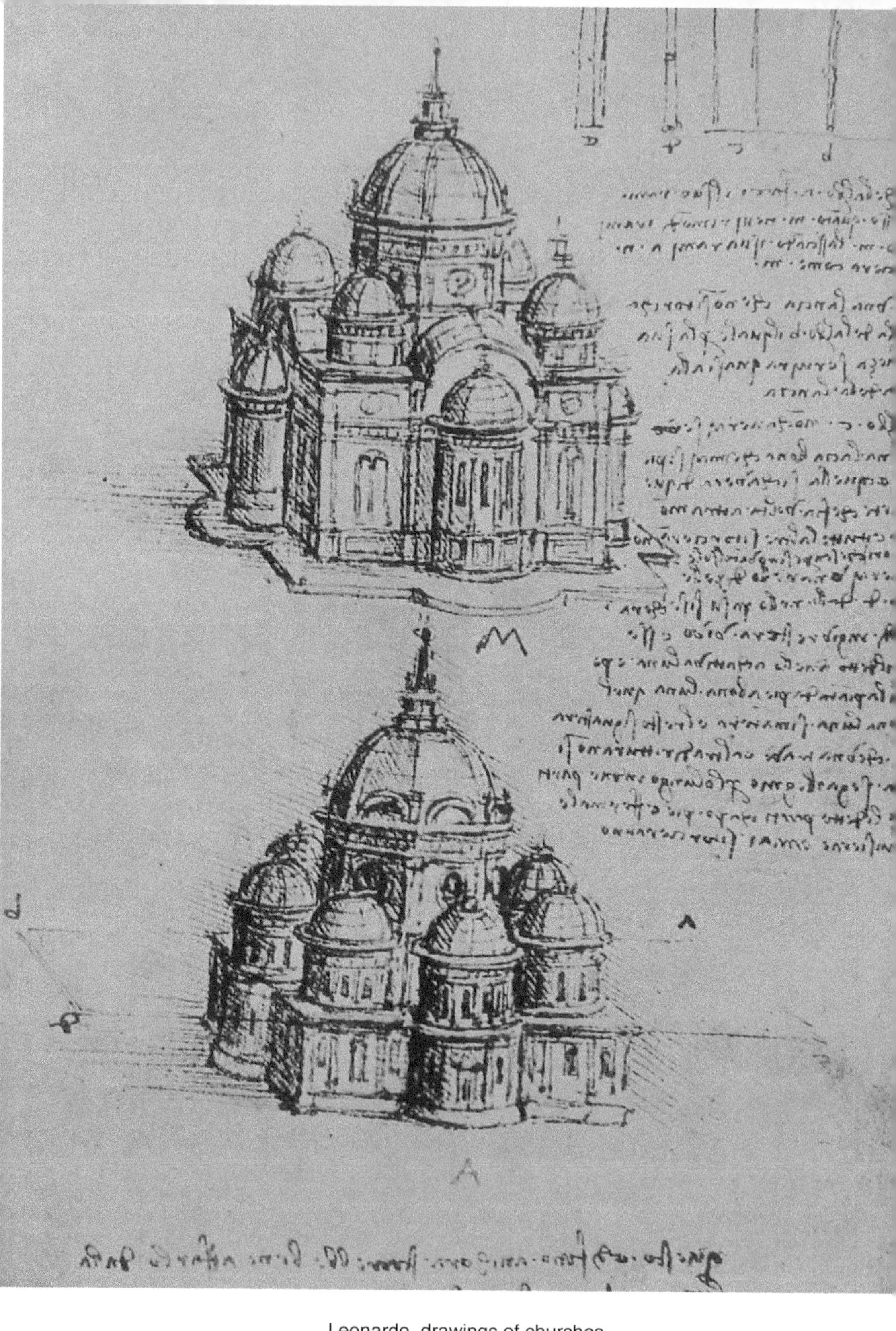

Leonardo, drawings of churches

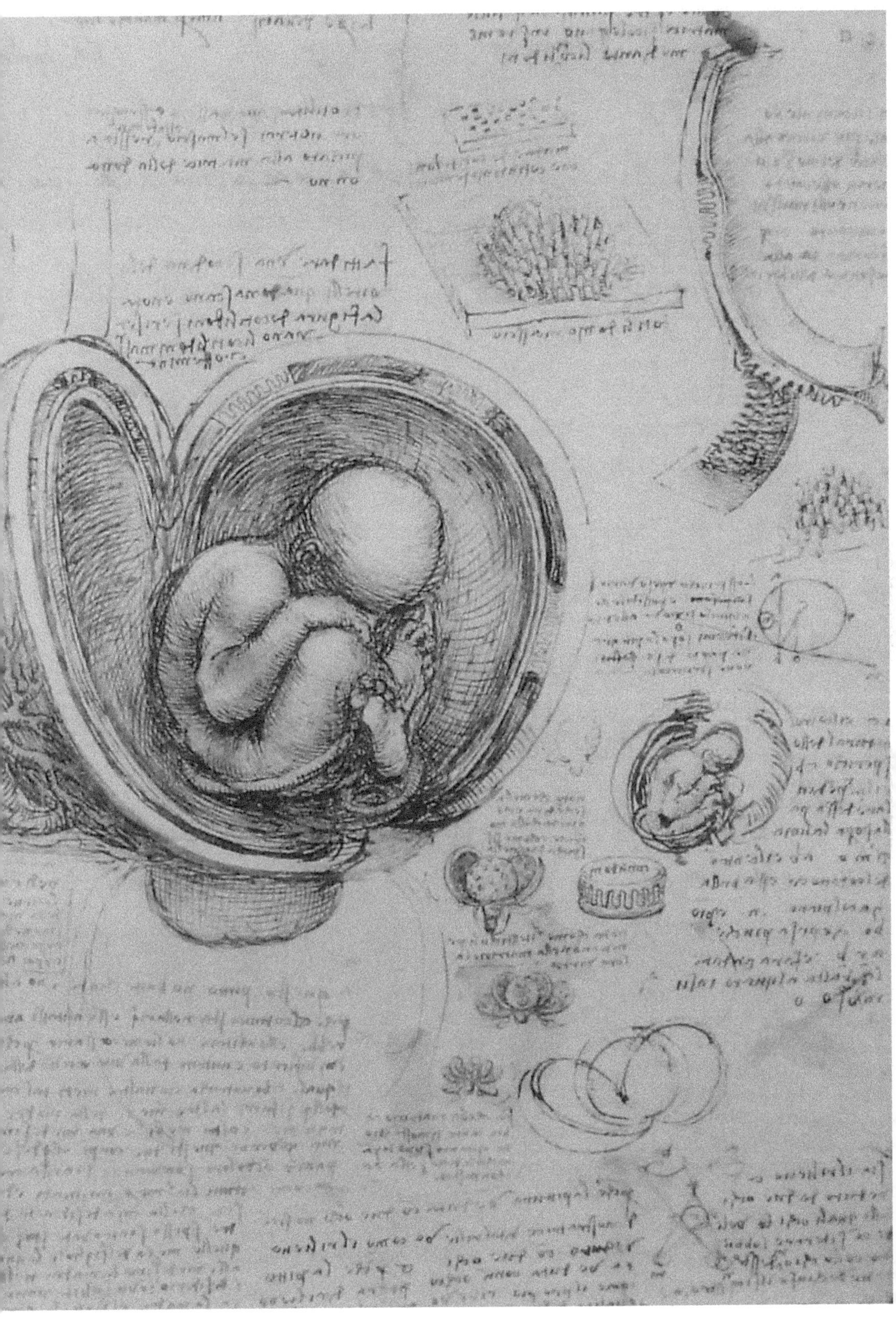

Leonardo, An Embryo In the Womb, c. 1512, Royal Collection, Windsor

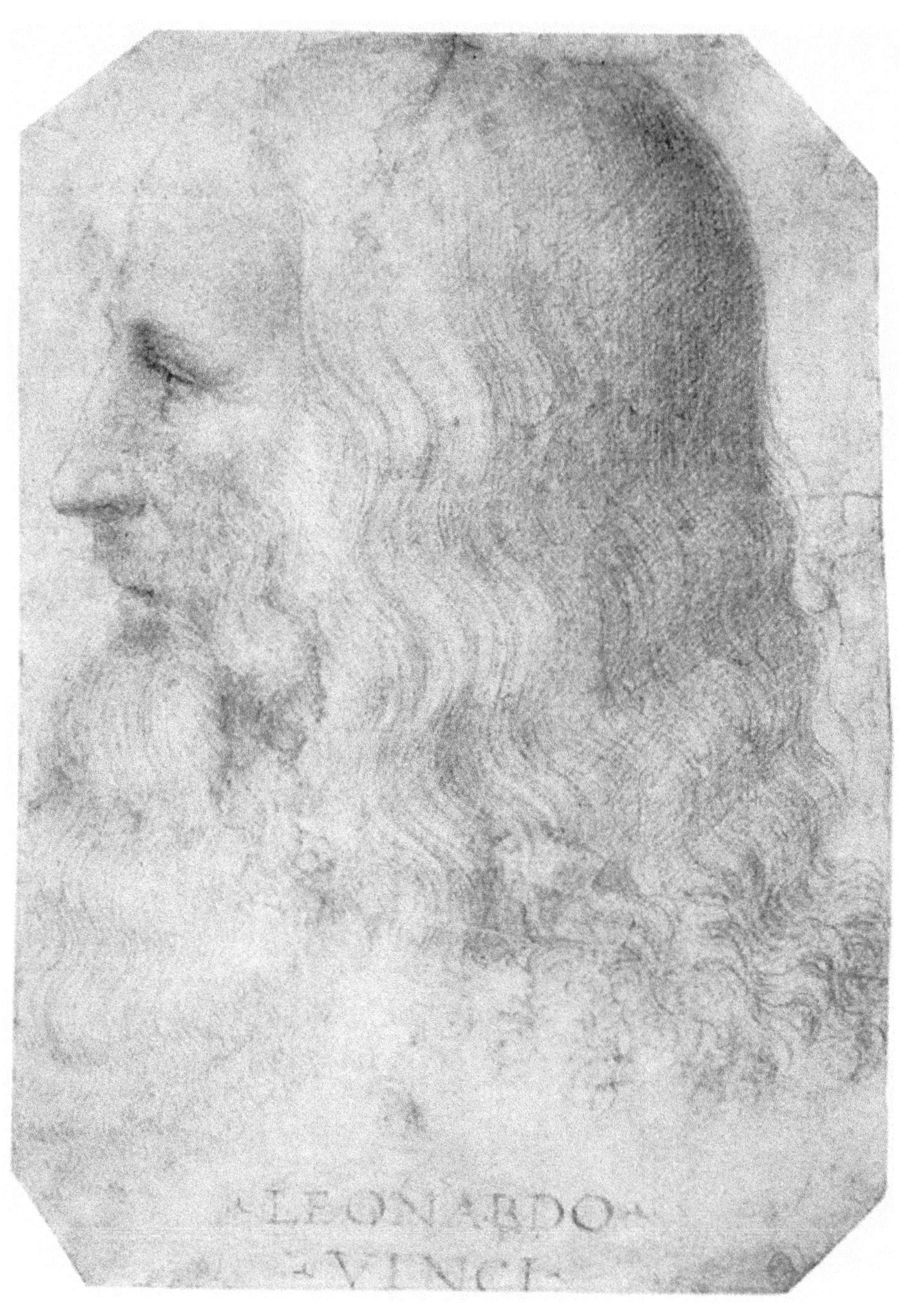

Francesco Melzi, Portrait of Leonardo, after 1510, Windsor

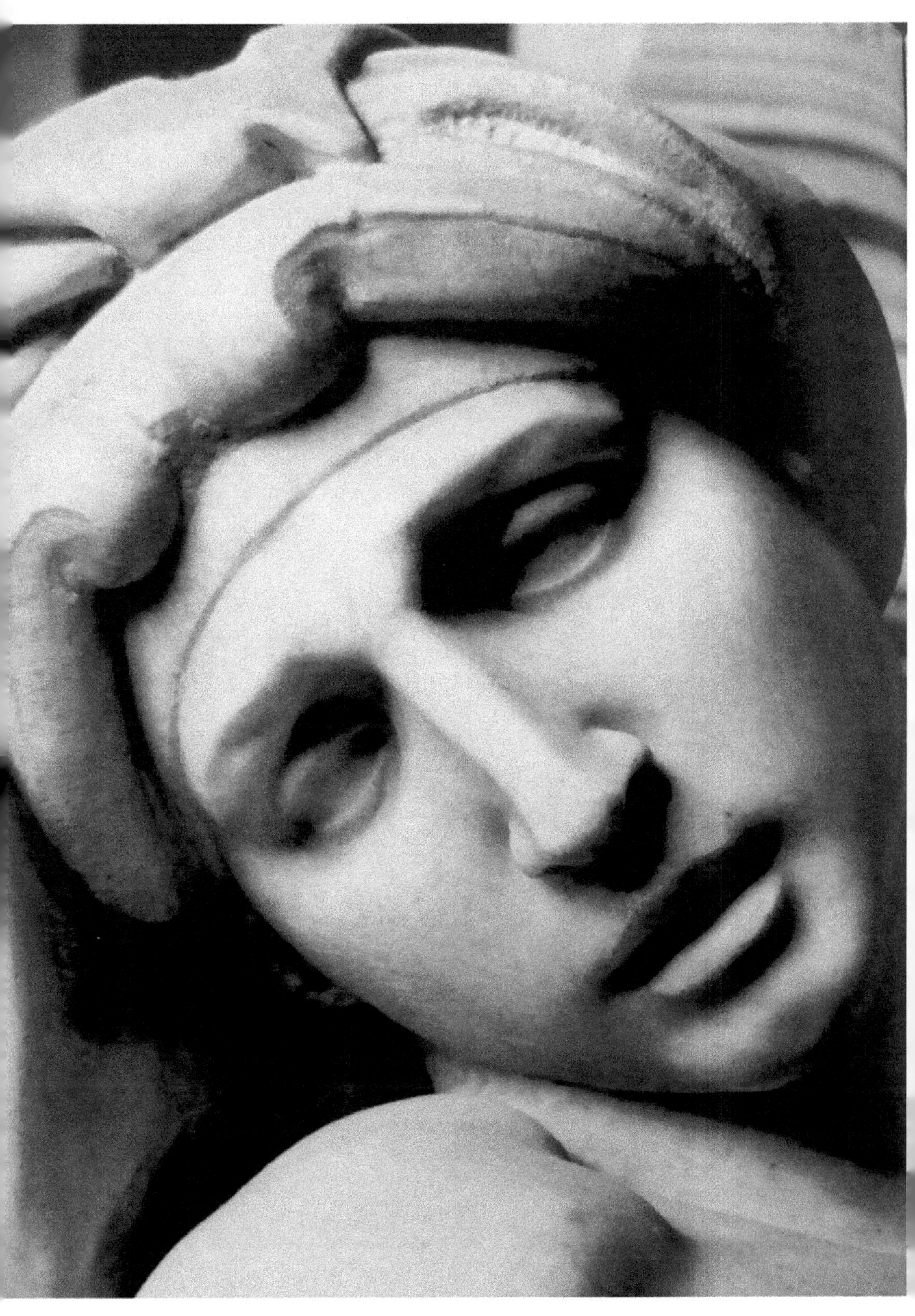

Michelangelo, Dawn, detail, Medici Chapel, Florence

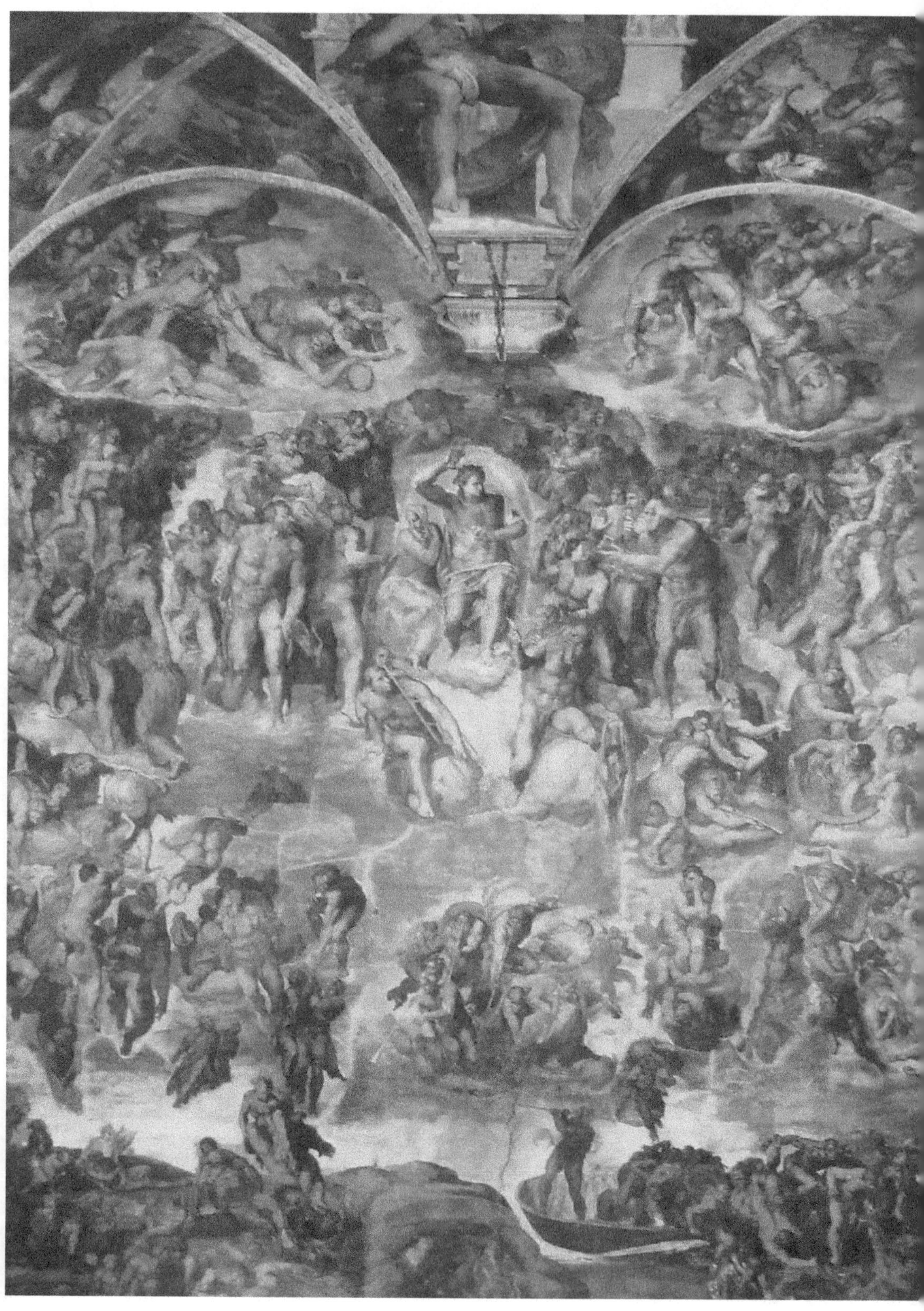

Michelangelo, The Last Judgement, Vatican, Rome

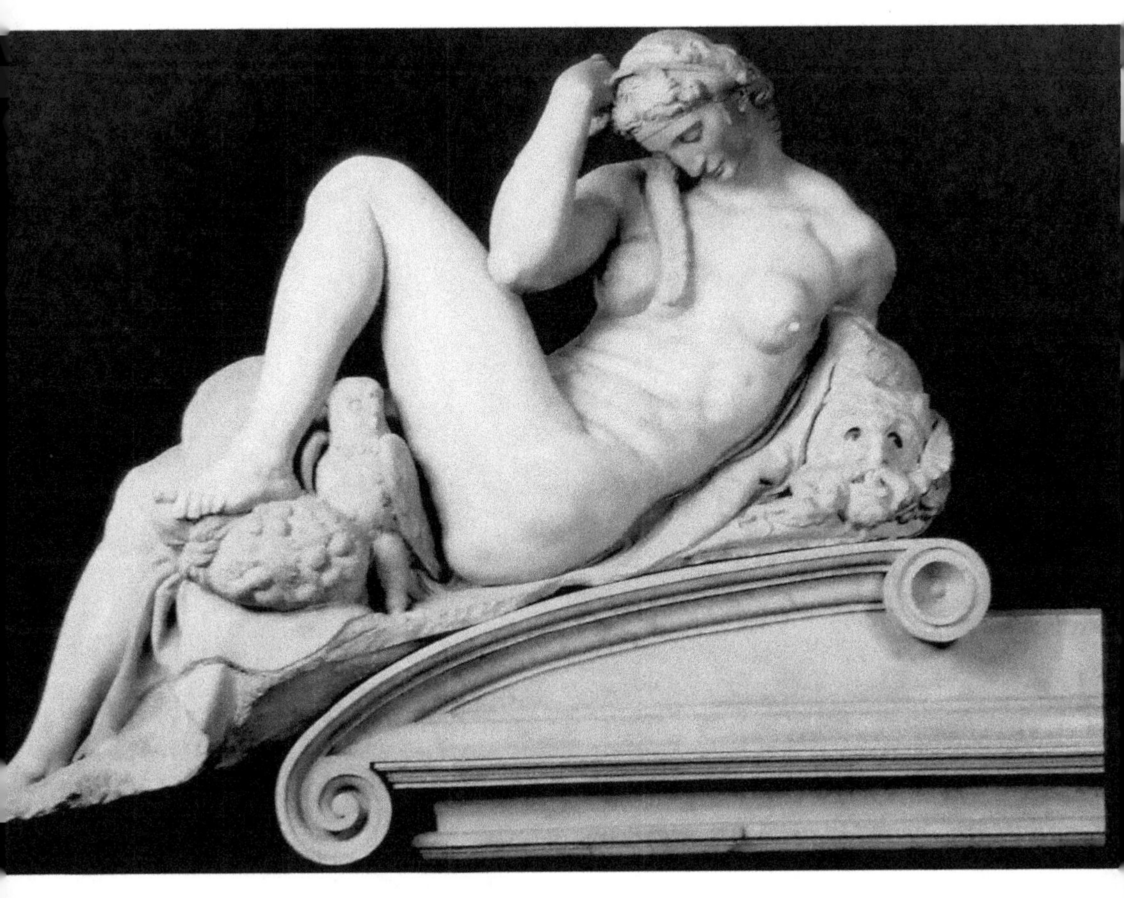

Michelangelo, Night, Medici Chapel, Florence

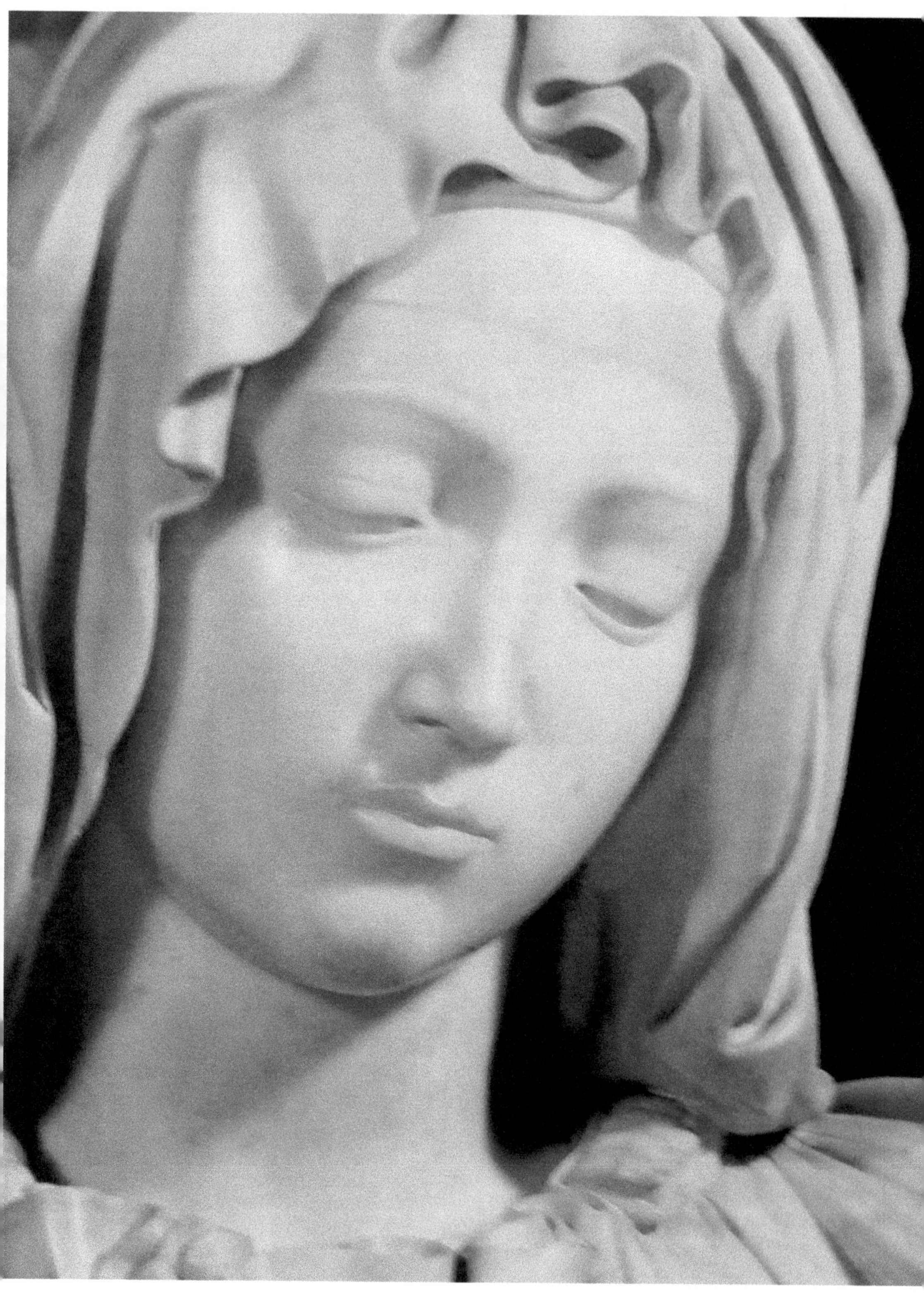

Michelangelo, Pietà, detail, Vatican, Rome

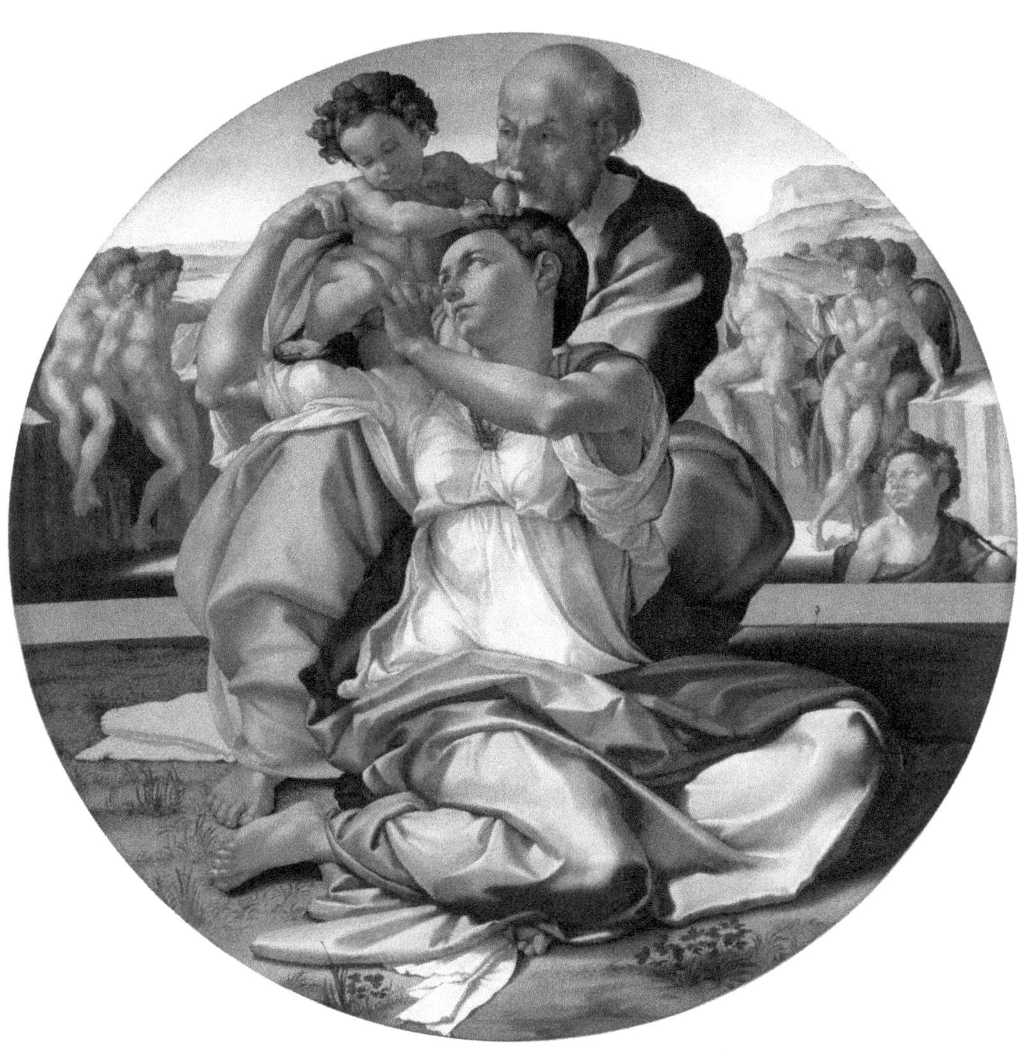

Michelangelo, Tondo, Uffizi Gallery

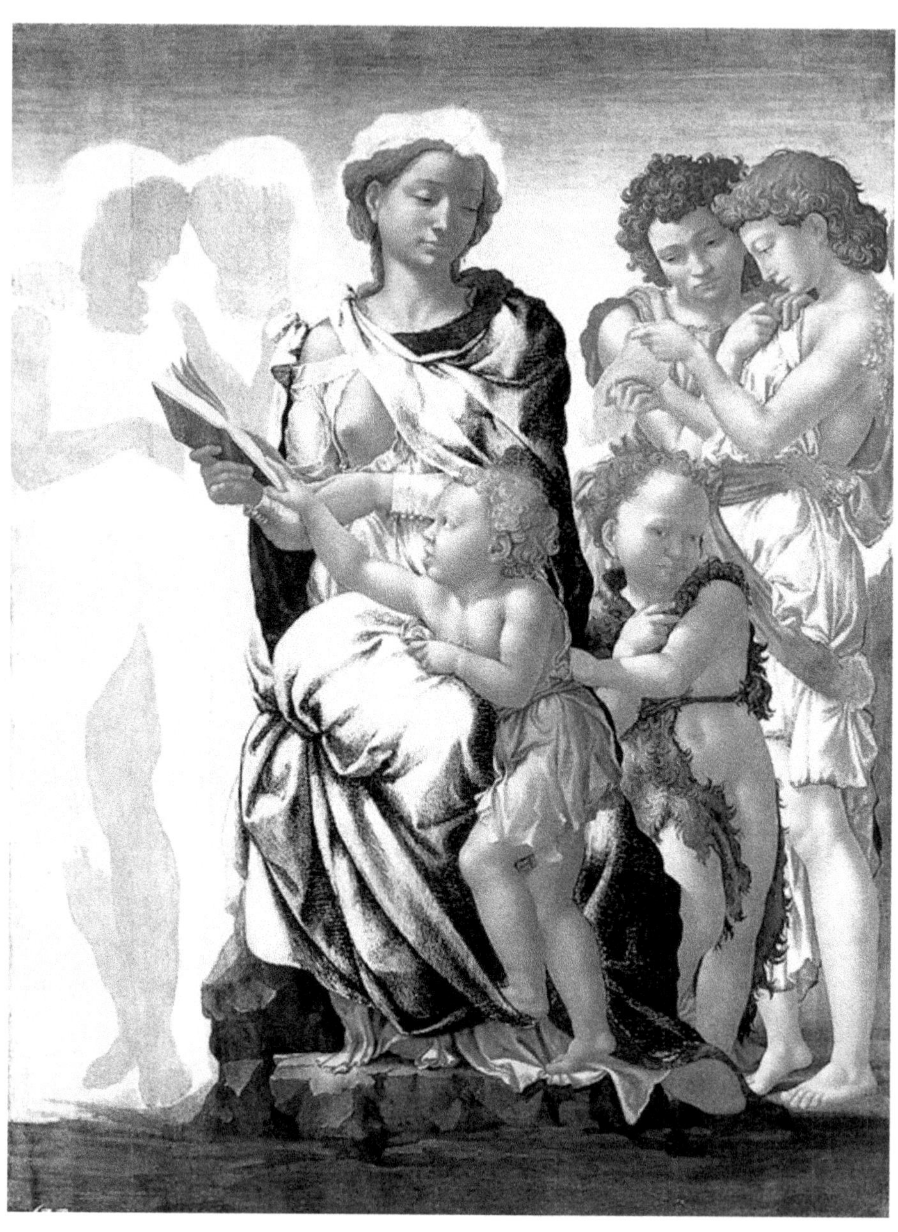

Michelangelo, The Madonna and Child With Saints, 1497.
National Gallery, London

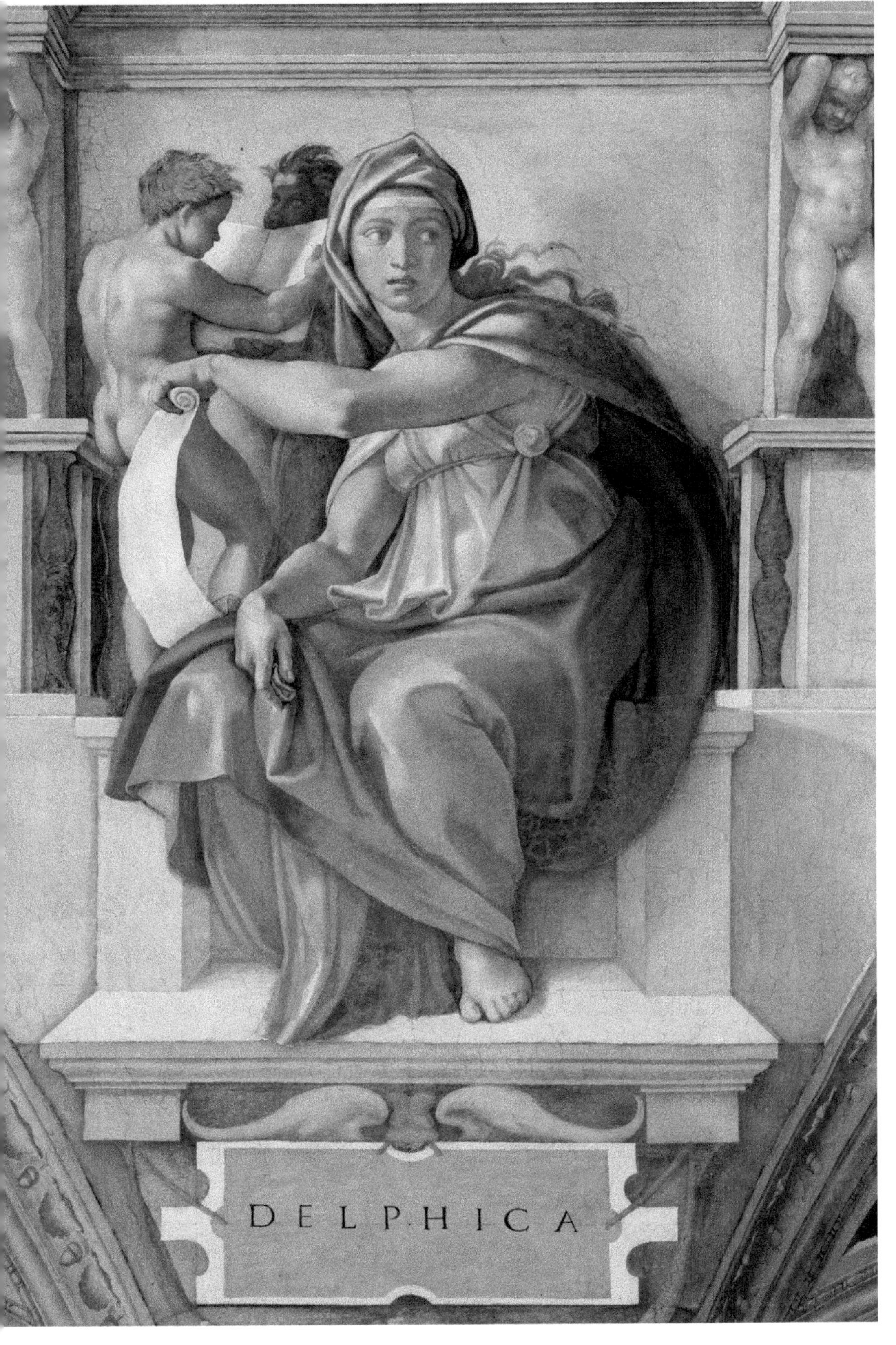

Michelangelo, Delphic Sibyl, Sistine Chapel (this page and over)

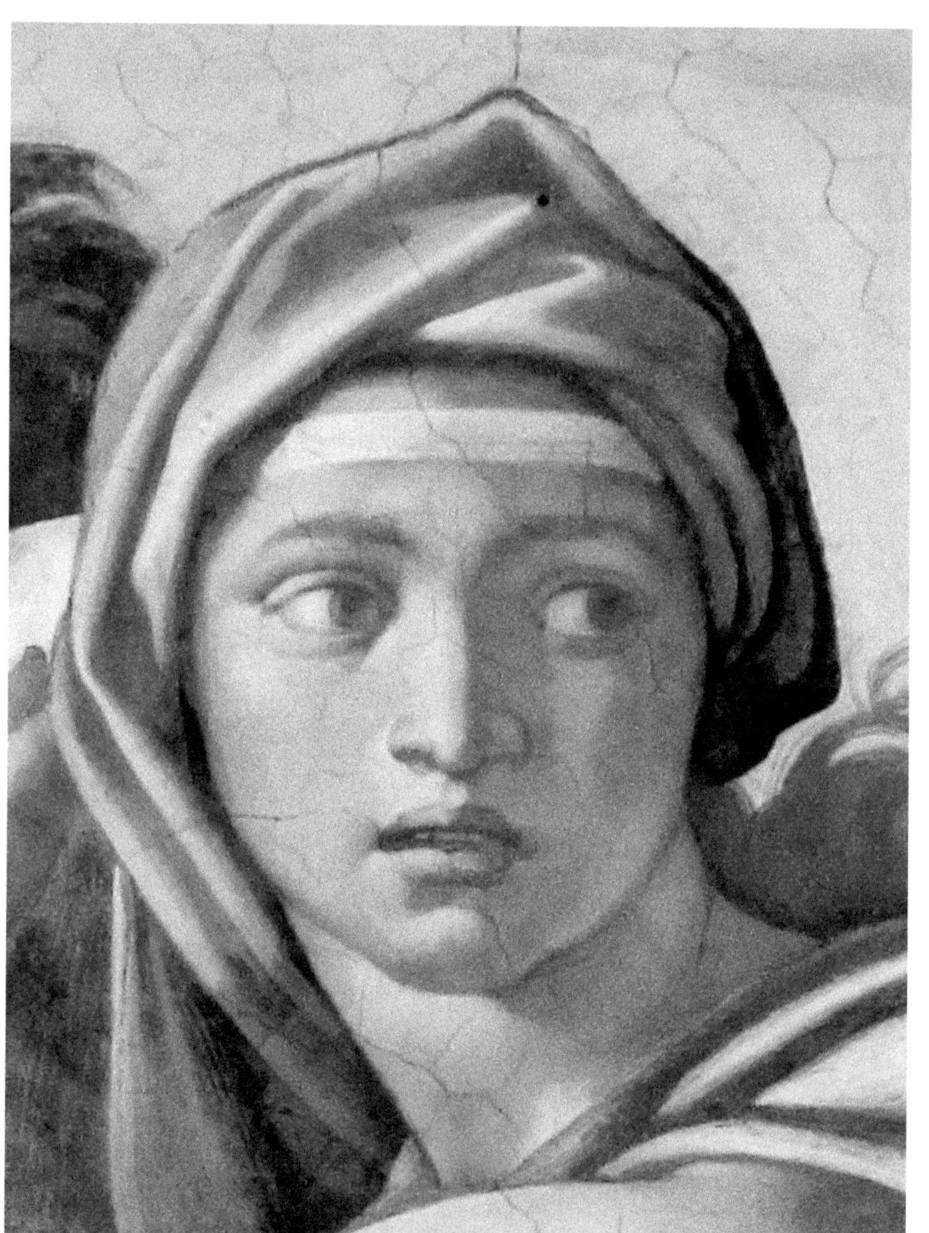

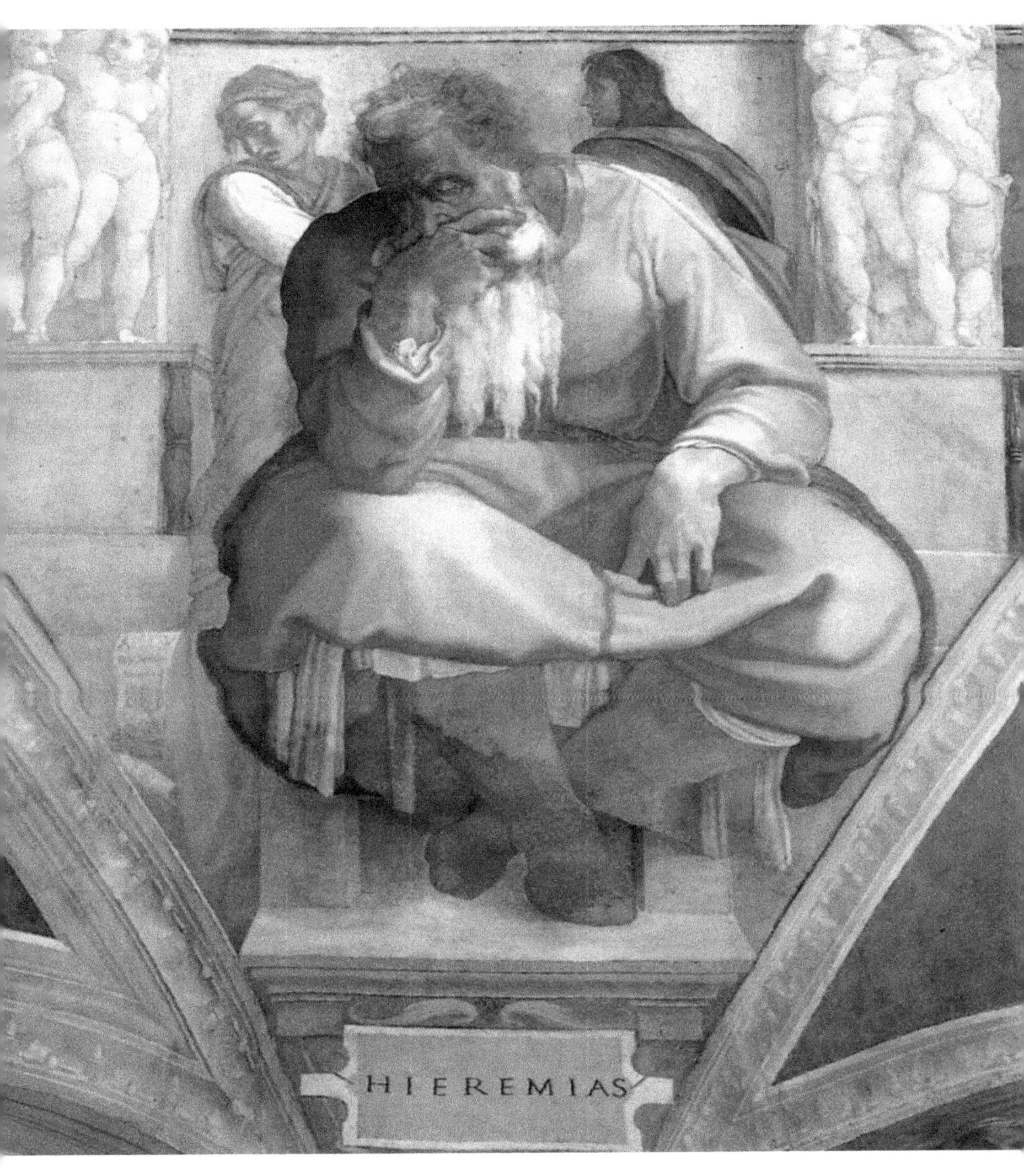

Michelangelo, Jeremiah, Sistine Chapel

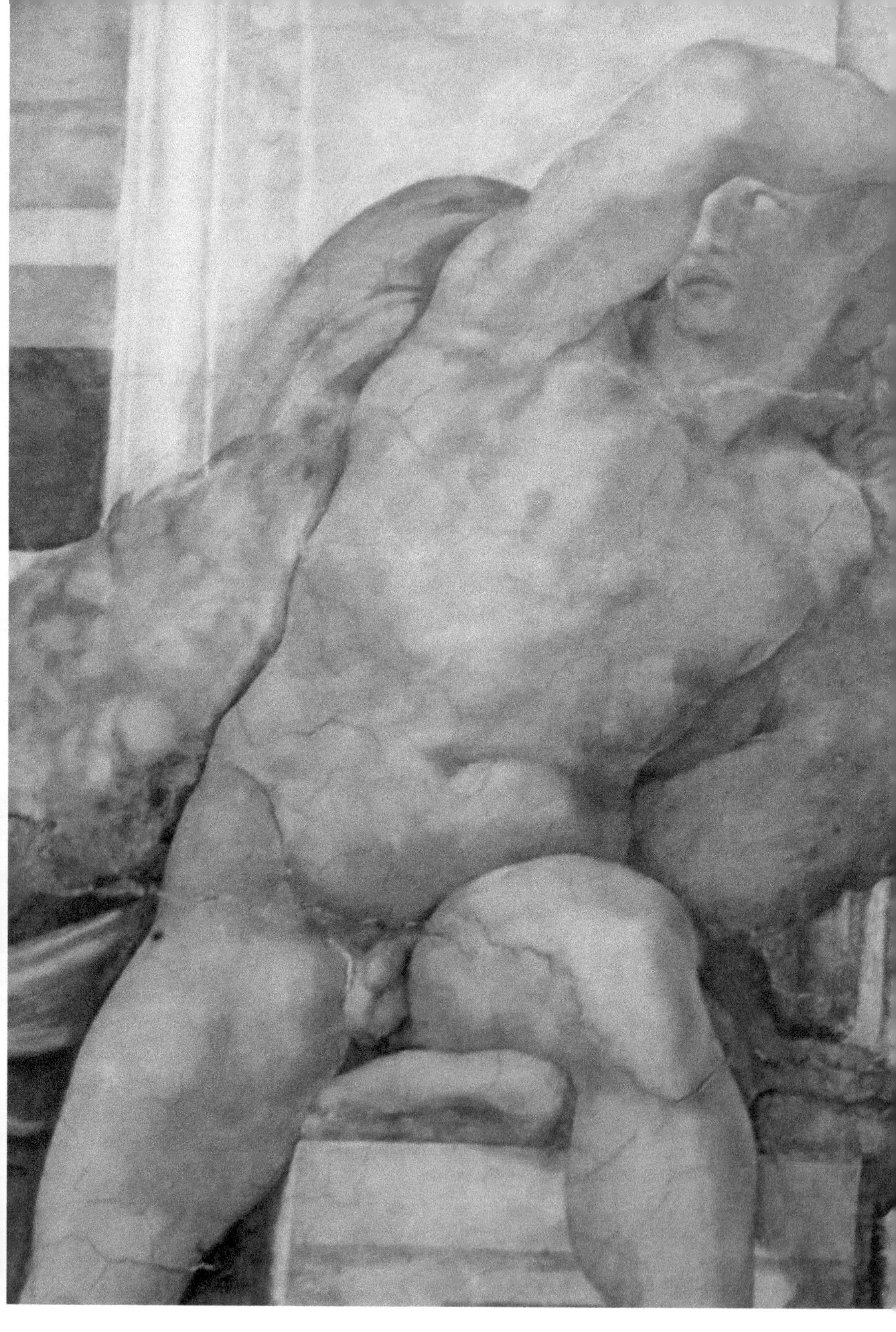

Michelangelo, Ignudi, Sistine Chapel

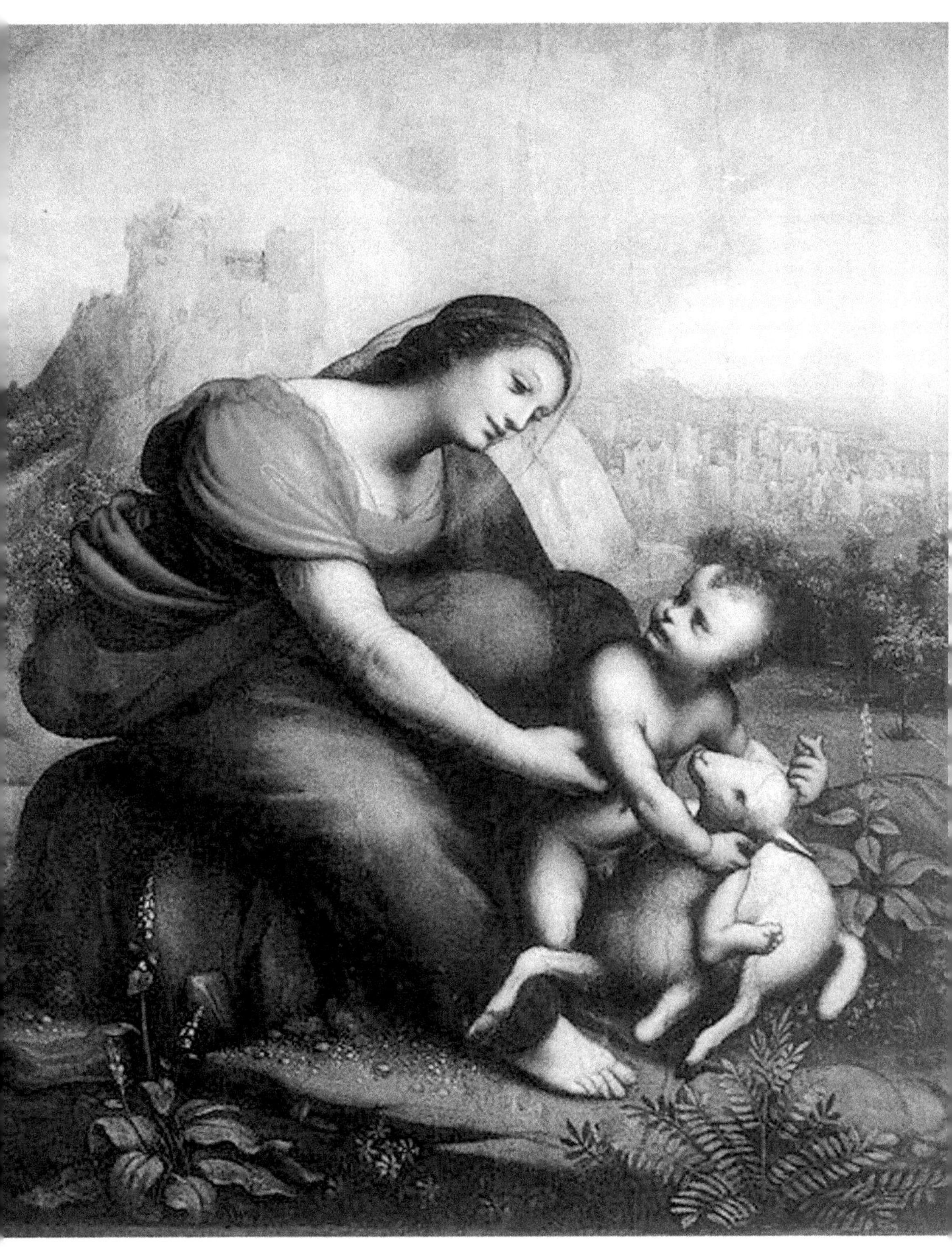

Cesare da Sesto, 1515, Madonna and Child,
Poldi Pezzoli Museum

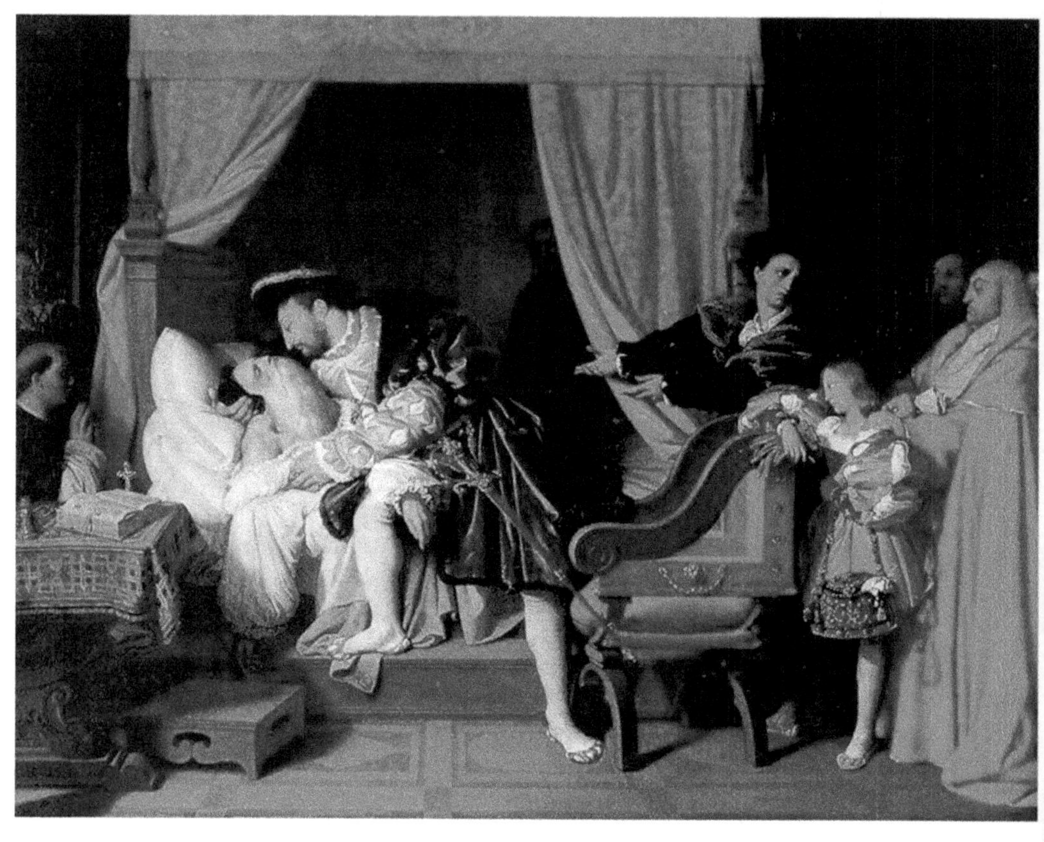

J.A.D. Ingres, The Death of Leonardo, 1818

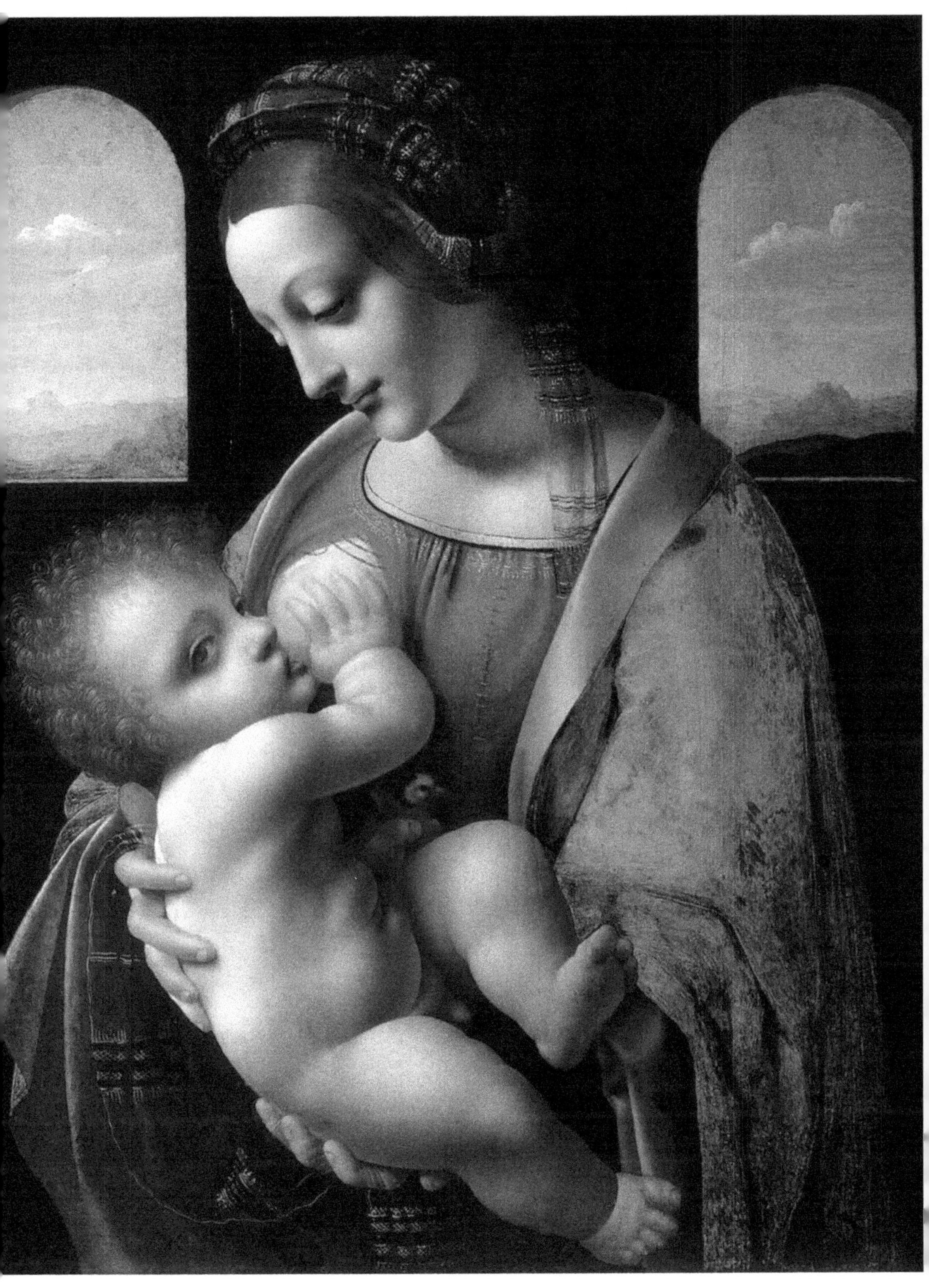

Leonardo da Vinci and others, The Litta Madonna,
Hermitage Museum, St Petersburg

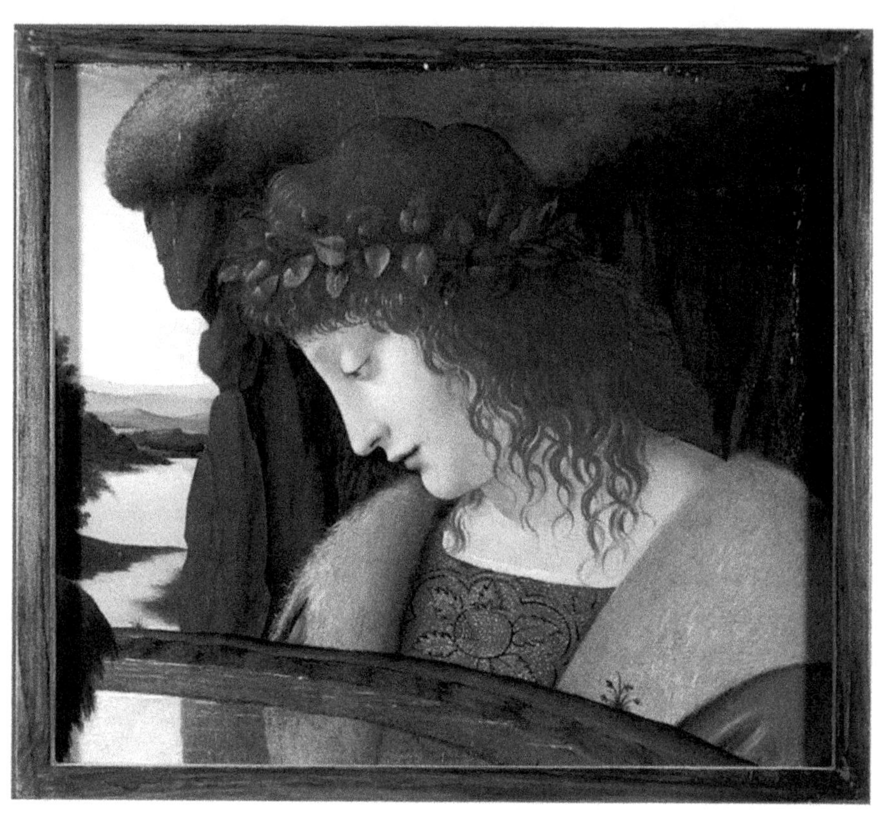

Follower of Leonardo, Narcissus, 1490,
National Gallery, London

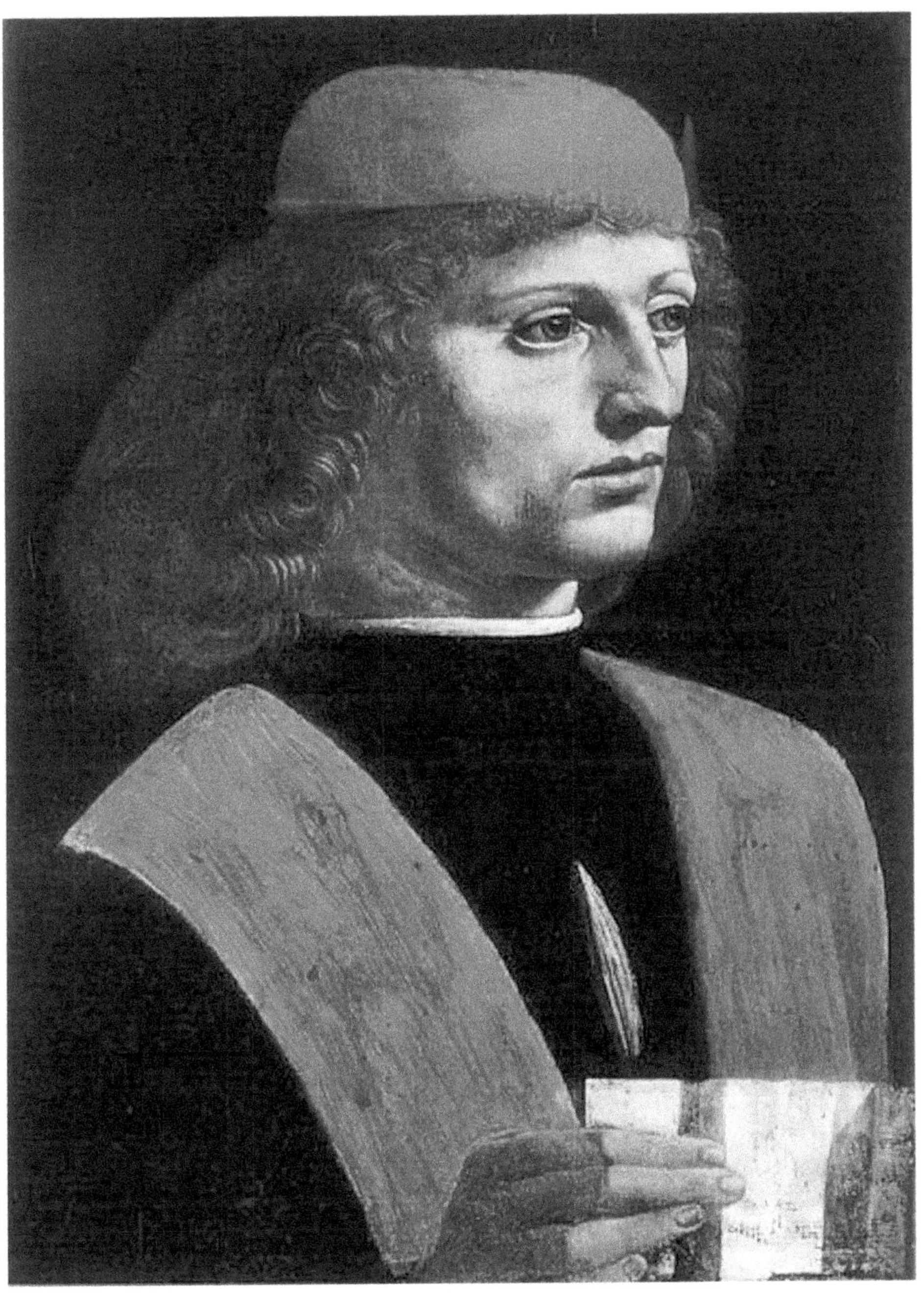

After Leonardo da Vinci, Portrait of a Musician,
1490, Milan

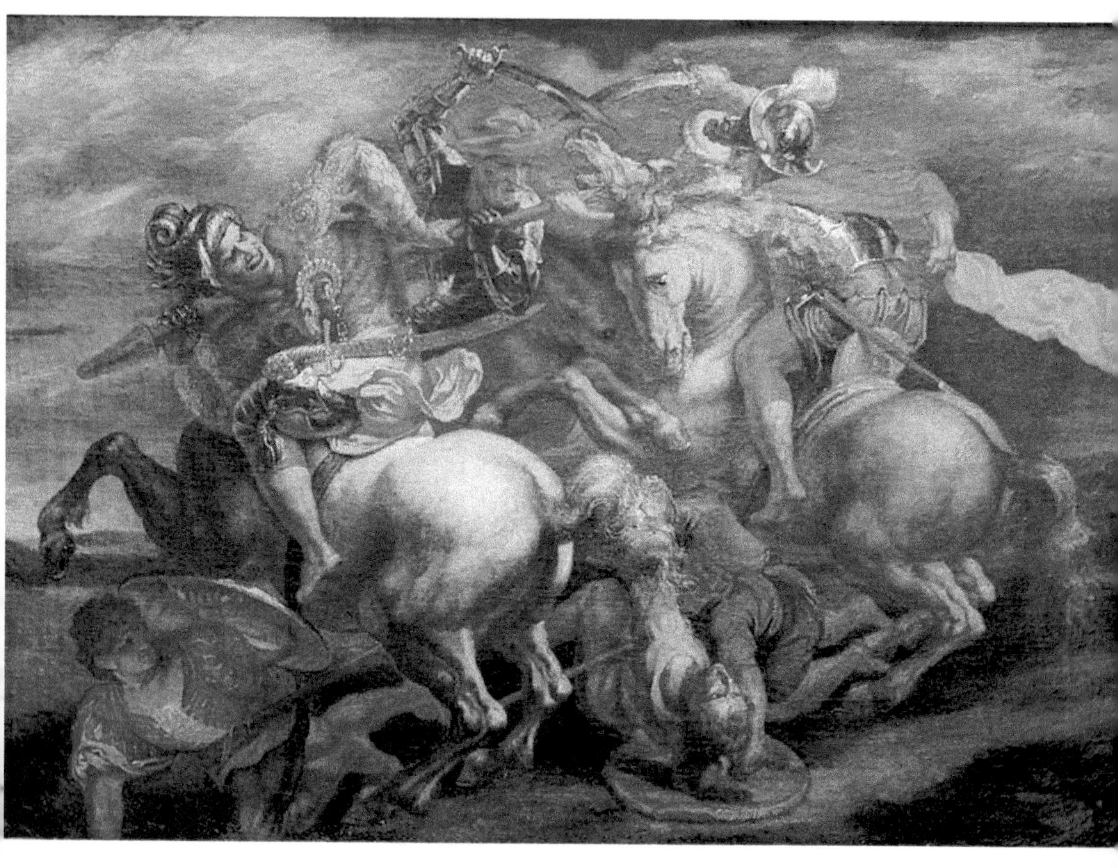

Peter Paul Rubens, The Battle of Anghiari, after
Leonardo da Vinci, Louvre, Paris

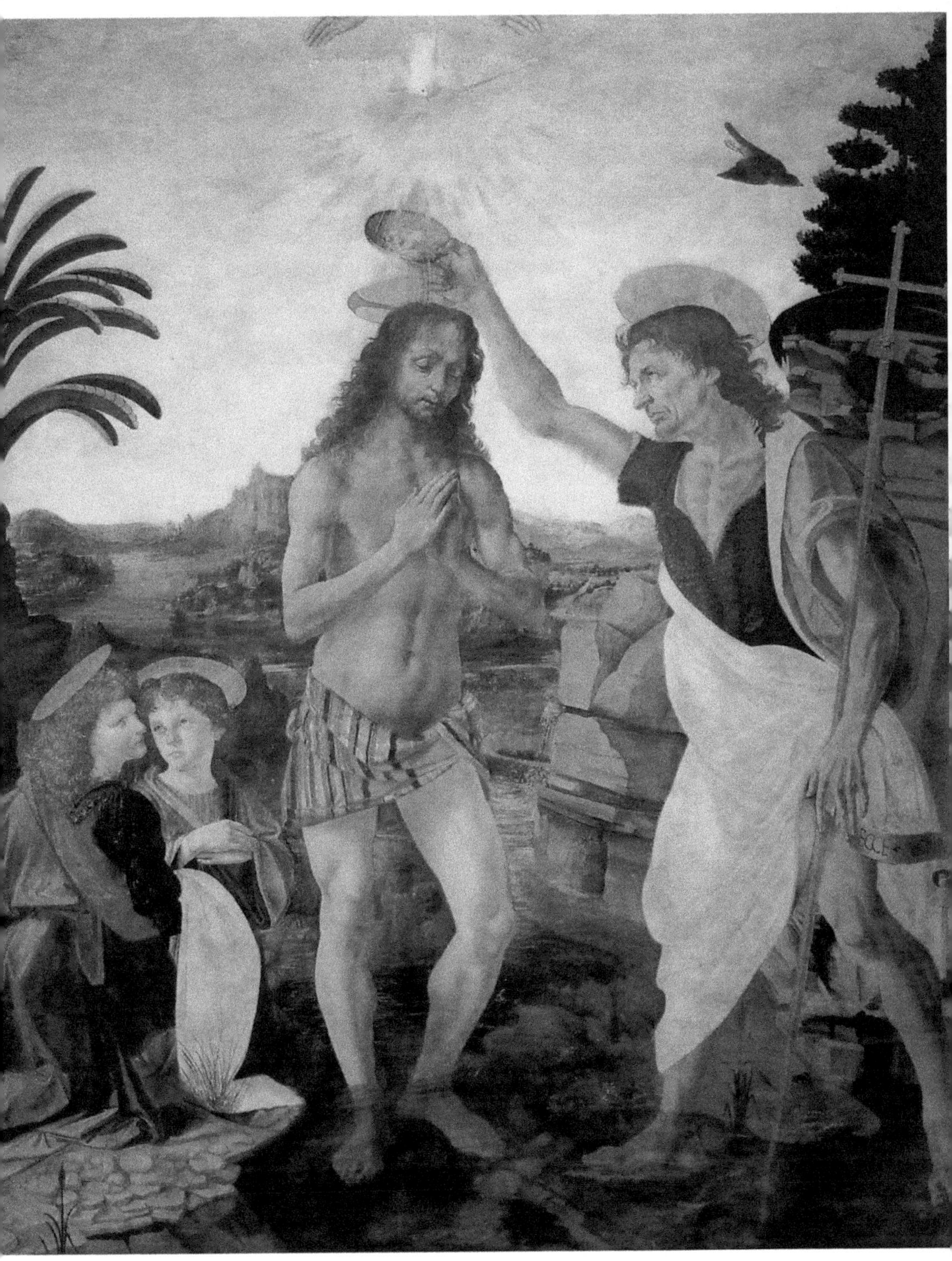

Andrea del Verrocchio, The Baptism of Christ

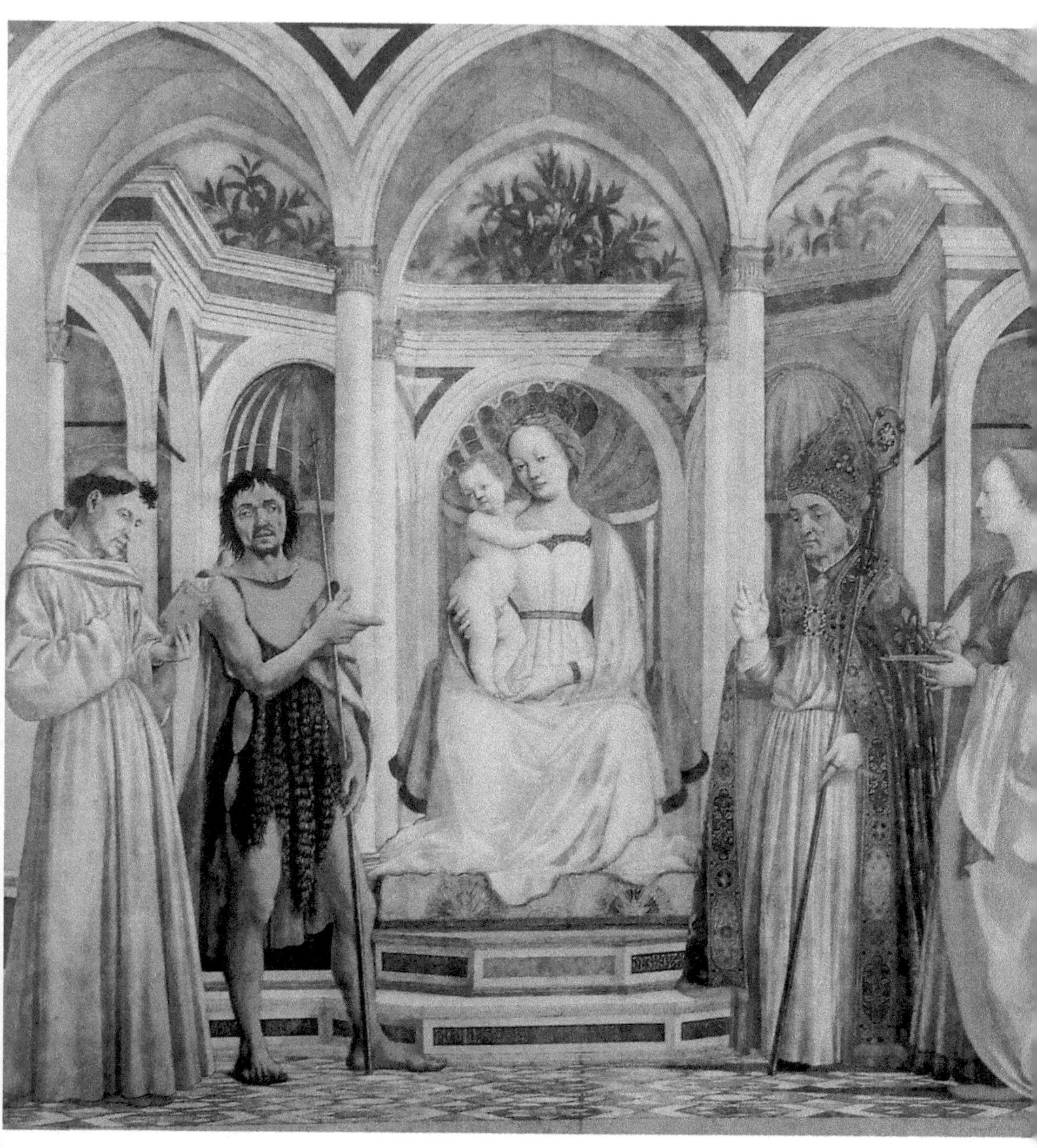

Domenico Veneziano, Madonna and Child With Saints, 1445, Uffizi Gallery

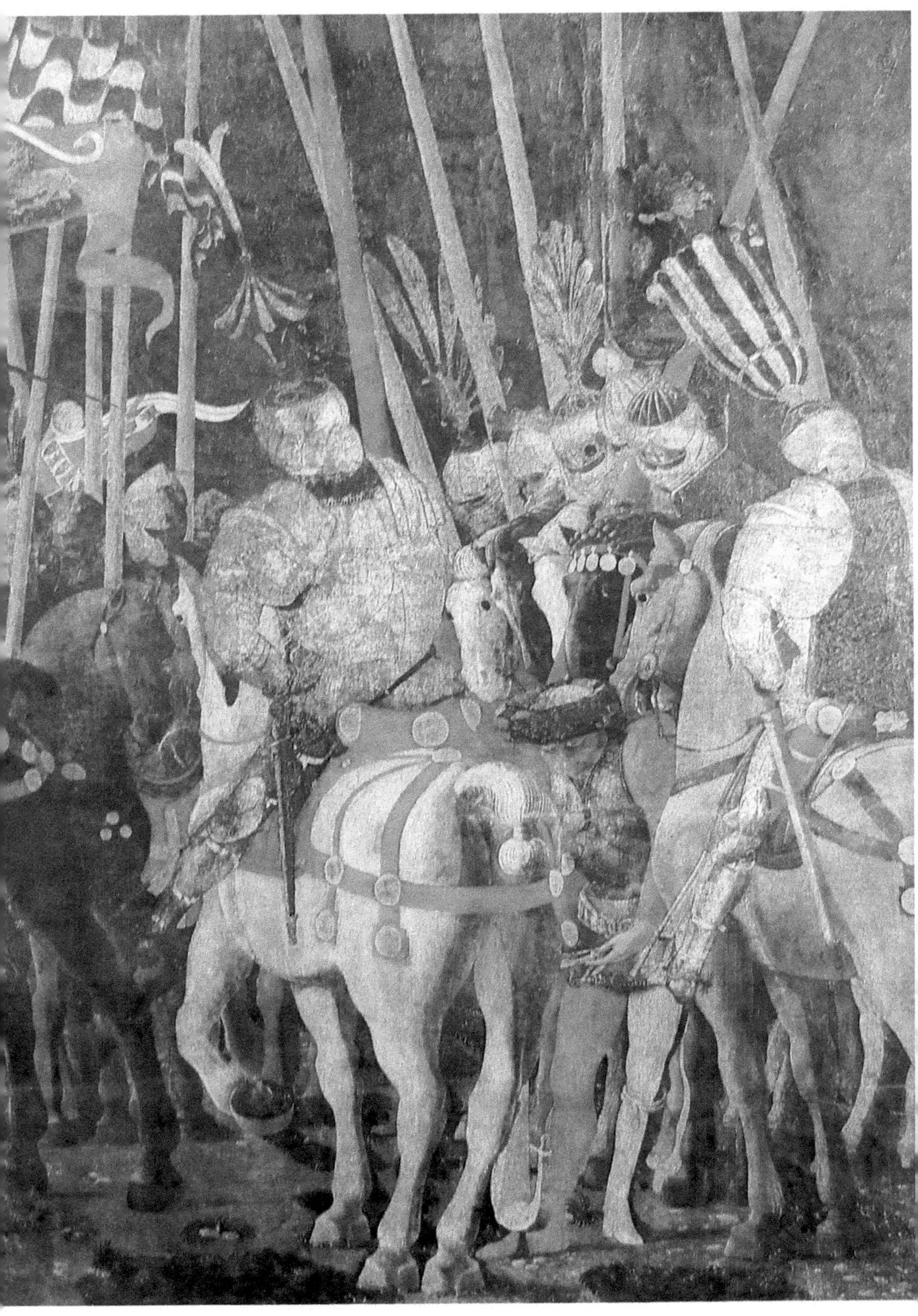

Paolo Uccello, The Battle of San Romano, Paris

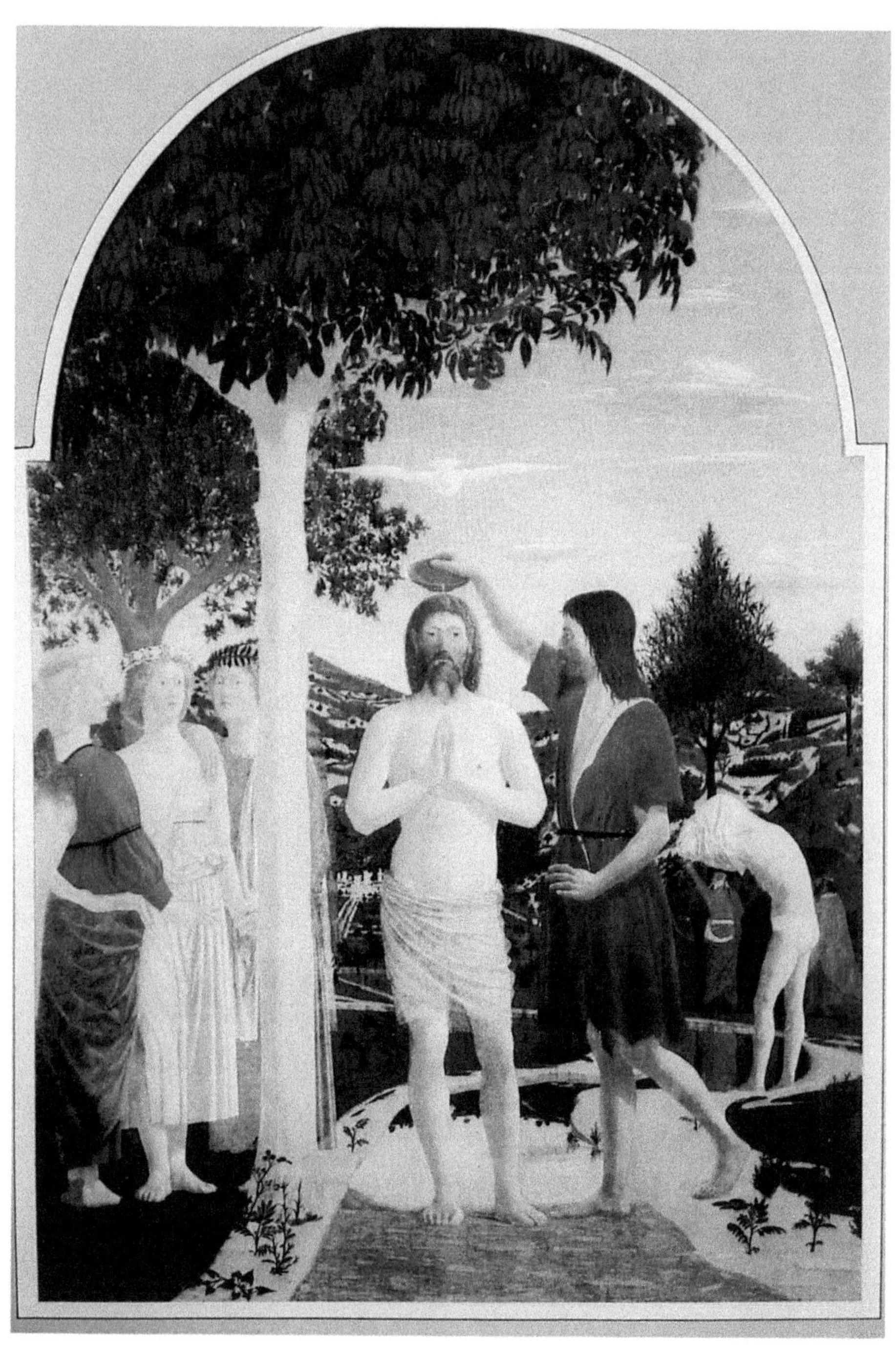

Piero della Francesca, *The Baptism of Christ*, National Gallery, London

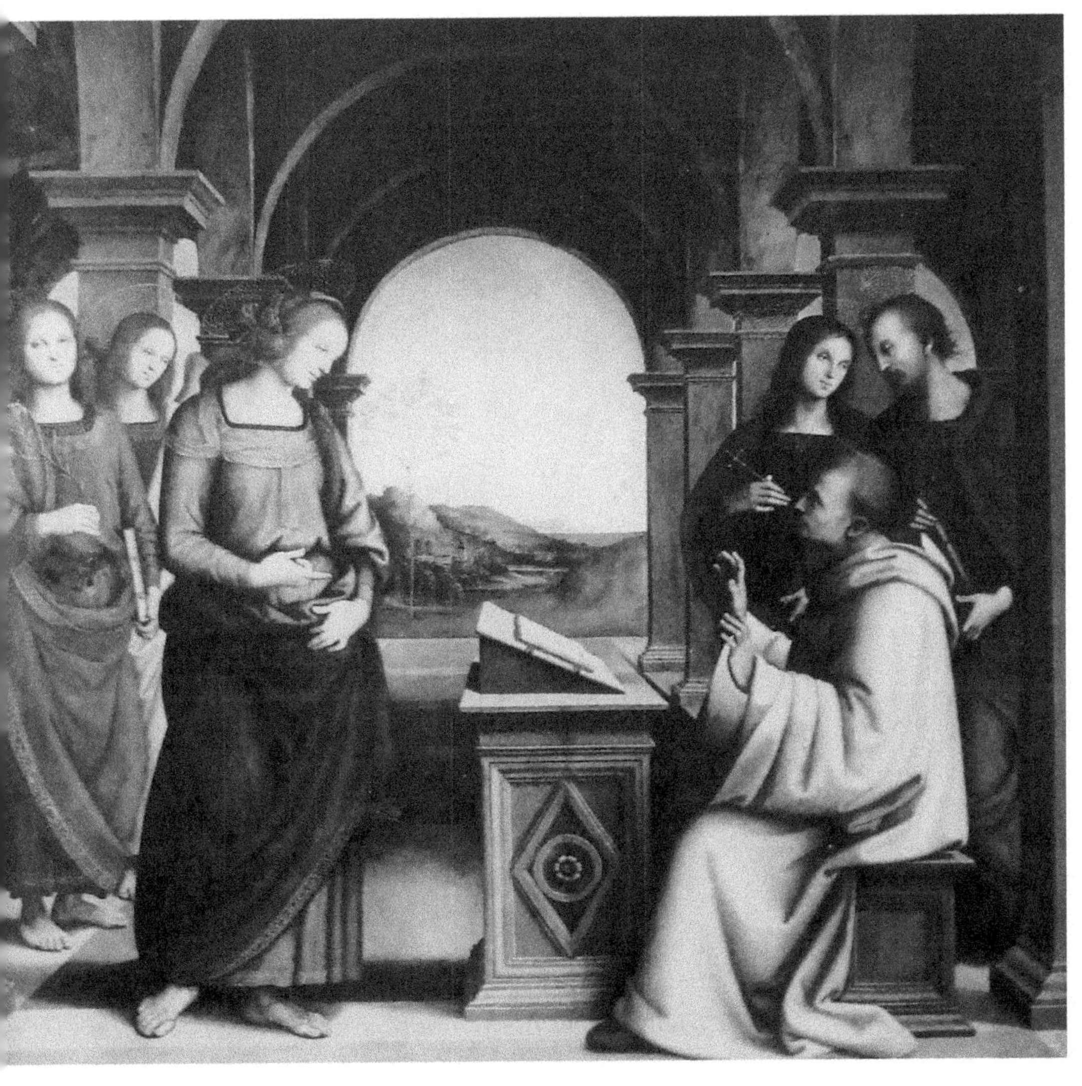

Perugino, Vision of St Bernard, 1488

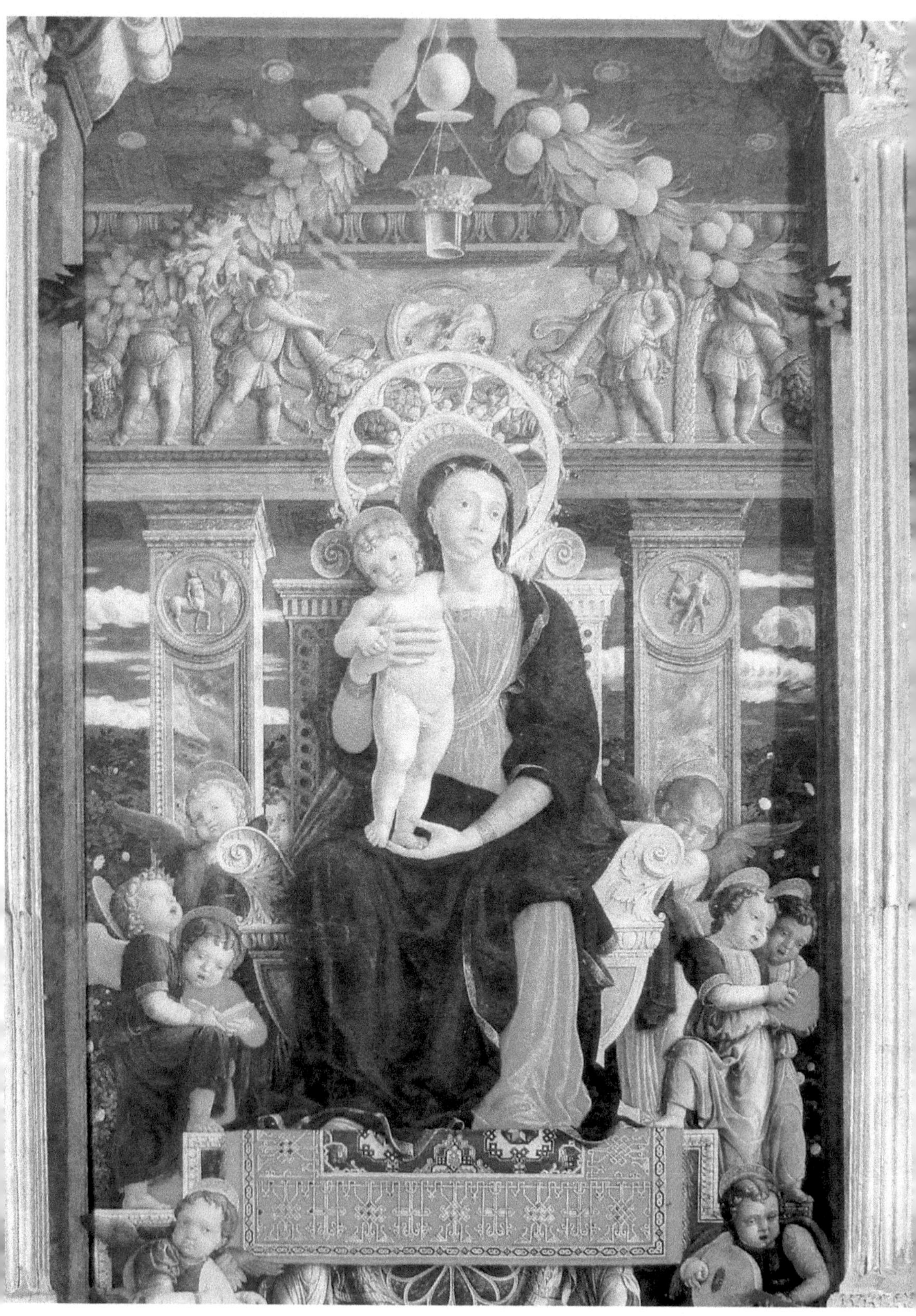

Andreas Mantegna, Madonna and Child Enthroned, 1457-60, Verona

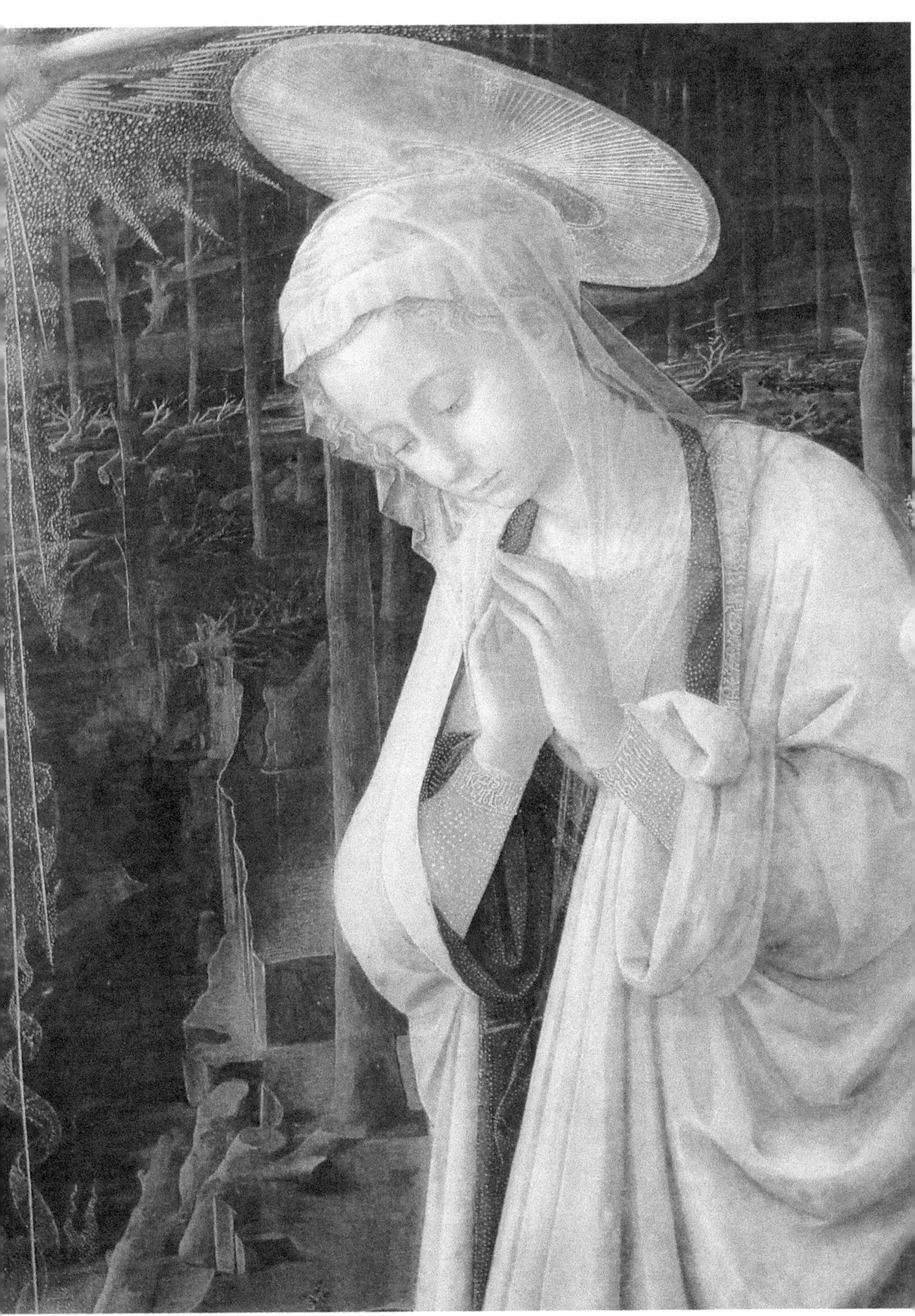

Fra Filippo Lippi, The Adoration of the Virgin, Berlin, detail

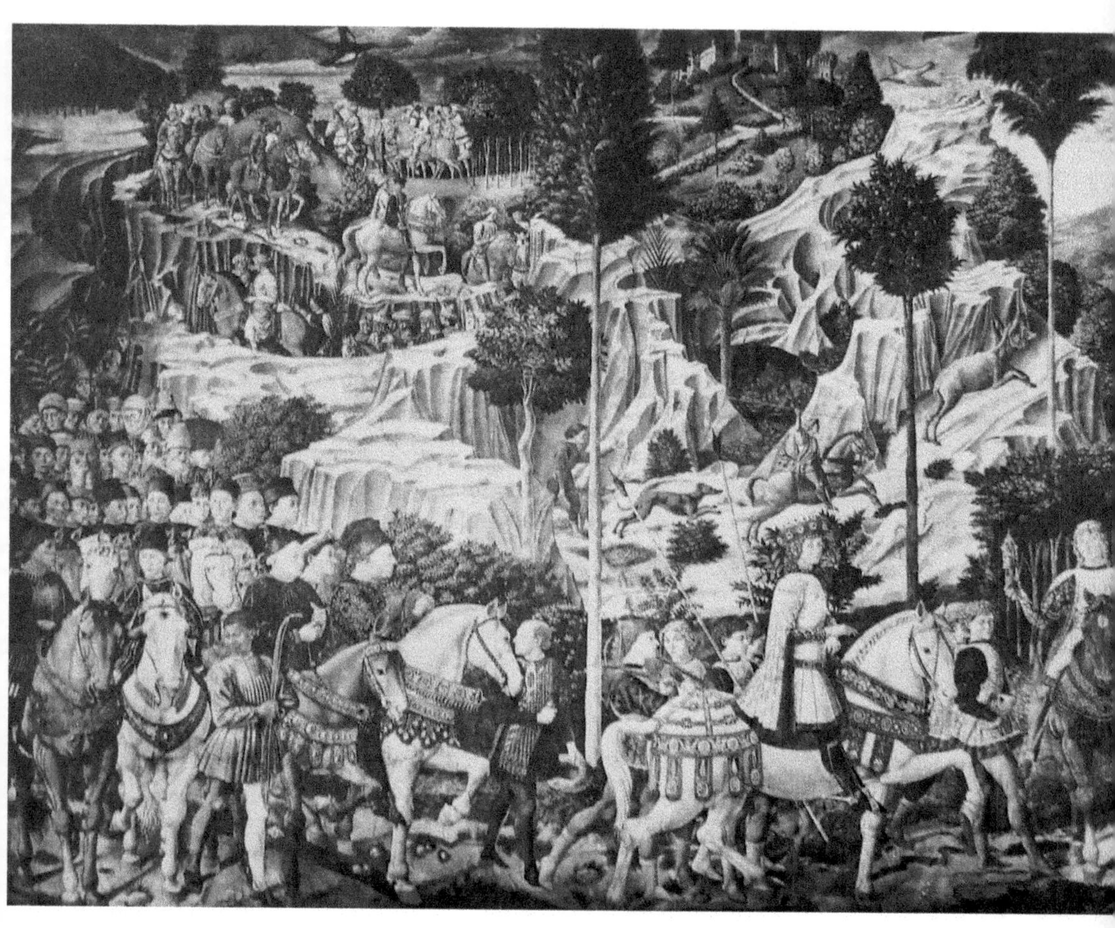

Benozzo Gozzoli, Journey of the Magi

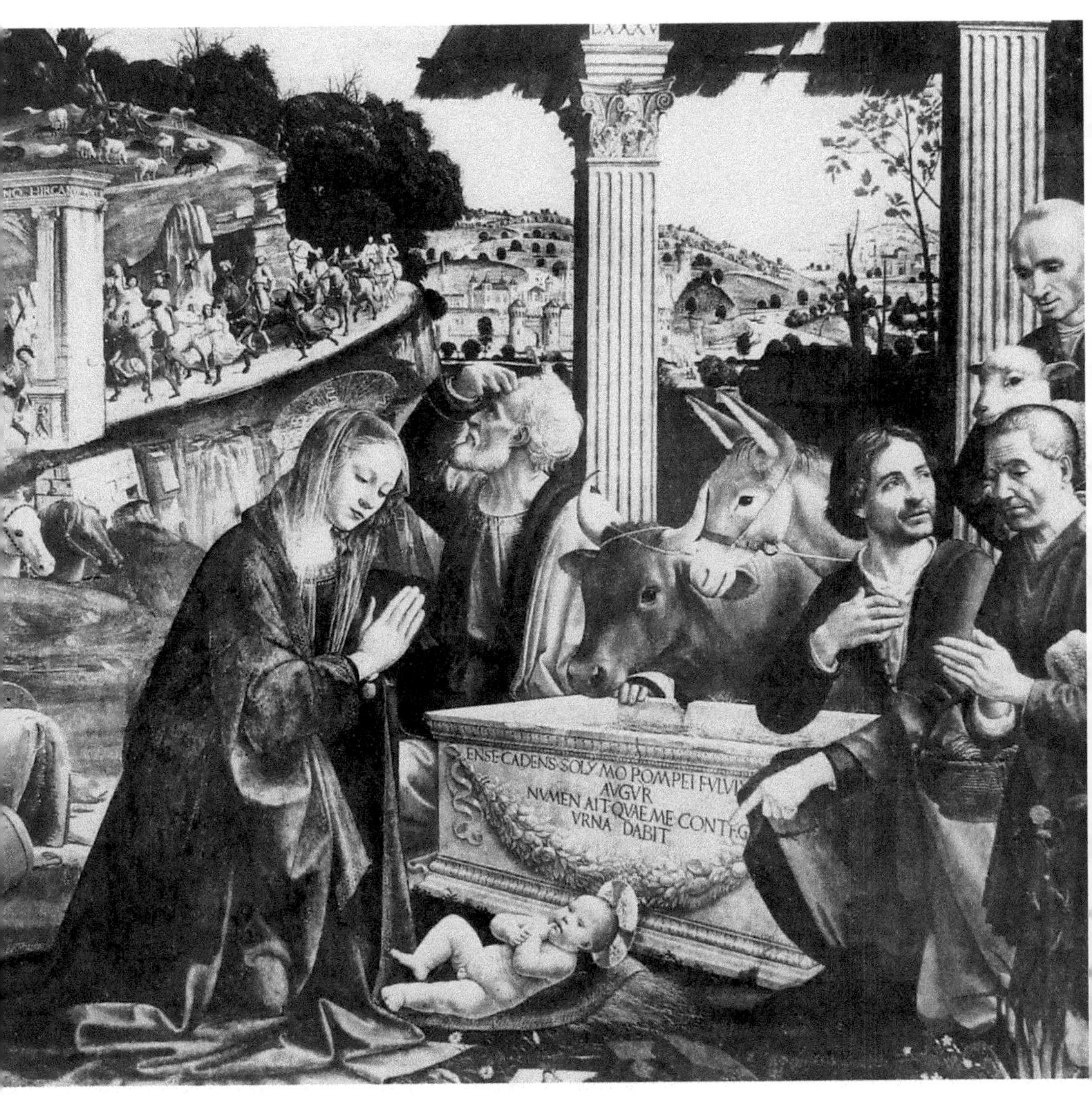

Domenico Ghirlandaio, Adoration of the Shepherds, 1485

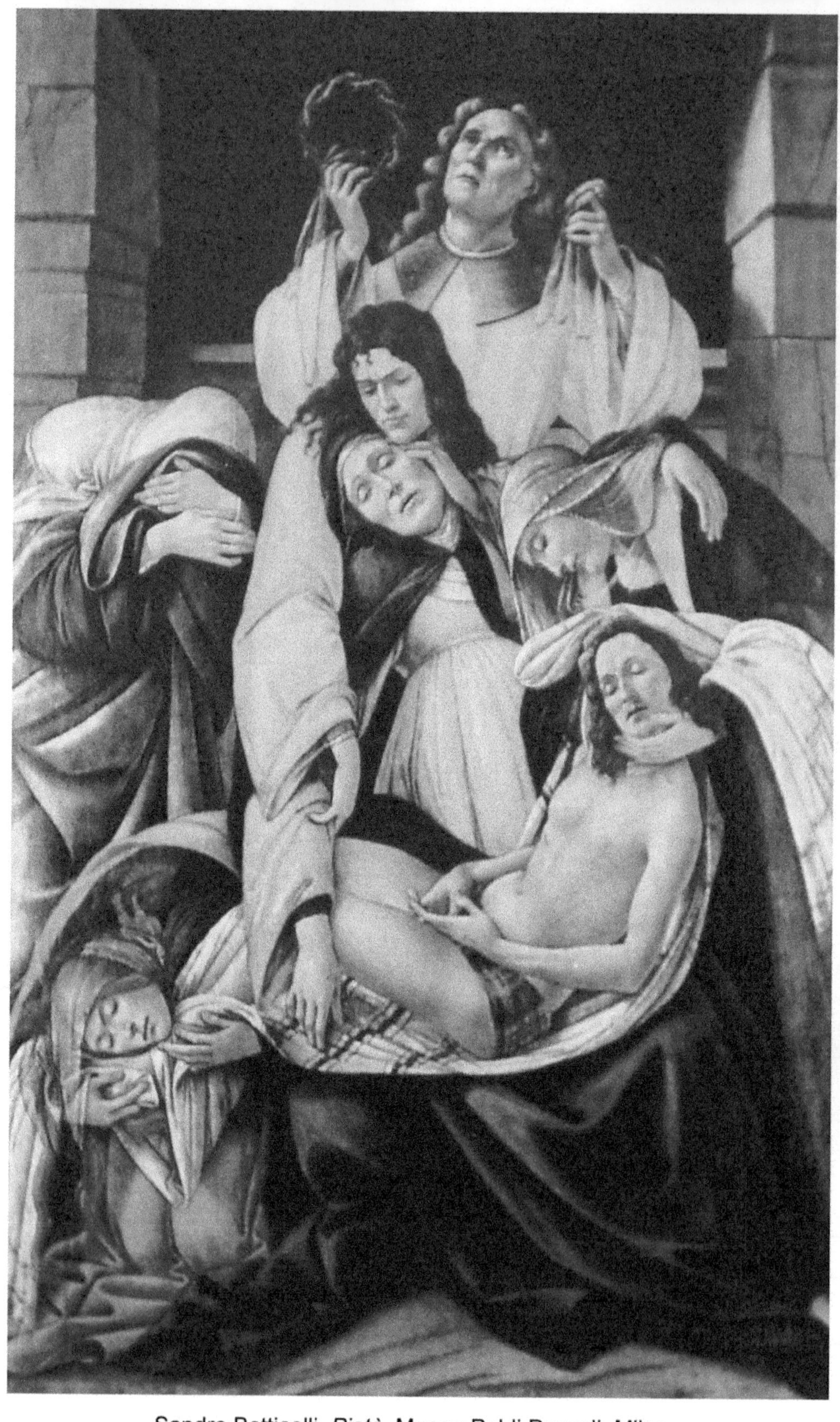

Sandro Botticelli, *Pietà*, Museo Poldi Pezzoli, Milan

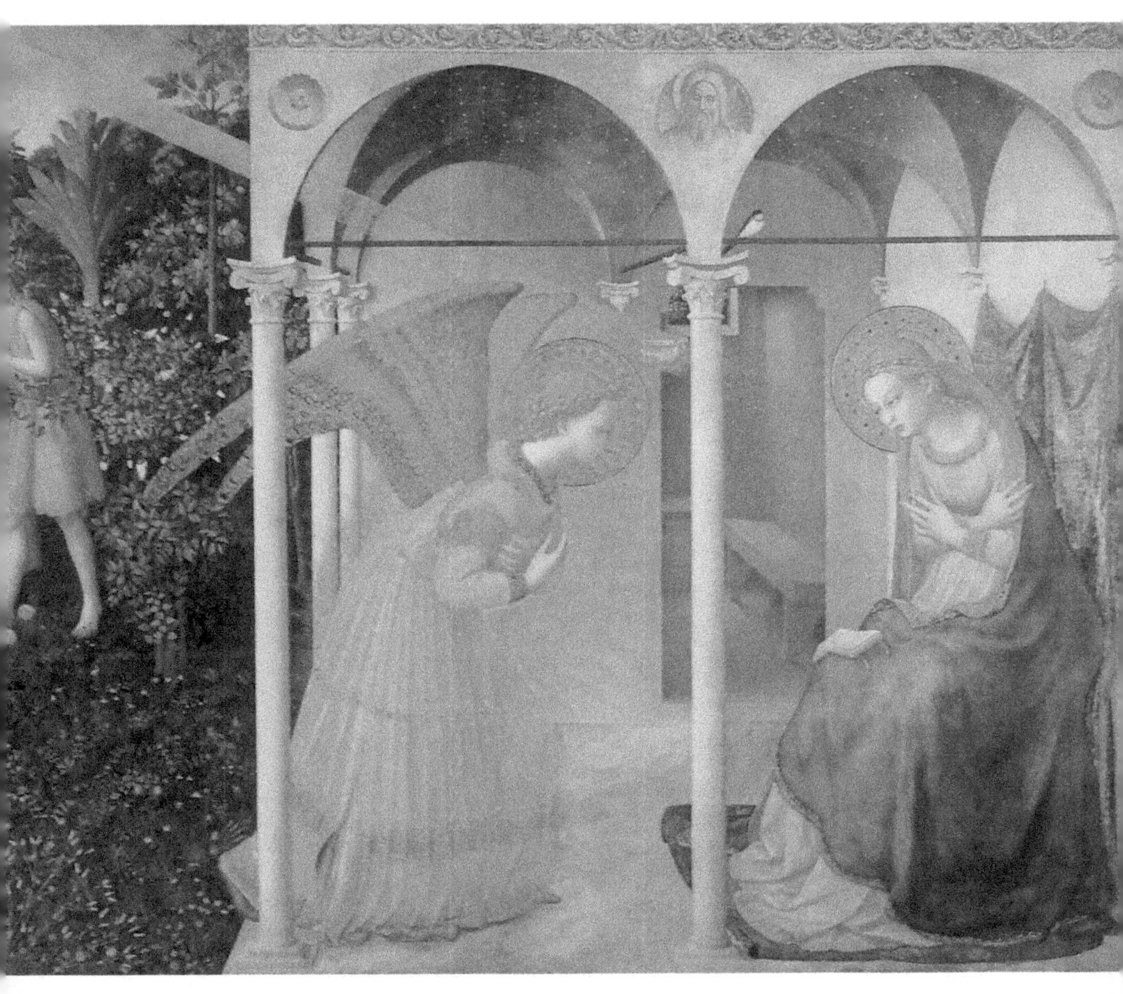

Fra Angelico, Annunciation, Prado, Madrid

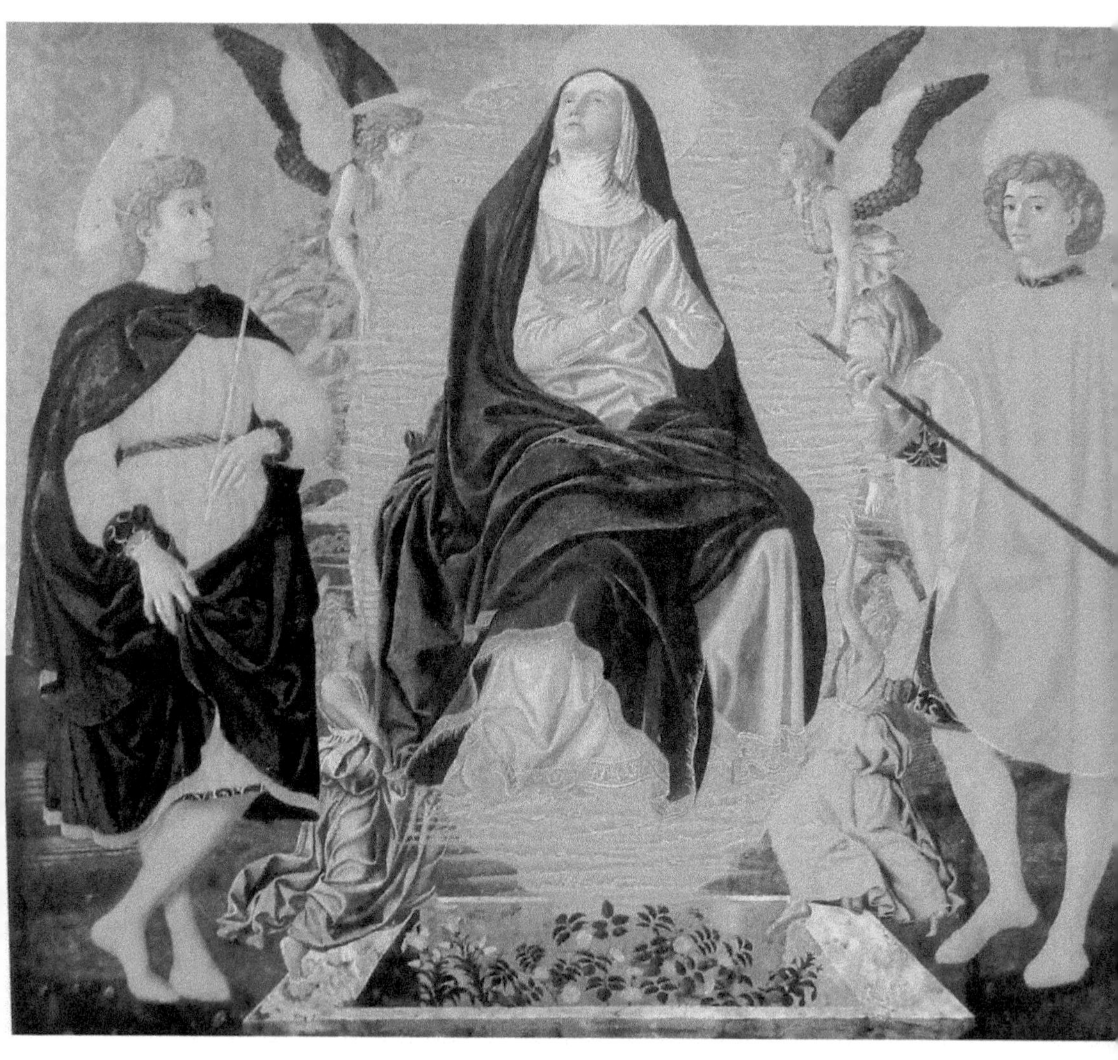

Andrea del Castagno, Assumption, Berlin

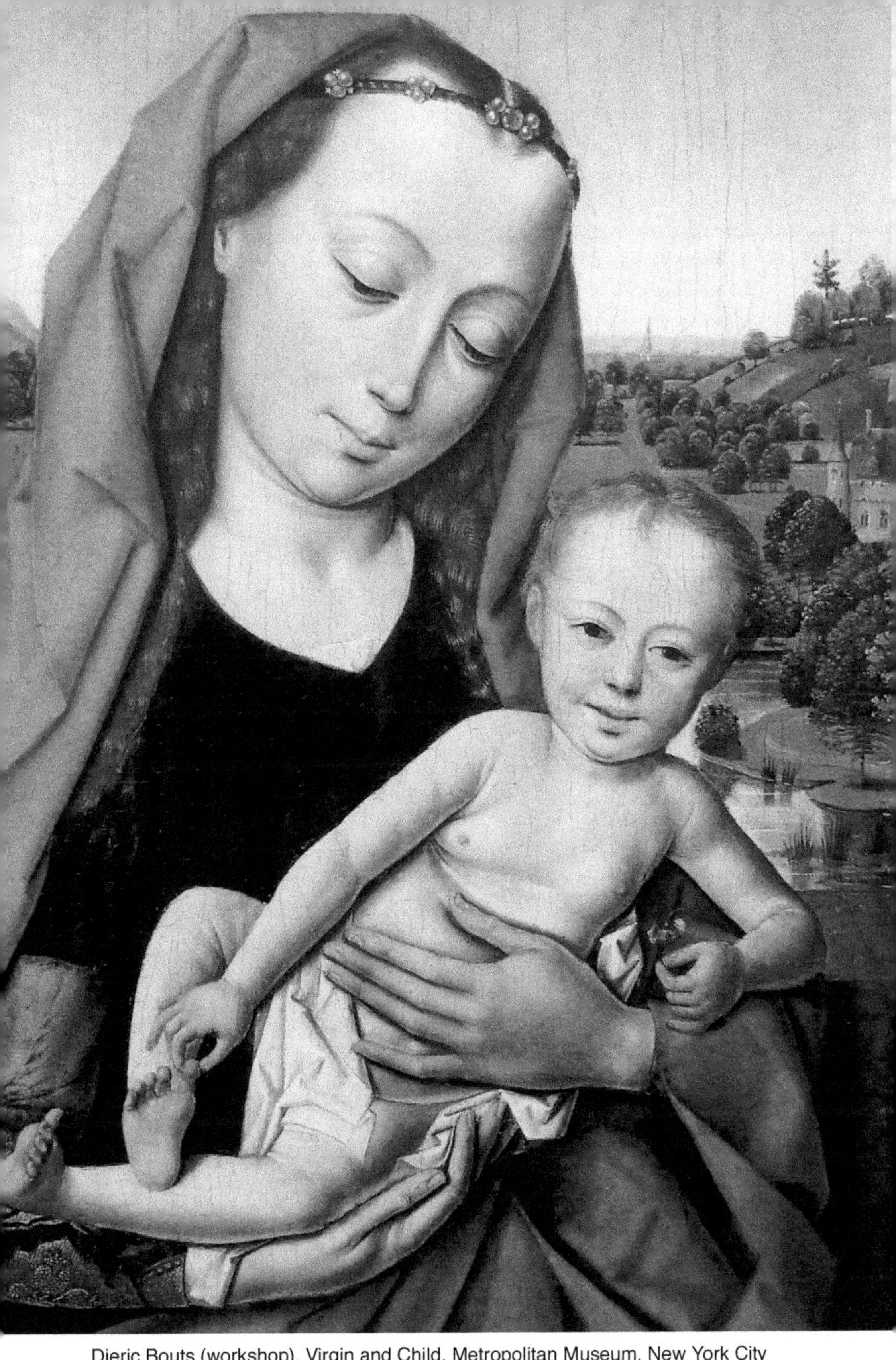

Dieric Bouts (workshop), Virgin and Child, Metropolitan Museum, New York City

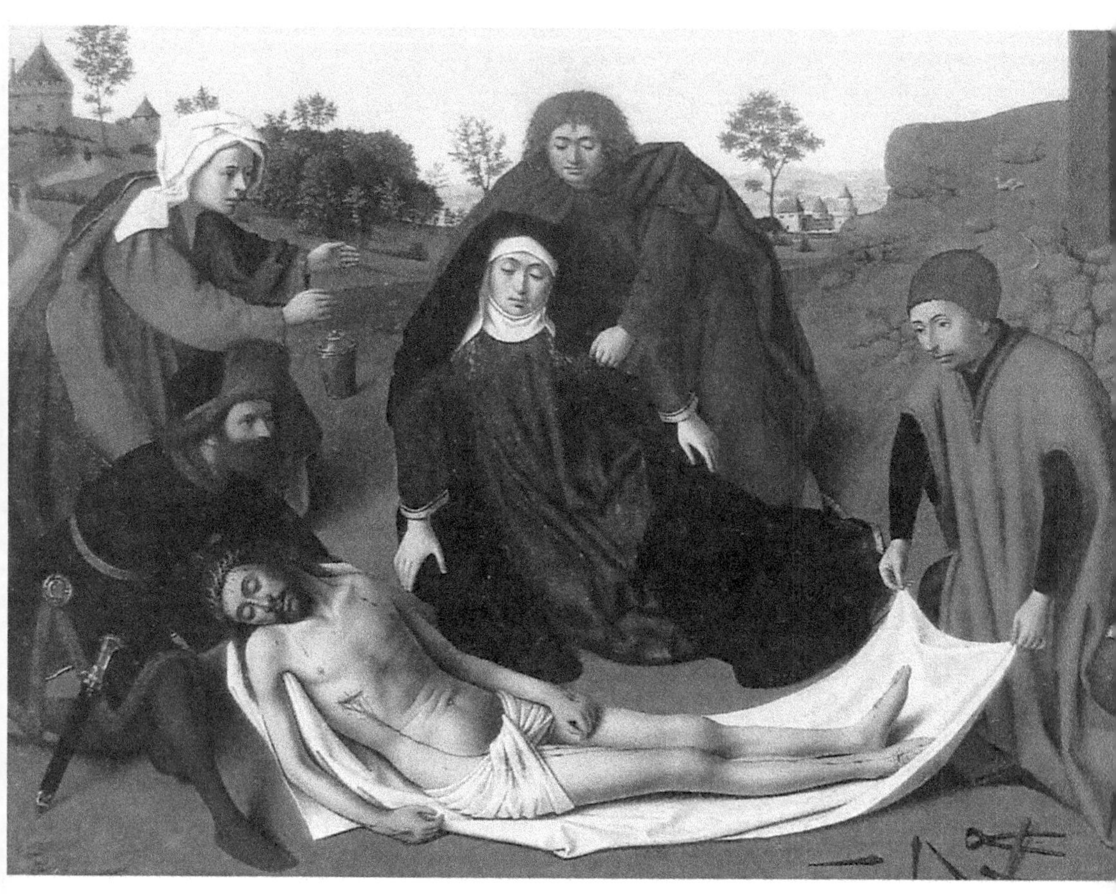

Petrus Christus, The Lamentation, Metropolitan Museum,
New York City

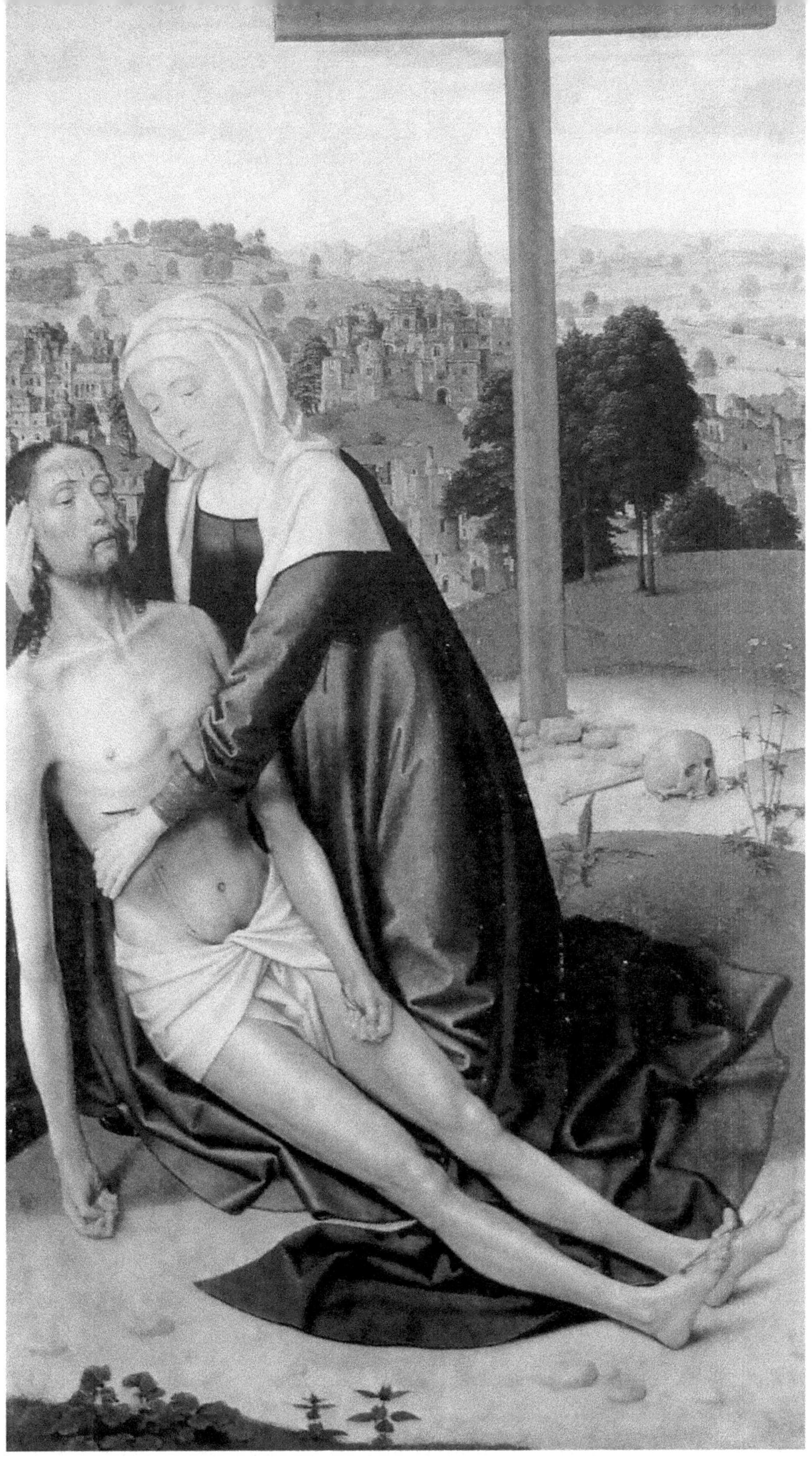

Gerard David, Pietà, Winterhur

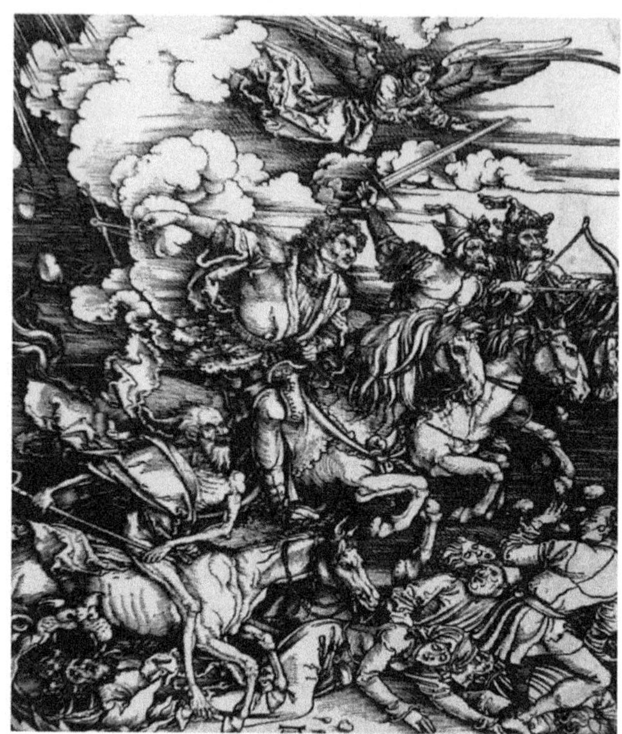

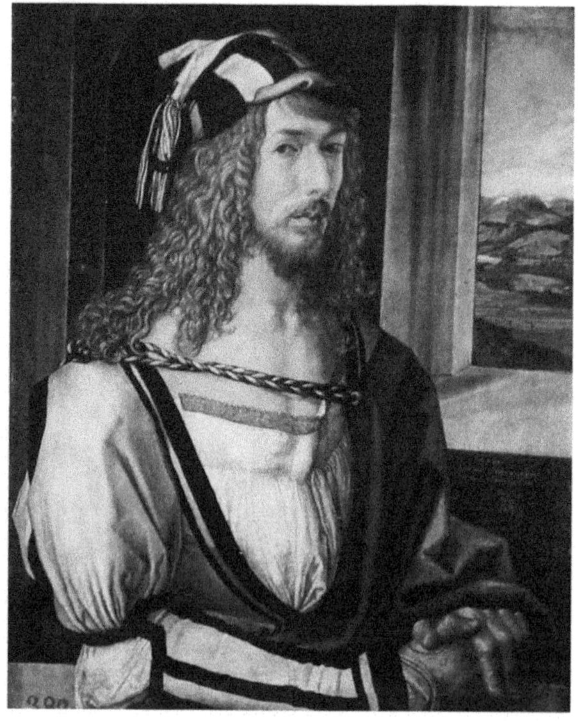

Albrecht Dürer

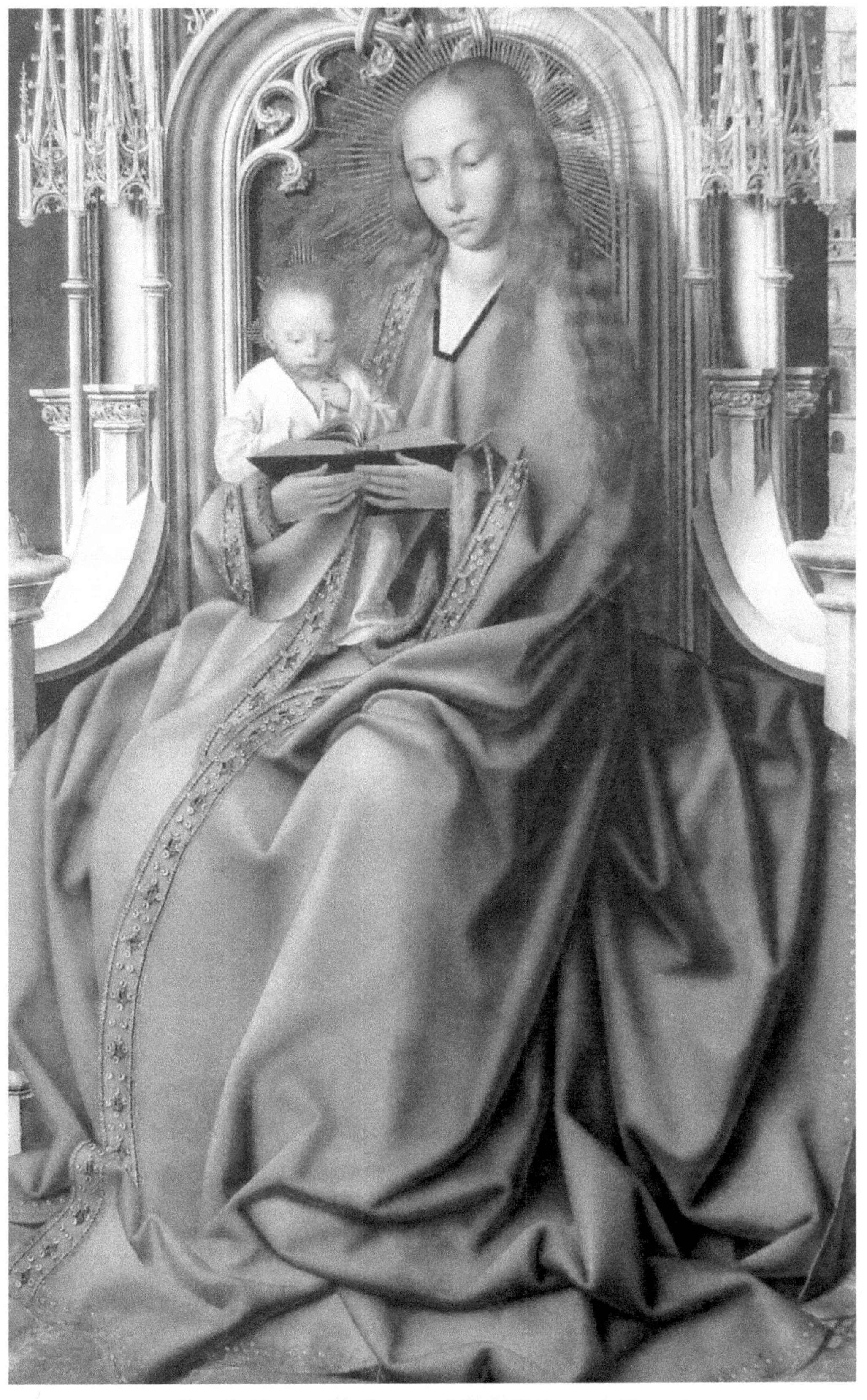

Quentin Massys, Madonna and Child Enthroned, Brussels

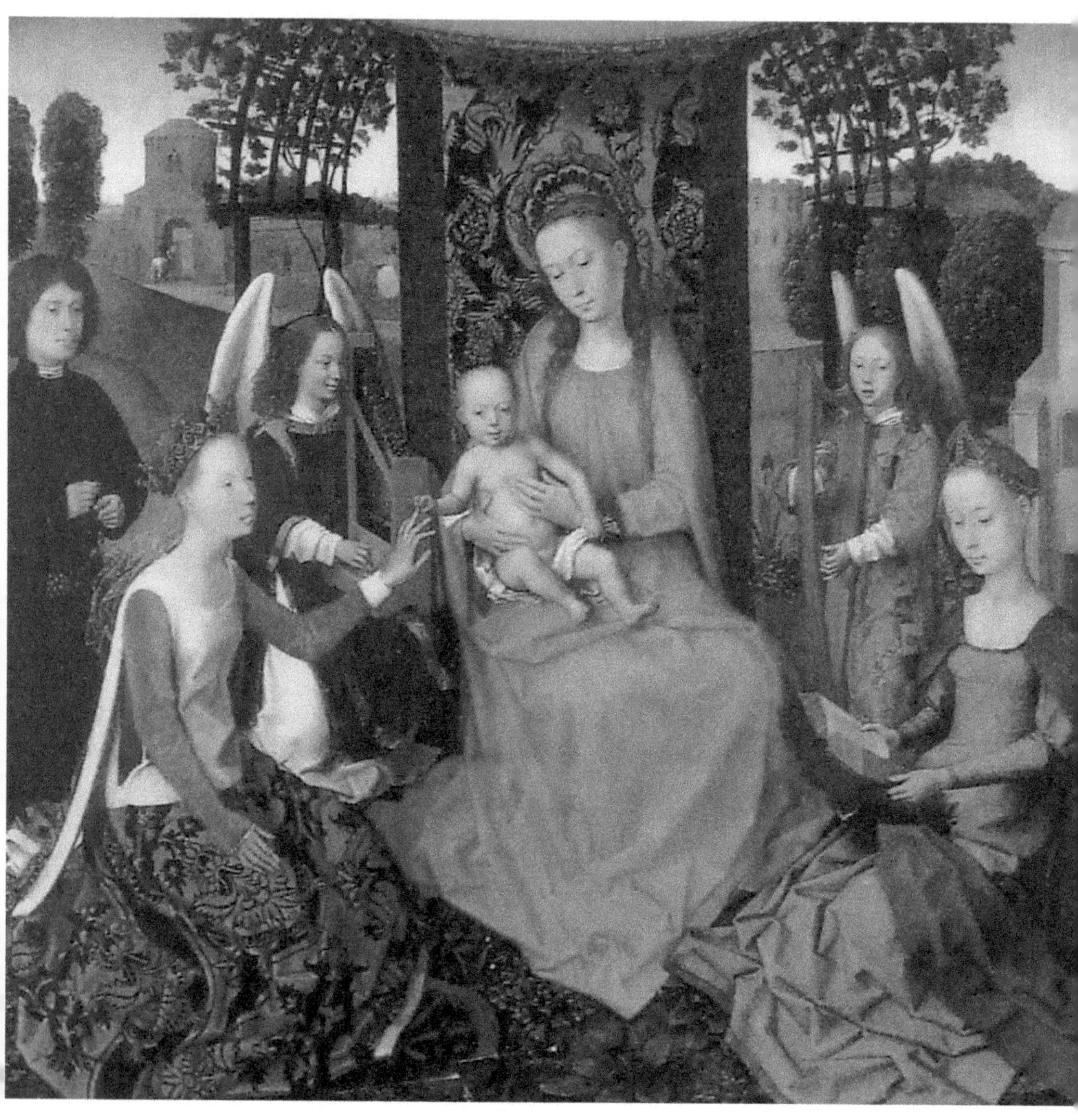

Hans Memling, The Mystic Marriage of St Catherine, Metropolitan Museum, New York City

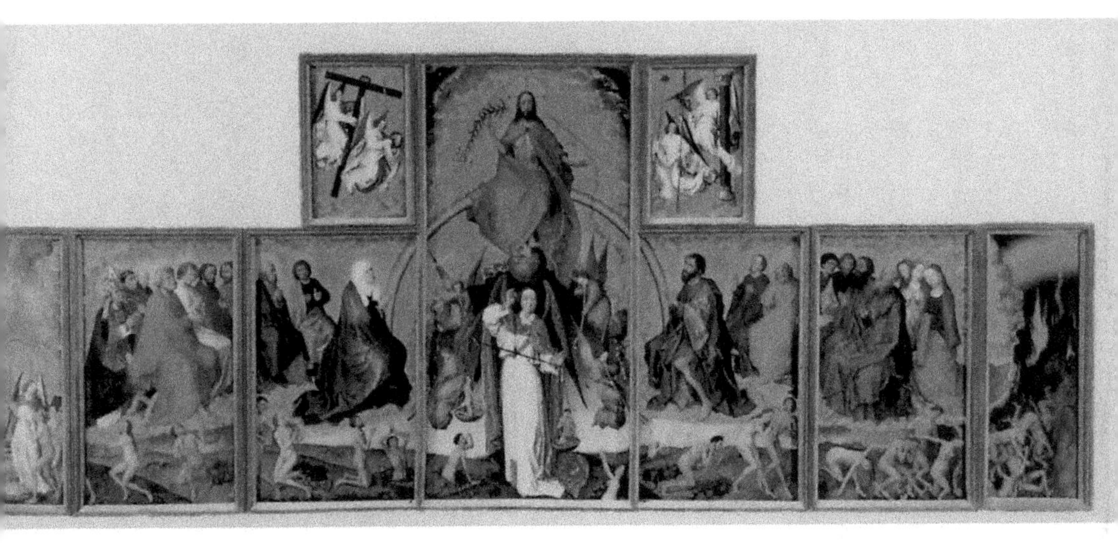

Rogier van der Weyden, The Last Judgement, 1445-49, Beaune

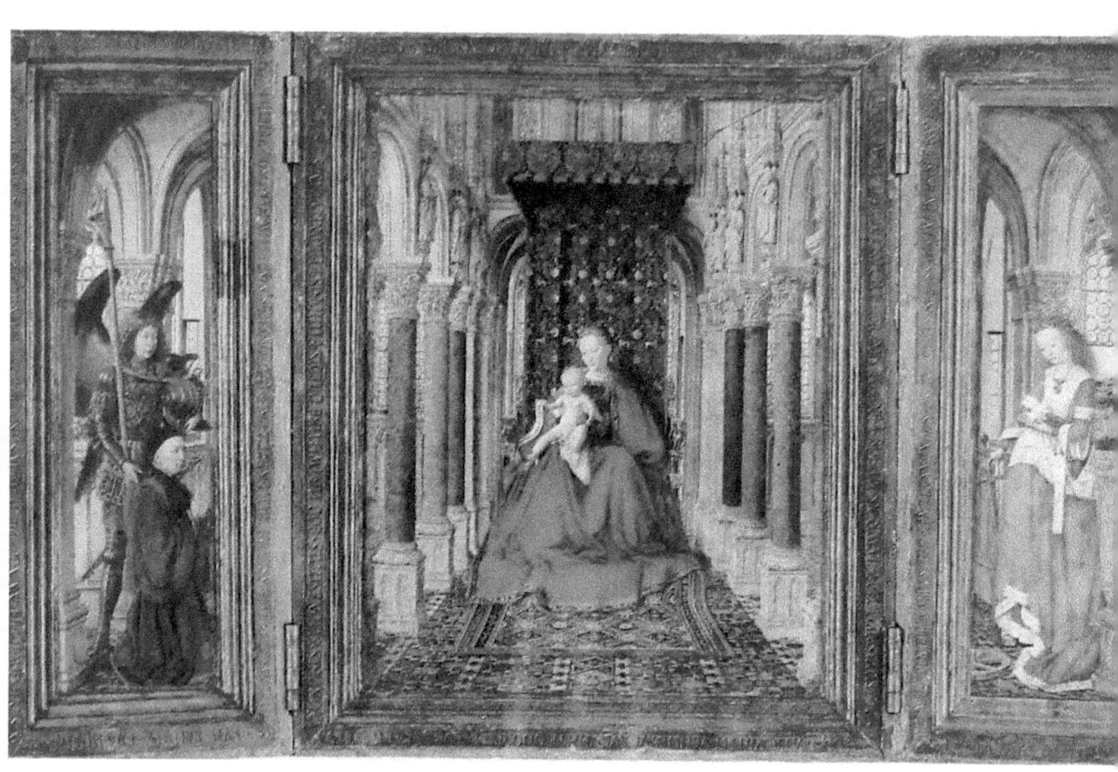

Jan van Eyck, The Dresden Triptych, 1437, Dresden

Works

Adoration of the Magi, 1481-2, panel, 246 x 243cm, Uffizi, Florence

The Virgin of the Rocks c.1503-6, oil, 189.5 x 120cm, National Gallery, London

The Virgin of the Rocks c.1483-6, oil, 198 x 123cm, Louvre, Paris

Study For the Head of an Angel, 1483-90, silverpoint on light brown prepared surface, 18.2cm x 16cm, Royal Library, Turin

Lady with the Ermine, c.1485-90, oil on panel, 54 x 39cm, Czartoryski Museum, Cracow

St John the Baptist, c. 1513-6, panel, 69 x 57cm, Louvre, Paris

Virgin and Child and St Anne, c. 1510, oil on panel, 168 x 112cm, Louvre, Paris

St Anne, the Virgin and Child with the Baptist c. 1498, black chalk and white on paper, 141.5 x 104.6cm, National Gallery, London

Annunciation, c. 1472-5, oil, 104 x 217cm, Uffizi Museum, Florence

The Benois Madonna, c. 1475-8, oil, Hermitage, St Petersburg

Madonna with Carnation, 1478-80, oil and panel, 62 x 47cm, Alte Pinakothek, Munich

with Verrocchio: *The Baptism of Christ*, 1472-5, panel, 177x 151cm, Uffizi Museum, Florence

Portrait of a Woman (Ginevra Benci?), 1474-6, oil on panel, 42 x 37cm, National Gallery of Art, Washington DC

St Jerome, 1481-2, panel, 246 x 243 cm, Louvre, Paris

The Last Supper, 1495-7, tempera on wall, 460 x 860cm, Convent of Ste Maria della Grazie, Milan

Female Portrait (La Belle Ferronnière), 1490-5, oil on panel, 62 x 44cm, Louvre, Paris

Mona Lisa, 1503-5, oil on panel, 77 x 53cm, Louvre Paris

Bacchus, 1511-5, 177 x 115cm, Louvre, Paris

Bibliography

ON LEONARDO DA VINCI

James Beck: *Leonardo's Rule of Painting*, Oxford University Press, 1979
Serge Bramly: *Leonardo: The Artist and the Man*, Michael Joseph 1992
Ritchie Calder: *Leonardo and The Age of the Eye*, Heinemann 1970
Kenneth Clark: *Leonardo da Vinci*, Cambridge University Press 1939
—*A Catalogue of the Drawings of Leonardo da Vinci in the Collection of His Majesty the King at Windsor Castle*, Cambridge University Press 1935
K.R. Eissler: *Leonardo da Vinci: Psychoanalytic Notes on The Enigma*, International Universities Press, New York, 1961
William A. Emboden: *Leonardo da Vinci: On Plants and Gardens*, Christopher Helm, Bromley, Kent, 1987
C. Gould: *Leonardo da Vinci, the Artist and the Non-Artist*, Boston 1975
L. Heydenreich: *Leonardo da Vinci*, New York 1954
Sigmund Freud: *Leonardo da Vinci*, tr Alan Tyson, Penguin 1963
Cecil Gould: *Leonardo: The Artist and the Non-Artist*, Weidenfeld & Nicholson 1975
K. Keele: *Leonardo da Vinci's Elements of the Science of Man*, New York 1983
Martin Kemp, ed: *Leonardo da Vinci*, Yale University Press/South Bank Centre 1987
Leonardo da Vinci: *The Drawings of Leonardo da Vinci*, introduction A.E. Popham, Cape, 1964
—*The Complete Paintings*, introduction by L.D. Ettinger, Weidenfeld & Nicolson 1969
—*Selections from the Notebooks*, Oxford University Press 1952
—*Leonardo on Painting*, ed Martin Kemp, Yale University Press, New Haven 1989

—*The Notebooks of Leonardo da Vinci*, Braziller, New York 1954
—*The Manuscripts of Leonardo da Vinci, at the Biblioteca Nacional of Madrid*, ed. L. Reti, 5 vols, New York 1974
—*Landscapes, Plants and Water Studies in the Collection of Her Majesty The Queen at Windsor Castle*, ed. C. Pedretti, New York 1982
—*C. Pedretti: Leonardo – Studies for the Last Supper*, Milan 1983
—*Leonardo da Vinci: Fragments at Windsor Castle from the Codex Atlanticus*, London 1957
—*Gabinetto disegni e stampe degli Uffizi. Inventario I. Disegni e esposti*, Florence 1986
—*Leonardo da Vinci,: Corpus of Anatomical Studies at Windsor Castle*, K.D. Keele & C. Pedretti, 3 vols, New York 1979-80
—*Treatise on Painting (Codex Urbinas Latinus 1270) by Leonardo da Vinci*, ed. A.P. McMahon, 2 vols, Princeton University Press, New Haven 1956
E. MacCurdy: *The Mind of Leonardo da Vinci*, London 1928
Alberti de Mazzeri: *Léonard de Vinci*, Paris 1984
C.D. O'Malley, ed: *Leonardo's Legacy: An International Symposium*,
Robert Payne: *Leonardo da Vinci*, Robert Hale 1979
C. Pedretti: *I Disegni di Leonardo da Vinci e della sua cerchia nel Gabinetto disegni e stampe della galleria degli Uffizii a firenze*, Florence 1985
—*Leonardo da Vinci, on Painting: A Lost Book*, California 1964
Morris Philipson, ed: *Leonardo da Vinci: Aspects of the Renaissance Genius*, Braziller, New York 1966
L. Retti: *Leonardo*, 1974
R.S. Stites: *The Sublimations of Leonardo da Vinci*, Washington DC, 1970
Victor I. Stoichita: *Leonardo da Vinci*, Abbey Library 1978
V.P. Zubov: *Leonardo da Vinci*, Cambridge, Mass., 1968

OTHERS

Emile de Antonio & Mitch Tuchman: *Painters Painting*, Abbeville Press, New York 1984
C.G. Argan: *The Renaissance*, Thames & Hudson 1969
Karen Armstrong: *The Gospel According to Woman; Christianity's Creation of the Sex War in the West*, Pan 1987
Geoffrey Ashe: *The Virgin: Mary's Cult and the Re-emergence of the Goddess*, Arkana 1987
Dore Ashton: *American Art Since 1945*, Thomas & Hudson 1982
Patrick Bade: *Femme Fatale: Images of evil and fascinating women*, Ash & Grant 1979
Michael Baxandall: *Painting and Experience in 15th Century Italy*, Oxford University Press 1988
—*Patterns of Intention: On the Historical Explanation of Pictures*, Yale University Press 1985
James Beck: *Italian Renaissance Painting*, Harper & Row, New York 1981
Ean Begg: *The Cult of the Black Virgin*, Routledge 1985

Bernard Berenson: *The Italian Painters of the Renaissance*, Phaidon 1952
—*Looking at Pictures with Bernard Berenson*, selected by Hann Kiel, Abrahams, New York 1974
Pamela Berger: *The Goddess Obscured*, Robert Hale 1988
Bruce Bernard: *The Queen of Heaven: A Selection of Painting the Virgin from the Twelfth to the Eighteenth Centuries*, Macdonald/ Orbis 1987
—*The Bible and Its Painters*, Orbis 1983
Carlo Bertelli: *Piero della Francesca*, Yale University Press, New Haven 1992
Anthony Bertram: *Piero della Francesca*, Studio Publications 1949
Frances Bonner, Lizbeth Goodman, Richard Allen, Linda Jones & Catherine King, eds: *Imagining Women Cultural Representations and Gender*, Polity Press, Cambridge 1992
Botticelli: *The Complete Paintings of Botticelli*, Granada 1980
Allan Brahama: *Italian Renaissance Painters of the Sixteenth Century*, National Gallery 1985
Robert Briffault: *The Mothers: A Study of the Origins of Sentiments and Institutions*, Allen & Unwin, 3 vols 1927
Helmut Brinker: *Zen in the Art of Painting*, Routledge & Kegan Paul 1987
Stephanie Brown: *Religious Painting*, Phaidon 1979
Jacob Burckhardt: *The Altarpiece in Renaissance Italy*, Phaidon 1988
Titus Burckhardt: *Sacred Art in East and West*, Perennial Book, Middlesex 1967
Robert Cafritz, Lawrence Gowring & David Rosand: *Places of Delight: The Pastoral Landscape*, Weidenfeld & Nicolson 1989
Nicolas & Elena Calas: *Icons and Image of the Sixties*, Dutton, New York 1971
Deborah Cameron, ed: *The Feminist Critique of Language: A Reader*, Routledge 1990
Joseph Campbell: *The Power of Myth*, with Bill Moyers, ed. Betty Sue Flowers, Doubleday, New York 1988
Michael P. Carroll: *The Cult of the Virgin Mary*, Princeton University Press, New Jersey 1986
Whitney Chadwick: *Women, Art, and Society*, Thames & Hudson 1990
—*Women Artists and the Surrealist Movement*, Thames & Hudson 1991
Andre Chastel: *Art of the Italian Renaissance*, tr Peter & Linda Murray, Alpine Fine Arts Collection 1985
—*The Studios and Styles of the Renaissance Italy 1460-1500*, tr Griffin, Thames & Hudson 1966
Gail Chester & Julienne Dickey, ed: *Feminism and Censorship: The Current Debate*, Prism Press, Bridport, Dorset 1988
Tom Chetwyd: *A Dictionary of Symbols*, Collins 1982
Herschel B. Chipp, ed. *Theories of Modern Art*, University Press of California, Los Angeles 1968
J.E. Cirlot: *A Dictionary of Symbols*, Routledge 1981
Hélène Cixous & Catherine Clément: *The Newly Born Woman*, tr Betsy Wing, Manchester University Press 1986
Kenneth Clark: *Landscape into Art*, Reader's Union 1965
—*Piero della Francesca*, Phaidon 1969
—*Rembrandt and the Italian Renaissance*, John Murray 1969
Bruce Cole: *The Renaissance Artist at Work*, John Murray 1983
—*Piero della Francesca: Tradition and Innovation in Renaissance Art*, Harper

Collins, New York 1991
J.C.Cooper: *An Illustrated Dictionary of Traditional Symbols*, Thames & Hudson 1978
Pierre Courthion: *Flemish Painting*, Thames & Hudson 1958
Jean-Luc Daval: *History of Abstract Painting*, Art Data 1989
Martin Davies: *Rogier van der Weyden*, Phaidon 1972
Lene Dresen-Coenders, ed: *Saints and She-Devils: Images of Women in the 15th and 16th Centuries*, Rubicon Press 1987
Steven C. Dubin: *Arresting Images: Impolitic Art and Uncivil Actions*, Routledge 1992
Georges Duby & Michele Perrot: *Power and Beauty: Images of Women in Art*, Tauris Parke Books,
Andrea Dworkin: *Intercourse*, Arrow 1988
—*Pornography: Men Possessing Women*, Women's Press 1984
Mary Eagleton, ed: *Feminist Literary Criticism*, Longman 1991
Colin Eisler: *Early Netherlandish Painting: The Thyssen-Bornemisza Collection*, Sotheby's Publications 1989
Mircea Eliade: *Ordeal by Labyrinth*, University of Chicago Press 1984
—*A History of Religious Ideas*, I, Collins 1979
—*Patterns in Comparative Religion*, Sheed & Ward 1958
—*Symbolism, the Sacred and the Arts*, Crossroad, New York 1985
Joan Evans, ed: *The Flowering of the Middle Ages*, Thames & Hudson 1966
Giorgio T. Faggin: *The Complete Paintings of the Van Eycks*, Wiedenfeld & Nicolson 1970
George Ferguson: *Signs and Symbols in Christian Art*, Oxford University Press 1961
John Ferguson: *An Illustrated Encyclopaedia of Mysticism*, Thames & Hudson 1976
Peter Fingesten: *The Eclipse of Symbolism*, University Press of California 1970
John Fletcher & Andrew Benjamin, ed; *Abjection, Melancholia and Love: the Work of Julia Kristeva*, Routledge 1990
Michel Foucault: *The History of Sexuality*, Penguin 1981
—*The Use of Pleasure: The History of Sexuality* vol. 2, Penguin 1987
S.J. Freedberg: *Painting of the High Renaissance in Rome and Florence*, Harper & Row, New York 1972
Max J. Friedlander: *From Van Eyck to Bruegel*, Phaidon 1969
Elinor Gadon: *The Once and Future Goddess*, Aquarian Press 1990
Niny Garavaghlia: *The Complete Paintings of Mantegna*, Weidenfeld & Nicholson 1971
Fred Gettings: *The Hidden Art: A Study of the Occult Symbolism in Art*, Studio Vista 1978
Matila Ghyka: *The Geometry of Art and Life*, Sheed & Ward, New York 1946
Pamela Church Gibson & Roma Gibson, ed: *Dirty Looks: Women, Pornography, Power*, British Film Institute 1993
Marija Gimbutas: *The Language of the Goddess*, Thames & Hudson 1989
Carlo Ginzburg: *The Enigma of Piero: Piero della Francesca, The Baptism, The Arezzo Cycle, The Flagellation*, Verso 1985
Rona Goffen: *Giovanni Bellini*, Yale University Press, New Haven 1989
Robert Goldwater & Marco Treves, eds. *Artists on Art*, John Murray 1975

E.H. Gombrich: *Norm and Form: Studies in the Renaissance I*,Phaidon 1985a
—*Symbolic Images, Renaissance Studies II*,Phaidon 1985b
—*New Light on Old Masters: Studies in the Art of the Renaissance*IV, Oxford 1986
Eugene Goodheart: *Desire and Its Discontents*, Columbia University Press, New York 1991
Michelangelo Buonarroti: *The Complete Paintings*, Granada 1980
Germaine Greer: *The Obstacle Race: The Fortunes of Women Painters and Their Work*, Secker & Warburg 1979; Picador 1981
John Hale: *Italian Renaissance Painting*, Phaidon 1977
James Hall: *A Dictionary of Subjects and Symbols in Art*John Murray 1984
F.C.Happold, ed. *Mysticism*, Penguin 1970
M. Esther Harding: *Women's Mysteries*,Rider 1989
Frederick Hartt: *History of Italian Renaissance Art: Painting, Sculpture, Architecture*, Thomas & Hudson 1987
—*Sandro Botticelli*, Collins 1954
Janet Hobhouse: *The Bride Stripped Bare: The Artist and the Nude in the Twentieth Century*, Cape 1988
Anne Hollander: *Seeing Through Clothes*, Viking Press, New York 1980
Maggie Humm: *Feminisms: A Reader*, Harvester Wheatsheaf, 1992
Michael Jacobs: *A Guide to European Painting*, David & Charles 1980
—*Mythological Painting* , Phaidon 1979
Waldemar Januszczak, ed: *Techniques of the World's Great Painters*, Phaidon 1980
C.G. Jung: *Memories, Dreams, Reflections*, Collins 1967
Diane Kelder: *Pageant of the Renaissance*, Pall Mall Press 1969
David Kinsley: *The Goddess's Mirror: Visions of the Divine From East and West*, State University of New York Press 1989
Julia Kristeva: *The Kristeva Reader*, ed Toril Moi, Blackwell 1986
—*Desire in Language: A Semiotic Approach to Literature and Art* ed Leon Roudiez, tr Thomas Gora, Alice Jardine & Leon Roudiez, Blackwell 1982
—Kristeva: "Motherhood According to Bellini", in *Desire in Language*
—*Revolution in Poetic Language*, tr Margaret Walker, Columbia University Press, New York 1984
—*Tales of Love*, tr Leon S. Roudiez, Columbia University Press, New York 1987
Weston La Barre: *The Ghost Dance*, Allen & Unwin 1972
—. *Muelos*, Columbia University Press, New York, 1985
Jacques Lacan and the *Ecole Freudienne: Feminine Sexuality*, ed. Juliet Mitchell and Jacqueline Rose, Macmillan 1982
Michael Levey: *High Renaissance*, Penguin 1975
—*Early Renaissance*, Penguin 1967
Lucy Lippard: *From the Center: feminist essays on women's art*, Dutton, New York 1976
Christopher Lloyd: *Fra Angelico*, Phaidon 1979
—*A Picture History of Art*, Phaidon 1979
Edward Lucie-Smith: *Symbolist Art*,Thames & Hudson, London, 1972
—. *Sexuality in Western Art*, Thames & Hudson, London, 1991
Fiona MacCarthy: *Eric Gill*, Faber 1989
Emile Male: *The Gothic Image*, Collins 1961

Elaine Marks & Isabelle de Courtivron, eds: *New French Feminisms: an Anthology*, Harvester Wheatsheaf 1981
K.B. MacFarlane: *Hans Memling*, Clarendon Press 1971
Roy McMullen: *Mona Lisa: The Picture and the Myth*, Macmillan 1975
J.C.J.Metford: *Dictionary of Christian Lore and Legend*, Thames & Hudson 1983
Toril Moi: *Sexual/Textual Politics: Feminist Literary Theory*, Routledge 1988
Joseph-Emile Muller: *Velasquez*, Thames Hudson 1976
Edward Mullins: *The Painted Witch: Female Body, Male Art*, Secker & Warburg 1985
Laura Mulvey: *Visual and Other Pleasures*, Macmillan 1989
Sally Munt, ed: *New Lesbian Criticism: Literary and Cultural Readings*, Harvester Wheatsheaf 1992
Peter & Linda Murray: *The Penguin Dictionary of Art and Artists*, Penguin 1976
Linda Murray: *High Renaissance*, Thames & Hudson 1977
Lynda Nead: *Female Nude: Art, Obscenity and Sexuality*, Routledge 1992
Erich Neumann: *The Great Mother*, Princeton University Press, New Jersey 1972
Shirley Nicholson, ed. *The Goddess Re-awakening: The Goddess Principle Today* Theosophical Publishing House, New York 1989
Novalis: *Pollen and Fragments: Selected Poetry and Prose*, tr. Arthur Versluis, Phanes Press, Grand Rapids, 1989
—. *Works* (Minor), Schlegel, Paris, 1837
—. *Novalis Schriften. Die Werke Friedrichs von Hardenberg*, ed. Richard Samuel, Hans–Joachim Mähl & Gerhard Schulz, Kohlhammer, Stuttgart, 1960–88
Rudolf Otto: *The Idea of the Holy*, Oxford University Press 1958
Erwin Panofsky: *Studies in Iconology*, Harper & Row, New York 1972
—*Early Netherlandish Painting*, Harvard University Press, Mass., 1953
Rozsika Parker & Griselda Pollock: *Old Mistresses: Women, Art and ideology* Routledge & Kegan Paul 1981
Geoffrey Parrinder: *Mysticism in the World's Religions*, Sheldon Press 1976
Walter Pater: *The Renaissance*, Oxford University Press 1980
Michael Payne: *Reading Theory: An Introduction to Lacan, Derrida, and Kristeva*, Blackwell 1993
Karen Petersen & J.J. Wilson: *Women Artists: Recognition and Reappraisal from the Early Middle Ages to the Twentieth Century*, Women's Press, 1978
Michael Phillipson: *Painting, Language and Modernity* , Routledge 1978
Piero della Francesca: *The Complete Paintings of Piero della Francesca*, intr. Peter Murray, notes by Pierluigi de Vecchi, Penguin, 1985
Griselda Pollock: *Vision and Difference: femininity, feminism and histories of art* Routledge 1988
John Pope-Hennessy: *Fra Angelico*, Phaidon 1974
Mario Praz: *The Romantic Agony*, tr Davidson, Oxford University Press 1933
Peter Redgrove: *The Black Goddess and the Sixth Sense*, Bloomsbury 1987 [BG]
Kathleen J. Reiger, ed: *The Spiritual Image in Modern Art*, Theosophical Publishing House, Wheaton, Illinois 1987
Ad Reinhardt: *Art as Art: The Selected Writings of Ad Reinhardt*, University of California Press, Berkeley, 1991
Jeremy Mark Robinson: *Glorification: Religious Abstraction in Renaissance and 20th Century Painting*, Crescent Moon 1994
—*The Madonna Glorified: The Paintings of Karen Arthurs and the Exhibition*

Hours of the Virgin, Based on Scenes From the Life of the Virgin Mary, Crescent Moon 1991
Robert Rosenblum: *Modern Painting and the Northern Romantic Tradition*,Thames & Hudson 1978
Mark Roskill: *What is Art History?* Thames & Hudson 1976
John Ruskin: *Works*, ed. E.T.Cook & A.Wedderburn, 39 vols, Allen 1903-12
Bertrand Russell: *A History of Western Philosophy*, Allen & Unwin 1971
Gill Saunders: *The Nude: a new perspective*, Herbert Press 1989
Elaine Showalter, ed: *The New Feminist Criticism*, Virago 1986
—*Sexual Anarchy: Gender and Culture at the* Fin de Siècle, Virago 1992
Monica Sjöo & Barbara Mor: *The Great Cosmic Mother*, Harper & Row, San Francisco 1987
Alistair Smith: *Early Netherlandish and German Painting*, National Gallery 1985
Sidney Spencer: *Mysticism in World Religion*, Penguin 1963
Oswald Spengler: *The Decline of the West*, Allen & Unwin 1961
Frank Stella: *Working Space*, Harvard University Press, Cambridge, Mass., 1986
Peter Streider: *Dürer: Paintings, Prints, Drawings* , F. Muller 1982
Susan Rubin Suleiman, ed: *The Female Body in Western Culture: Contemporary Perspectives*, Harvard University Press, Cambridge, Mass., 1986
Patrick Trevor-Roper: *The world blunted through sight: An inquiry into the influence of defective vision on art and character*, Thames & Hudson 1970
Nicholas Usherwood: *The Bible in 20th Century Art*, Pagoda Books 1987
Maurice Valency: *In Praise of Love: An Introduction to the Love-Poetry of the Renaissance*, Macmillan, New York 1961
Paul Valéry: *An Introduction to the Method of Leonardo da Vinci*,1894, in *An Anthology*, selected by James Lawler, Routledge 1977
Lionello Venturi: *Renaissance Painting, from Leonardo to Dürer*, Skira/ Macmillan 1979
—*Italian Paintings*, Zwemmer 1950
—*Botticelli*, Phaidon 1964
Benjamin Walker: *Body Magic*, Paladin 1979
Marina Warner: *Alone Of All Her Sex: The Myth and Cult of the Virgin Mary* Picador 1985
—*Monuments and Maidens*, Weidenfeld & Nicholson 1985
Alan Watts: *The Myth and Ritual of Christianity*, Thames & Hudson 1983
Peter Webb: *The Erotic Arts*, Secker & Warburg 1983
Margaret Whinney: *Early Flemish Painters*, Faber 1966
John White: *The Birth and Rebirth of Pictorial Space*, Faber 1957/87
Frank Whitford: *Egon Schiele*, Thames & Hudson 1981
Edward C.Whitmont: *Return of the Goddess*, Routledge 1987
Peter Lamborn Wilson: *Angels*, Thames & Hudson 1980
Heinrich Wolfflin: *Classic Art*, Phaidon 1952/80
Manfred Wudram: *Art of the Renaissance*, Weidenfeld & Nicolson 1985

CRESCENT MOON PUBLISHING

web: www.crmoon.com e-mail: cresmopub@yahoo.co.uk

ARTS, PAINTING, SCULPTURE

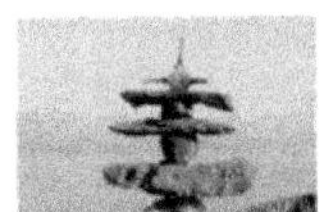
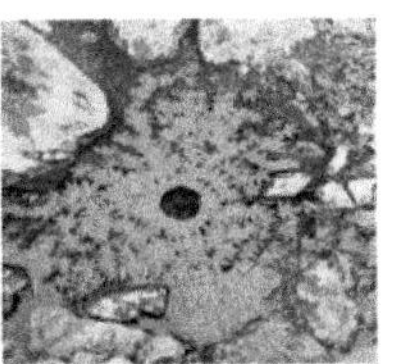

The Art of Andy Goldsworthy
Andy Goldsworthy: Touching Nature
Andy Goldsworthy in Close-Up
Andy Goldsworthy: Pocket Guide
Andy Goldsworthy In America
Land Art: A Complete Guide
The Art of Richard Long

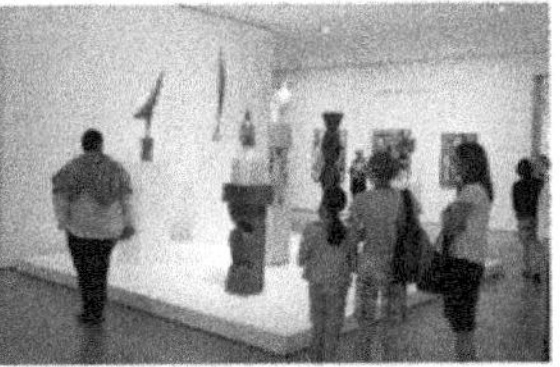
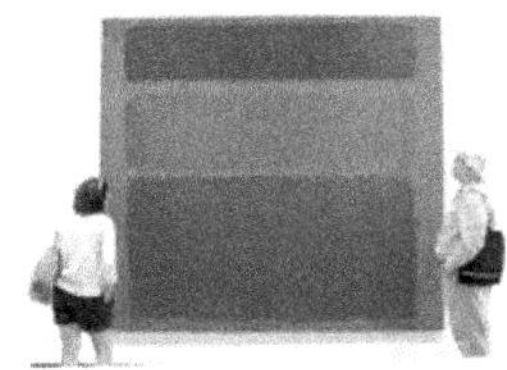

Richard Long: Pocket Guide
Land Art In the UK

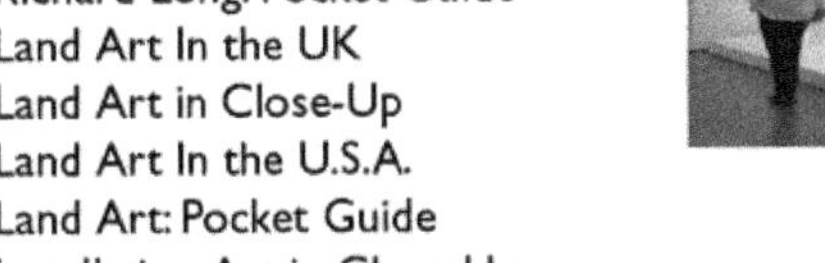

Land Art in Close-Up
Land Art In the U.S.A.
Land Art: Pocket Guide
Installation Art in Close-Up
Minimal Art and Artists In the 1960s and After
Colourfield Painting
Land Art DVD, TV documentary
Andy Goldsworthy DVD, TV documentary
The Erotic Object: Sexuality in Sculpture From Prehistory to the Present Day
Sex in Art: Pornography and Pleasure in Painting and Sculpture
Postwar Art
Sacred Gardens: The Garden in Myth, Religion and Art
Glorification: Religious Abstraction in Renaissance and 20th Century Art

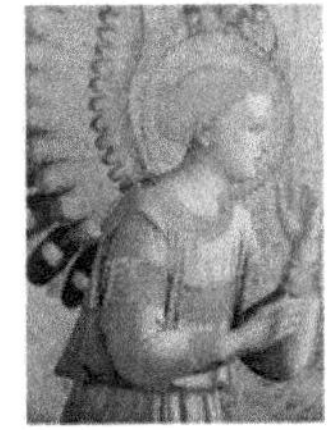

Early Netherlandish Painting
Leonardo da Vinci
Piero della Francesca
Giovanni Bellini
Fra Angelico: Art and Religion in the Renaissance
Mark Rothko: The Art of Transcendence
Frank Stella: American Abstract Artist

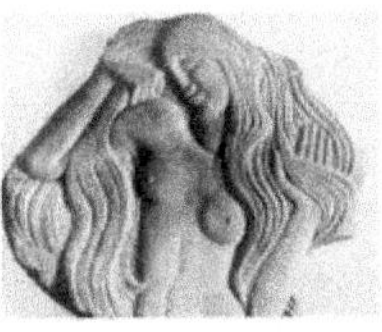
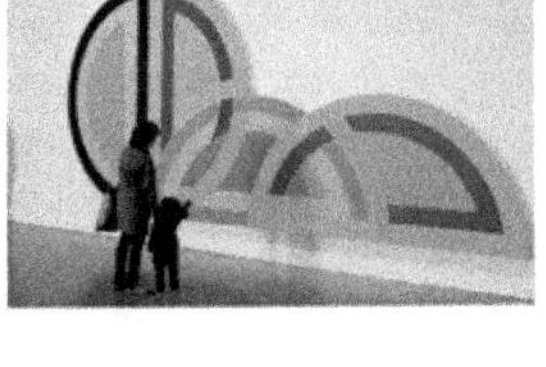

Jasper Johns
Brice Marden
Alison Wilding: The Embrace of Sculpture
Vincent van Gogh: Visionary Landscapes
Eric Gill: Nuptials of God

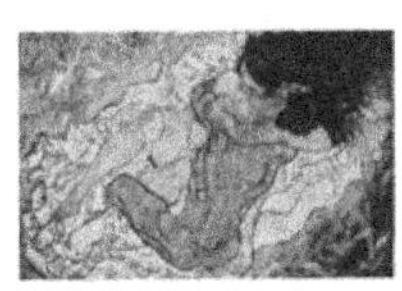
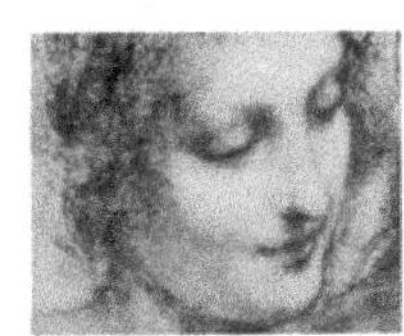

Constantin Brancusi: Sculpting the Essence of Things
Max Beckmann
Caravaggio
Gustave Moreau
Egon Schiele: Sex and Death In Purple Stockings
Delizioso Fotografico Fervore: Works In Process 1
Sacro Cuore: Works In Process 2
The Light Eternal: J.M.W. Turner
The Madonna Glorified: Karen Arthurs

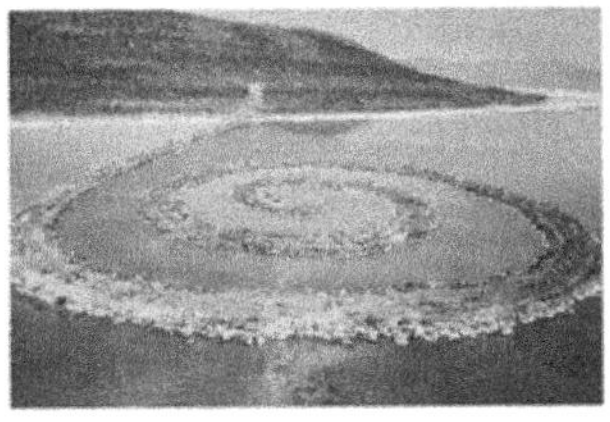

LITERATURE

J.R.R. Tolkien: The Books, The Films, The Whole Cultural Phenomenon
J.R.R. Tolkien: Pocket Guide
Tolkien's Heroic Quest
The *Earthsea* Books of Ursula Le Guin
Beauties, Beasts and Enchantment: Classic French Fairy Tales
German Popular Stories by the Brothers Grimm
Philip Pullman and *His Dark Materials*
Sexing Hardy: Thomas Hardy and Feminism
Thomas Hardy's *Tess of the d'Urbervilles*
Thomas Hardy's *Jude the Obscure*
Thomas Hardy: The Tragic Novels
Love and Tragedy: Thomas Hardy
The Poetry of Landscape in Hardy
Wessex Revisited: Thomas Hardy and John Cowper Powys
Wolfgang Iser: Essays and Interviews
Petrarch, Dante and the Troubadours
Maurice Sendak and the Art of Children's Book Illustration
Andrea Dworkin
Cixous, Irigaray, Kristeva: The *Jouissance* of French Feminism
Julia Kristeva: Art, Love, Melancholy, Philosophy, Semiotics and Psychoanalysis
Hélene Cixous I Love You: The *Jouissance* of Writing
Luce Irigaray: Lips, Kissing, and the Politics of Sexual Difference
Peter Redgrove: Here Comes the Flood
Peter Redgrove: Sex-Magic-Poetry-Cornwall
Lawrence Durrell: Between Love and Death, East and West
Love, Culture & Poetry: Lawrence Durrell
Cavafy: Anatomy of a Soul
German Romantic Poetry: Goethe, Novalis, Heine, Hölderlin
Feminism and Shakespeare
Shakespeare: Love, Poetry & Magic
The Passion of D.H. Lawrence
D.H. Lawrence: Symbolic Landscapes
D.H. Lawrence: Infinite Sensual Violence
Rimbaud: Arthur Rimbaud and the Magic of Poetry
The Ecstasies of John Cowper Powys
Sensualism and Mythology: The Wessex Novels of John Cowper Powys
Amorous Life: John Cowper Powys and the Manifestation of Affectivity (H.W. Fawkner)
Postmodern Powys: New Essays on John Cowper Powys (Joe Boulter)
Rethinking Powys: Critical Essays on John Cowper Powys
Paul Bowles & Bernardo Bertolucci
Rainer Maria Rilke
Joseph Conrad: *Heart of Darkness*
In the Dim Void: Samuel Beckett
Samuel Beckett Goes into the Silence
André Gide: Fiction and Fervour
Jackie Collins and the Blockbuster Novel
Blinded By Her Light: The Love-Poetry of Robert Graves
The Passion of Colours: Travels In Mediterranean Lands
Poetic Forms

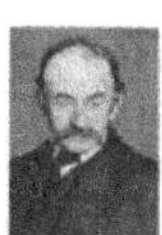
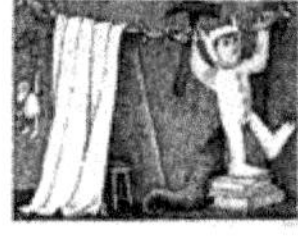
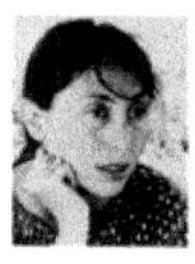
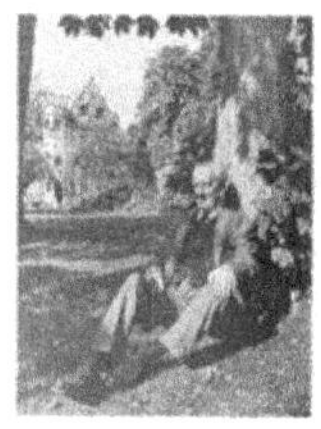
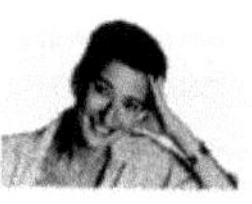
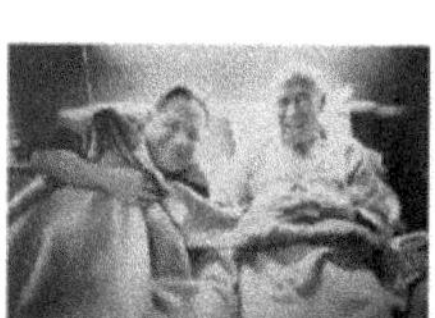
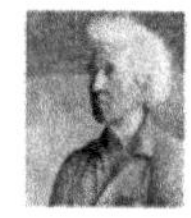
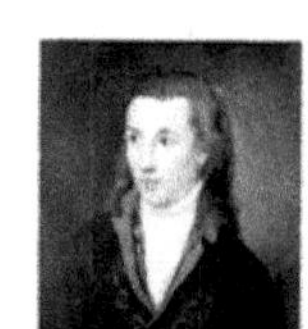

POETRY

Ursula Le Guin: Walking In Cornwall
Peter Redgrove: Here Comes The Flood
Peter Redgrove: Sex-Magic-Poetry-Cornwall
Dante: Selections From the Vita Nuova
Petrarch, Dante and the Troubadours
William Shakespeare: Sonnets
William Shakespeare: Complete Poems
Blinded By Her Light: The Love-Poetry of Robert Graves
Emily Dickinson: Selected Poems
Emily Brontë: Poems
Thomas Hardy: Selected Poems
Percy Bysshe Shelley: Poems
John Keats: Selected Poems
Joh n Keats: Poems of 1820
D.H. Lawrence: Selected Poems
Edmund Spenser: Poems
Edmund Spenser: Amoretti
John Donne: Poems
Henry Vaughan: Poems
Sir Thomas Wyatt: Poems
Robert Herrick: Selected Poems
Rilke: Space, Essence and Angels in the Poetry of Rainer Maria Rilke
Rainer Maria Rilke: Selected Poems
Friedrich Hölderlin: Selected Poems
Arseny Tarkovsky: Selected Poems
Arthur Rimbaud: Selected Poems
Arthur Rimbaud: A Season in Hell
Arthur Rimbaud and the Magic of Poetry
Novalis: Hymns To the Night
German Romantic Poetry
Paul Verlaine: Selected Poems
Elizaethan Sonnet Cycles
D.J. Enright: By-Blows
Jeremy Reed: Brigitte's Blue Heart
Jeremy Reed: Claudia Schiffer's Red Shoes
Gorgeous Little Orpheus
Radiance: New Poems
Crescent Moon Book of Nature Poetry
Crescent Moon Book of Love Poetry
Crescent Moon Book of Mystical Poetry
Crescent Moon Book of Elizabethan Love Poetry
Crescent Moon Book of Metaphysical Poetry
Crescent Moon Book of Romantic Poetry
Pagan America: New American Poetry

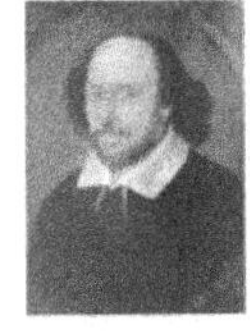
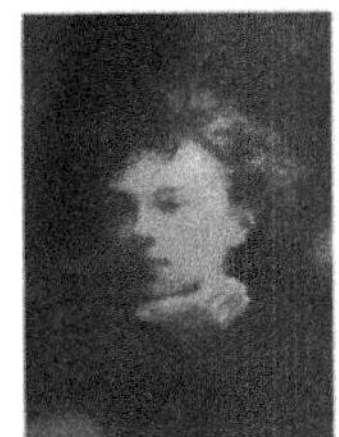
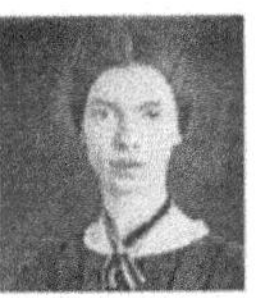
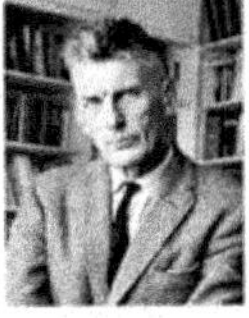
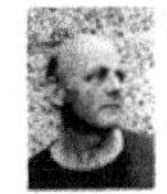
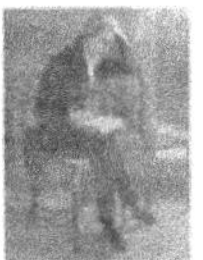
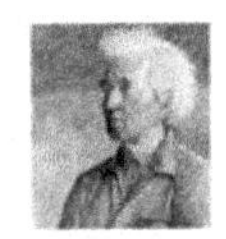
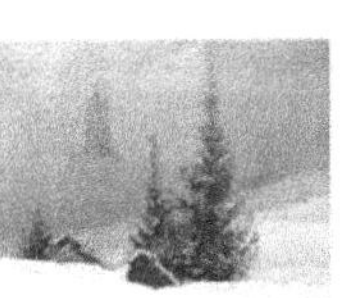
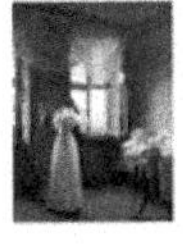
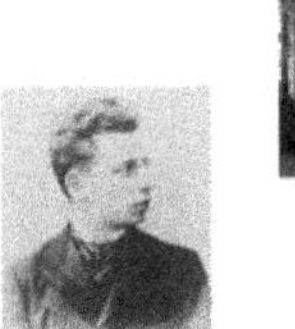
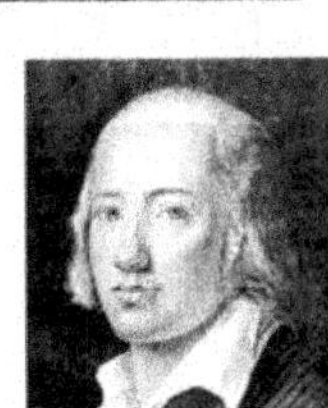
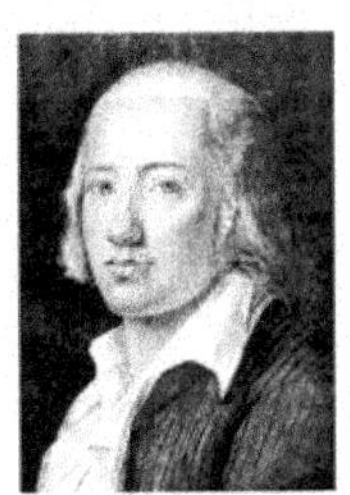

MEDIA, CINEMA, FEMINISM and CULTURAL STUDIES

J.R.R. Tolkien: The Books, The Films, The Whole Cultural Phenomenon
J.R.R. Tolkien: Pocket Guide
The *Lord of the Rings* Movies: Pocket Guide
The Cinema of Hayao Miyazaki
Hayao Miyazaki: *Princess Mononoke*: Pocket Movie Guide
Hayao Miyazaki: *Spirited Away*: Pocket Movie Guide

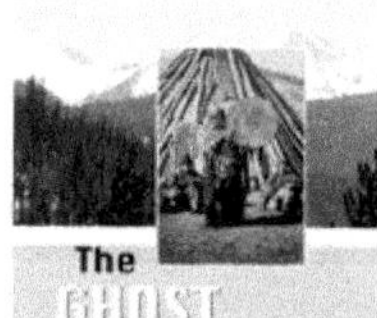

Tim Burton : Hallowe'en For Hollywood
Ken Russell
Ken Russell: *Tommy*: Pocket Movie Guide
The Ghost Dance: The Origins of Religion
The Peyote Cult

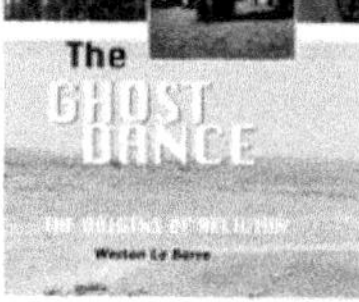

Cixous, Irigaray, Kristeva: The *Jouissance* of French Feminism
Julia Kristeva: Art, Love, Melancholy, Philosophy, Semiotics and Psychoanalysis
Luce Irigaray: Lips, Kissing, and the Politics of Sexual Difference
Hélene Cixous I Love You: The *Jouissance* of Writing
Andrea Dworkin
'Cosmo Woman': The World of Women's Magazines

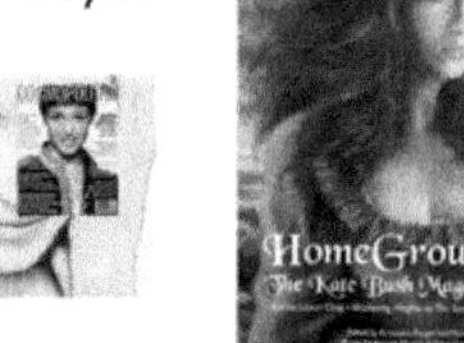

Women in Pop Music
HomeGround: The Kate Bush Anthology
Discovering the Goddess (Geoffrey Ashe)
The Poetry of Cinema
The Sacred Cinema of Andrei Tarkovsky
Andrei Tarkovsky: Pocket Guide
Andrei Tarkovsky: *Mirror*: Pocket Movie Guide

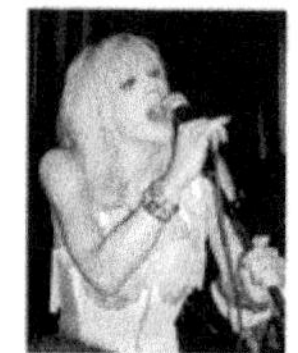

Andrei Tarkovsky: *The Sacrifice*: Pocket Movie Guide
Walerian Borowczyk: Cinema of Erotic Dreams
Jean-Luc Godard: The Passion of Cinema
Jean-Luc Godard: *Hail Mary*: Pocket Movie Guide
Jean-Luc Godard: *Contempt*: Pocket Movie Guide
Jean-Luc Godard: *Pierrot le Fou*: Pocket Movie Guide
John Hughes and Eighties Cinema

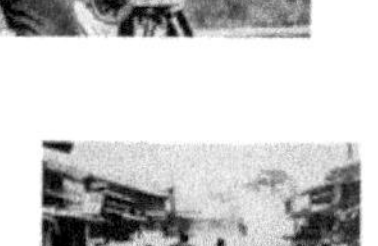

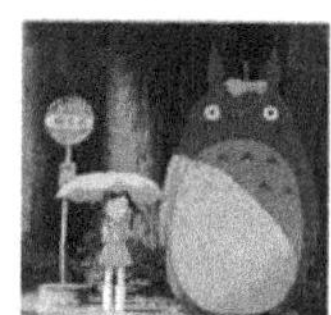

Ferris Bueller's Day Off: Pocket Movie Guide
Jean-Luc Godard: Pocket Guide
The Cinema of Richard Linklater
Liv Tyler: Star In Ascendance
Blade Runner and the Films of Philip K. Dick
Paul Bowles and Bernardo Bertolucci
Media Hell: Radio, TV and the Press
An Open Letter to the BBC

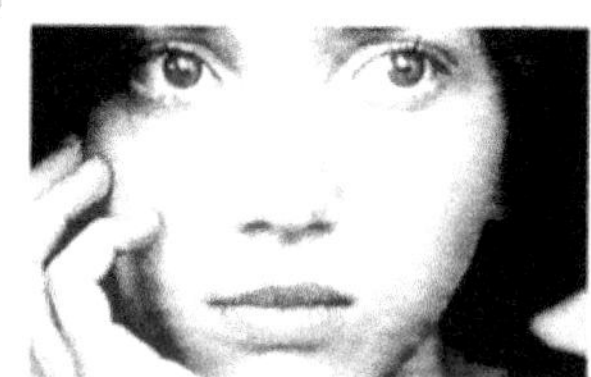

Detonation Britain: Nuclear War in the UK
Feminism and Shakespeare
Wild Zones: Pornography, Art and Feminism
Sex in Art: Pornography and Pleasure in Painting and Sculpture
Sexing Hardy: Thomas Hardy and Feminism

The Light Eternal is a model monograph, an exemplary job. The subject matter of the book is beautifully organised and dead on beam. (Lawrence Durrell)
It is amazing for me to see my work treated with such passion and respect. (Andrea Dworkin)

CRESCENT MOON PUBLISHING
P.O. Box 1312, Maidstone, Kent, ME14 5XU, Great Britain. www.crmoon.com

cresmopub@yahoo.co.uk www.crescentmoon.org.uk

www.ingramcontent.com/pod-product-compliance
Ingram Content Group UK Ltd.
Pitfield, Milton Keynes, MK11 3LW, UK
UKHW020426250726
13967UKWH00007B/2834

9 781861 717429